Primal
MANAGEMENT

Primal
MANAGEMENT

Unraveling the Secrets of

Human Nature to

Drive High Performance

Paul Herr

᠎AMACOM

American Management Association

New York • Atlanta • Brussels • Chicago • Mexico City • San Francisco
Shanghai • Tokyo • Toronto • Washington, D.C.

Special discounts on bulk quantities of AMACOM books are available to corporations, professional associations, and other organizations. For details, contact Special Sales Department, AMACOM, a division of American Management Association, 1601 Broadway, New York, NY 10019.
Tel: 212-903-8316. Fax: 212-903-8083.
E-mail: specialsls@amanet.org
Website: www.amacombooks.org/go/specialsales
To view all AMACOM titles go to: www.amacombooks.org

This publication is designed to provide accurate and authoritative information in regard to the subject matter covered. It is sold with the understanding that the publisher is not engaged in rendering legal, accounting, or other professional service. If legal advice or other expert assistance is required, the services of a competent professional person should be sought.

Quotes from Plain Talk: Lessons from a Business Maverick by Ken Iverson (©1998 John Wiley & Sons, Inc.) on pages 98, 113–114, 195–196, 218, 219, and 220 are reprinted with permission of John Wiley & Sons Ltd.

Library of Congress Cataloging-in-Publication Data

Herr, Paul, 1955–
    Primal management : unraveling the secrets of human nature to drive high performance / Paul Herr.
        p.   cm.
    Includes bibliographical references and index.
    ISBN-13: 978-0-8144-1396-8 (hbk.)
    ISBN-10: 0-8144-1396-X (hbk.)
    1. Employee motivation.   2. Performance—Psychological aspects.
3. Management—Psychological aspects.   I. Title.

    HF5549.5.M63H466   2009
    658.3'14—dc22

                                                            2008053759

Printing number

10   9   8   7   6   5   4   3   2   1

CONTENTS

Primal
MANAGEMENT

INTRODUCTION

THE RISE OF THE SUPERORGANISM

In biology, a superorganism is a group of individual organisms that act as one—like a colony of army ants. Ant colonies, working as coordinated units, can defeat creatures hundreds of times their size. Corporate superorganisms are similar. They are composed of individual human beings who think and act as one, much like a tribe. They are as formidable in the corporate ecosystem as army ants are in their ecosystems.

I don't mean to imply that human beings should cooperate like mindless insects. Human beings possess a sophisticated form of social bonding that some psychiatrists refer to as *cathexis*. This social bonding mechanism underlies relationships of all types, and corporations, unfortunately, are not aware of it. Traditional corporate hierarchies rely, instead, on rules, regulations, bureaucratic structures, hard-fisted competition, and fear to coordinate human beings.

A superorganism, on the other hand, is held together organically and naturally by invested relationships and doesn't need an artificial shell to force cooperation and coordination. If you remove the bureaucratic shell from a traditional hierarchy, the humans inside would mostly scatter like marbles because there is nothing fundamental holding them together. If you remove the shell from a superorganism, it will continue to function because its individual members are interconnected, self-motivated, self-organizing, and self-managing—just as nature intended.

Any company can become a superorganism if it learns how to work harmoniously with human nature rather than against it. Superorganisms,

I predict, will someday dominate the corporate landscape because they create maximum wealth for the corporate ecosystem. They create a win-win scenario where everyone benefits—shareholders, managers, employees, and customers.

A HARD APPROACH TO THE
SOFT SIDE OF BUSINESS

The secret to aligning with human nature, and thereby creating a corporate superorganism, lies in understanding the motivational mechanism that powers human achievement. I've been researching the motivational mechanism from a hard, biologic/engineering perspective for thirty years. I started pondering emotions and motivation in 1977 when I was an engineering student at the University of Wisconsin, Madison. I had always been impressed by the elegant design of the human body—the human hand, for example, is an elegant mechanism that engineers have yet to duplicate. The same goes for the human eye or circulatory system. Then the thought occurred to me, "What about human emotions? Where is the elegance in a system that causes people to jump off bridges, go postal, and experience road rage?" I felt, deep down, however, that our motivational mechanism should be just as elegant as the rest of our design—and so began my odyssey to reverse engineer nature's motivational mechanism.

This hard approach reveals emotions and feelings for what they are—the fundamental forces that make us go. I hope to demonstrate that emotions are involved in every decision and every move we make. This claim may seem audacious and far-fetched now, but, by the end of the book, it will hopefully make perfect sense. I hope you enjoy this tough, logical, engineering approach to the soft side of business.

Emotions, as the word implies, put us into motion. They are the forces that move us from the moment we wake up in the morning to the moment we go to bed. As forces, they obey laws similar to the laws of physics. Newton's first law of motion states that an object at rest will remain at rest unless acted upon by a force. I will prove something similar—a human being at rest will remain at rest unless acted upon by an emotional force—a feeling! Taken as a group, these forces are responsible for essentially everything going on inside corporations everywhere. In other words, they are *fundamental*. *Primal Management* proposes a methodology to measure, manage, and harness these vital forces to create a high-performance workplace.

I aim to shake the business community out of its wrong-headed approach to emotion. It has pretended that emotions and feelings are irrational and unimportant. This is simply wrong. I intend to turn this kind of thinking on its head by proving that subtle emotional incentives lie at the core of economic decision making, the core of economic utility, the core of employee satisfaction and engagement, and the core of organizational excellence. Emotions lie at the vital core of the human condition because we are universally motivated to seek emotional pleasure and to avoid emotional pain. We will discover that making a few deep changes at an emotional level will radiate organically throughout an organization and empower it—somewhat like turning on a light switch.

How many times have you heard someone say something like, "I don't care how they feel. I just want them to get their work done." I intend to demonstrate, in *Primal Management*, that this macho "Who cares about feelings?" attitude may work in the short term to get a project out the door, but it is downright unbusinesslike and harmful in the long term. Ignoring the intrinsic rewards that power human performance is equivalent to a race car driver ignoring his engine—it's not a good idea if you want to win races.

THE DEEP ARCHITECTURE OF MOTIVATION

During my thirty years of exploring the murky subject of emotion, the deep architecture of the human motivational mechanism gradually came into focus for me. This mechanism is easy to understand once you understand nature's design theme—survival. This is the main idea throughout this book—that nature does not leave the necessities of life to chance. Rather, it evolves circuits to make sure the necessities get done. The main behaviors that ensure our physical survival, and the feelings of pleasure and pain that encourage them, are as follows:

1. Acquiring nutrition: enforced with feelings of hunger, thirst, and satiation

2. Energy conservation (rest): enforced with feelings of fatigue and relaxation

3. Protection of one's physical body: enforced with sensory pain and pleasure

4. Oxygen intake: enforced with the pain of holding one's breath

5. Reproduction: enforced through romantic pleasure and sexual pleasure

These biologic appetites, and the feelings associated with them, are simple and straightforward. Nobody would question their existence because they are self-evident. What is less self-evident, however, are the feelings that regulate our social needs. I will argue throughout *Primal Management* that our social needs are just as tightly regulated as our biologic needs—and with similar appetite-like circuits that generate pleasurable and painful feelings.

Here are the social appetites that complement the biologic appetites to create a comprehensive bio/social survival system:

1. Cooperation: enforced by the warm feelings we experience when we are with the persons, places, and things that are important to us and painful feelings of alienation when we are excluded from the tribe

2. Skill mastery or competency: enforced with feelings of high and low self-esteem

3. Skill deployment and goal attainment: enforced with the euphoria of a win and the dysphoria (pain) of a loss

4. Innovation: enforced with curiosity and the eureka pleasure when we get an idea

5. Self-protection: enforced with pleasant feelings when we achieve security and fearful and anxious feelings when our survival is at risk

Once nature chose to traverse the slippery slope of using feelings of pleasure and pain to regulate biologic needs like reproduction, energy conservation, and nutrition, there was no turning back. Once one behavior was rewarded in this way, then, logically, every other survival behavior needed to be similarly rewarded or human beings would have overindulged in the rewarding behaviors at the expense of the ones without rewards.

I propose that positive feelings emanating from the motivational mechanism, taken as a group, constitute the emotional paycheck (intrinsic rewards) that drives human achievement. We will learn how to measure and track this important paycheck in Chapter 2.

THOUGHT EXPERIMENT

Perhaps the social appetite concept will make more sense if we conduct a little thought experiment. Imagine that you, and ten of your neighbors, volunteer for an experiment at a local university to assess the role of emotions in human survival. Step 1 of the experiment involves entering a chamber where your memories are erased except for a rudimentary vocabulary and basic motor skills like walking, running, and throwing. You and your neighbors emerge from the chamber disoriented and able to neither recognize one another nor recall any previously acquired knowledge, skills, or experiences. In other words, you are all suffering from debilitating mass amnesia. Now imagine that your group is dropped into the middle of the Amazon rain forest with just the clothes on your backs. What would happen to your group? Are you doomed?

The Innovation Appetite

You are initially befuddled and clueless. Some of your neighbors are terrified by the strange surroundings and jungle noises and huddle together for protection. The risk takers in your group, coaxed by curiosity, the pleasure of novelty, begin to cautiously explore the new environment. During the course of these explorations, observations are made regarding the types of plants, animals, and resources in the forest that might come in handy later on.

After a period of exploration, one of your neighbors, a woman, notices fruit hanging from a tree. She also recalls seeing a patch of bamboo growing next to a nearby river. In a flash of insight, these observations congeal into an idea, a simple innovation—knock the fruit down with long, lightweight, bamboo poles. This eureka moment announces itself with a brief burst of pleasure. The eureka pleasure serves a couple of functions. First, it informs the innovator that she has made a potentially important discovery that may help her group survive. Furthermore, the eureka pleasure motivates her to share her discovery with the group.

Curiosity (the pleasure of novelty) and the eureka moment (the pleasure of ideation) emanate from what I call the innovation appetite. This appetite encourages human beings to explore their environment and invent survival technologies. In the modern context, this appetite motivates everything from family vacations to exploring novelty-rich (exotic) destinations to innovation on the cutting edge of scientific research.

The Competency Appetite

The female neighbor returns to the group with an armful of ripe figs. The famished group applauds her discovery, and pays careful attention as she demonstrates how she used the pole to knock down fruit. This fruit-collecting technology is unanimously seen as valuable and worth copying and perfecting and is thereby added to the tribe's embryonic trove of survival knowledge—its culture.

The group, by applauding the new fig-harvesting technology, unwittingly triggers the next appetite—the competency appetite. This appetite locks on to applauded skills, like the fig-harvesting skill, and makes them feel desirable and worth mastering. Everyone who subsequently masters the new skill will experience improved feelings of self-esteem and self-confidence. These rewarding feelings lie at the core of the competency appetite and at the core of human culture.

Additional innovations occur over the next several months as the group develops hunting, gathering, tool-making, shelter-making, and food-preparation skills. Group members who master these skills experience higher and higher levels of self-esteem and feel and act the most confident. They also become esteemed and relied-upon by other members of the group. Members of the tribe who fail to master these skills are internally punished with painful and persistent feelings of worthlessness and incompetence and sulk around on the periphery of the group.

Over time, feelings of high and low self-esteem motivate individuals in the group to master a shared toolbox of survival knowledge and skills. This vital social appetite gets the entire group marching in a common direction with a shared survival technology. In the modern context these powerful feelings motivate us to master the survival skills of our nation-tribes by attending college, learning trades, and becoming skillful in sports, hobbies, and artistic endeavors.

The Skill-Deployment Appetite

Mastering skills is not enough. It is equally important for the group to be productive by deploying their skills on a daily basis. Motivating day-to-day achievement falls on the next social appetite, the skill-deployment appetite.

Imagine that you are assigned the task of putting meat on the table tonight. When you accomplish this task, say, by trapping a capybara, the skill-deployment appetite will detect your achievement and reward you with a brief, but highly rewarding, euphoria. This sort of reward motivates everyone in the group to be active and productive in the many tasks of everyday life. If a member of the group sits for too long without completing a task, the skill-deployment appetite will detect this inactivity and punish him/her with a gnawing sense of boredom.

In the modern context, the skill-deployment appetite is hugely important. It motivates a rich swath of productive, goal-directed behavior. Without this appetite there would be no pleasure associated with a win. Winning and losing would feel exactly the same—nothing. Fans at football games would no longer cheer when touchdowns are scored and golfers would stop playing golf because a good shot would feel exactly the same as a bad shot. Competitive sports, card games, hobbies, home-improvement projects, and all other goal-directed behaviors would cease because success and failure in these activities would feel exactly the same.

I think you can see where I am going with this discussion of the social appetites. Emotions are not as soft, irrational, or irrelevant as we have all been taught. Rather, they are absolutely vital for our survival and without these subtle incentives the group of neighbors in our thought experiment would be dead. The biologic and social appetites, taken as a group, constitute a sophisticated autopilot that stealthily points us in the direction of survival.

Anyone attempting to lead a group of human beings should understand the primal appetites all human beings possess to innovate, master skills, deploy skills to achieve goals, work as a highly coordinated and bonded team, and feel protected. If corporations are smart, they will reject dispassionate rationalism and learn to feed the social appetites that drive high performance.

The implications of the social appetite approach are enormous. Advertising professionals, for example, must evoke positive emotions to sell their products and services. If *Primal Management* can clarify how these emotions function, then it can deliver tremendous value to the advertising community. The application pursued in *Primal Management* is not advertising, but employee motivation—how to evoke positive emotion to create an optimally productive workforce. The suggestions contained in this book should work as well today as 1,000 years from today. They should work until scientists reengineer human nature. I have worked diligently to simplify the vast and murky subject of human motivation to its crystalline essence. Simplicity and clarity are therefore my value-added propositions.

This book should help executives, managers, and supervisors everywhere bring out the very best in their employees. I hope to change your view of yourself, your employees, and the society you live in. You and I have been brainwashed by Western culture to look at human beings as fundamentally rational creatures. This is simply wrong. We are fundamentally emotional creatures who devise rational strategies to serve our emotional (survival) needs.

RESPECTING YOUR WORLDVIEW

As you've probably noticed, this is a science-based book with an evolutionary perspective. When I say "nature designed" or "nature made," this is shorthand for saying, "the impersonal process of natural selection, operating across thousands or millions of years of human evolution, caused the motivational mechanism to evolve slowly and organically to its current state."

If recent surveys about religion are accurate, I'm in grave risk of alienating the 45 percent of the U.S. population that believes in the biblical, creationist worldview. Another 38 percent of the population accepts the idea of evolution but believes that human evolution was divinely guided.[1] Pope John Paul II, one of the most scientific popes in recent memory, believed that humans evolved but that God inserted a soul at some point in the process.

I don't want to threaten or disrespect anyone's belief system, but I'm a scientist and this book takes a scientific perspective. Perhaps we can resolve this issue by agreeing that the motivational design ought to be logical and serve our survival, regardless of who, or what, "designed" it. I will henceforth refer to the designer simply as "nature."

Since we are having this heart-to-heart, I also want to broach another sensitive issue—respecting one another's investments. I promise to respect you, the reader, as an expert on human nature—particularly your own nature. We are all lifelong users of human nature and we've all built a worldview brick by brick around our personal experiences. I don't want to topple anyone's hard-won edifice of understanding. I therefore suggest that readers look at this book as an organizational framework on which to hang your hard-won wisdom regarding human nature. Think of my social appetite theory as a Christmas tree and your hard-won insights as the ornaments. Let's face it, emotions and motivation are complex and confusing so an organizational framework that is simple and clear is a good thing—a valuable thing!

ACKNOWLEDGING OUR ANCESTRY

Human beings today are physically, intellectually, and emotionally similar to our Upper Paleolithic ancestors, who hunted big game in small bands 40,000 years ago. Human beings today, like then, are fundamentally designed to live in small, tightly knit tribal communities. The tribe is therefore the best unit of analysis for thinking about human behavior. If companies want to align themselves with human nature they must understand, and conform to, a survival mechanism designed for small tribal groups.

Another benefit of the tribal perspective is its simplicity. It is far easier to wrap one's mind around a group of 150 individuals with a unitary culture and shared identity than it is to contemplate today's megasocieties and megacorporations. The tribal perspective is not only scientifically correct, but it also makes our journey much easier.

I use the terms *tribe* and *tribal* throughout this book.[2] Whenever I use the word *tribe*, I'm talking about something serious—ancestors who triumphed in the difficult struggle for survival and therefore made our existence possible. The latest thinking in genetics suggests that evolution can occur at both the individual and group level (group selection). In this case, it is often the fittest group that survives (the tribe), not necessarily the fittest individual.

We don't think of ourselves as tribal people because we abandoned that lifestyle long ago, yet it still affects every aspect of our minds, emotions, personalities, and organizations. The motivational mechanism, we will discover, is a distinctively tribal apparatus that often malfunctions within the context of modern complex societies. Hierarchically organized corporations are not united or tribal and do not take full advantage of nature's motivational mechanism. Rather, they starve the social appetites and end up with motivationally malnourished employees.

A smattering of contrarian companies, like Google, Quad/Graphics, W. L. Gore, Whole Foods Market, Nucor Steel, and Herman Miller in the United States and Semco SA in Brazil, have achieved spectacular productivity and growth by trying something radically different. They created structurally flat organizations that meshed with the underlying emotional architecture that all human beings share. These corporate superorganisms are unusual by Western standards, but are relatively common in East Asia, where the cultures are more "we" focused than "me" focused.[3] Chinese family-owned companies, for example, are based on *guanxi*, or trust networks, and have many of the same qualities as the Western superorganisms.[4]

HOW STERILE IS YOUR CAGE?

What do human beings and zoo-raised tigers have in common? Answer: We both live outside our natural habitats. Tigers are native to the jungles of Asia. Human beings are originally native to a wide variety of ecosystems where we survived by hunting and gathering.

What do you suppose happens to a tiger after it is plucked from its natural environment and placed into a sterile zoo setting? Before the 1960s, zoos kept animals in simple enclosures surrounded by iron bars. These impoverished environments created stress and profoundly abnormal behavior. The animals were often aggressive and self-destructive.

Our cousins, the great apes, also did not react well to sterile captivity. They would often sit in a stupor and rock back and forth, just like mentally ill human beings often do. Animals would generally not breed under such unnatural conditions. The brains of both animals and humans exhibit reduced neuronal branching and increased cell death, especially in the hippocampus region, after long-term exposure to stressful conditions. In other words, keeping an animal in an unnatural and stressful environment will result in brain damage.[5]

Beginning in the 1960s, zoos were pressured to treat their animals more humanely. In response to this pressure, zoos started designing enclosures that mimicked the animals' natural habitats. Bars were replaced by moats and zoo curators went to great lengths to research the ecosystem requirements of their animals.

Human beings today face precisely the same plight as the abused zoo animals, yet nobody in corporate America is researching the habitat needs of their employees. We were also plucked from our ancestral hunter-gatherer habitat and placed into a gilded cage of our own making. In a very real sense, we are like fish out of water.

Human beings are small-group creatures. Our motivational systems function best in groups of 150 or fewer individuals.[6] Human beings, just like the zoo animals, often malfunction in the unnatural "cages" provided by today's megasocieties because our brains were designed to operate within small, intimate groups.

Companies often lock employees in sterile cages by treating them in a cool, impersonal manner. This unnatural, hyperrational approach to management creates an impoverished work environment in which human beings battle one another instead of cooperating. Human beings have a deep-seated need to be imbedded within a close-knit group to function at their best; and this need is often frustrated within the modern work world.

A cool, impersonal approach to management ignores the motivational mechanism and is therefore harmful to everyone involved—management, shareholders, customers, and employees. Hyperrational management tries to jam a square peg into a round hole. I propose a more balanced, ecosystem approach to management that embraces both the rational and emotional sides of human nature. Employees, I will demonstrate, function much better when companies craft a natural workplace ecosystem that mimics the closely knit tribal communities of our ancestors. This is the truly rational and efficient thing to do.

MEET THE MAVERICKS

I profile three contrarian leaders, and their unconventional companies, in *Primal Management*. Each of these leaders worked harmoniously with human nature and achieved spectacular success in the process:

1.   Ken Iverson, the chairman of Nucor Steel (deceased)

2.   Harry Quadracci, the founder, president, and CEO of Quad/Graphics (deceased)

3.   Ricardo Semler, the CEO and main shareholder of Semco SA, a Brazilian company that provides a diverse array of products and services

I refer to, and quote from, this threesome often because they are my management heroes. All three of them detected something rotten in traditional management dogma and had the guts to do something about it. Traditional, hierarchical, bureaucratic management didn't feel right to these guys so they broke all the rules and created something natural and marvelous in the process—thriving egalitarian companies that were self-managing, self-motivated, and self-organizing. In other words, they spawned the first generation of superorganisms.

All three of my heroes described themselves as business mavericks and two of them wrote books with *maverick* in the title. They earned the moniker *maverick* because they turned right when the rest of the corporate world turned left. By turning right, however, they aligned themselves with human nature and enjoyed spectacular business success on account of it. In *Primal Management* we discover the method behind their madness and hopefully convince you to turn right too. By the end of the book I intend to show the mavericks for what they were—brilliant management innovators who were well ahead of their time.

All three mavericks used a similar formula to align with human nature. There is nothing complicated about their formula because it boils down to treating employees with dignity and respect. Here is how Ricardo Semler describes his democratic (egalitarian) approach to management:

> The first of Semco's three values is democracy, or employee involvement. Clearly, workers who control their working conditions are going to be happier than workers who don't. Just as clearly, there is no contest between the company that buys the grudging compliance of its work force and the company that enjoys the enterprising participation of its employees.[7]

Semler, by the way, is a Harvard-trained MBA who was named a "Global Leader of Tomorrow" by the World Economic Forum; was twice named as Brazil's "Business Leader of the Year"; was voted "Latin American Businessman of the Year" by Gazeta Mercantil, Latin America's equivalent of the *Wall Street Journal*[8]; and his company, Semco SA, is often referred to as the best place to work in Brazil by management associations, labor unions, and the press.

Here are several of the principles all three mavericks profiled in *Primal Management* shared:

- They were all aggressive hierarchy-busters so their organizations were flat and based upon egalitarian—nobody is better than anybody else—principles. Hierarchy, they felt, creates barriers to communication, concentrates decision making in the few rather than the many, and makes the folks on the bottom feel small, insignificant, disrespected, and, hence, demotivated.

- All three mavericks believed in the motto "small is beautiful." They managed to maintain a sense of interpersonal intimacy by keeping individual plants, offices, and teams small, even as they grew into large organizations with thousands of employees. Harry Quadracci summarized this philosophy with his oft-used phrase—"think small."[9] The modular design of the superorganisms resulted in some redundant overhead costs and lost economies of scale, but these losses were more than compensated for by the improved motivation and productivity realized within intensely bonded work groups.

- All three mavericks created companies that were almost completely devoid of bureaucracy, rules, regulations, organizational charts, and other systems of control. They achieved much of their efficiency from the simple notion that human beings will make good decisions, and will not need to be monitored by an army of overseers, if you treat them with respect and dignity and let them manage themselves.

Harry Quadracci and the other mavericks, I argue, aligned their companies with human nature by feeding the five social appetites that are the topic of this book. Quadracci's employee-centric approach resulted in both spectacular growth for the company and seven consecutive years on *Fortune* magazine's 100 Best Companies to Work For list. Quad/Graphics is a social experiment that succeeded spectacularly!

Quadracci's approach worked because it meshed with the emotional architecture of his workers. In other words, human beings function best in intensely personal, committed, and invested work groups. This sort of tribal setting is the natural habitat for a social species such as ours.

So what was the outcome of Quadracci's employee-centric behavior? It was a printing company that stunned the competition with its innovation and productivity. Quad/Graphics was also nimble. It could erect a printing plant in half the time of its competitors, run the presses faster than their rated capacity, and out-innovate the competition. Quad/Graphics produced a superior product at a reasonable cost.

Quadracci's formula resulted in a fantastic growth rate. Quad/Graphics went from a shoestring start-up operation in 1971 to a company with $500 million in yearly revenues in 1984. It now employs 12,000 people and has yearly revenues of nearly $2 billion.[10] *Inc.*, *Forbes*, and other national business magazines featured Harry in their publications between 1980 and 2002. Quadracci's success was remarkable by any measure, but more so considering that he triumphed in a mature, slow-growth industry with entrenched competitors and with a management team dominated by high school graduates.[11] Quad/Graphics is a classic example of a superorganism. It is also a personal favorite because I worked there for six months while I was getting my MBA at the University of Chicago. Harry hit on something fundamental about human nature. He put a round peg in a round hole and discovered that human beings will manage themselves if they are part of a committed, tight-knit group. His ideas will work in any industry—service or manufacturing, profit or nonprofit—that is populated with human beings. If you want to create a productive superorganism filled with dedicated employees, follow Quadracci's example.

Ken Iverson was the business maverick who created the largest superorganism, Nucor Steel. Nucor has grown into a $14 billion dynamo in the steel industry based on Iverson's simple idea, ". . . aligning worker interests with management and shareholder interests through an egalitarian meritocracy largely devoid of class distinctions."[12] In other words, Nucor's path to dominance in the steel industry was to become a very large tribe—a superorganism just like Quad/Graphics and Semco SA. I quote Iverson often because he eloquently describes the essence of egalitarian, trust-based management.

My hat goes off to the three mavericks. They pulled it off. They proved that companies that align themselves with human nature are both incredibly productive and incredibly rewarding places to work. Ricardo Semler, the South American maverick, describes management that aligns with human nature as "the third way" or "natural business"—not capitalism, not socialism, but something that is simultaneously more trusting, productive, exhilarating, and, in every sense, rewarding.[13] Semler believes that the purpose of business is not to make money, but to make the workers, whether working stiffs or top executives, feel good about life. This is similar to the main tenet of *Primal Management*—that nature wants human beings to feel good (experience the five productive pleasures) when they do good work.

Semler's contrarian, employee-centric approach attracted tremendous interest in the business community. He has given hundreds of speeches at companies, conferences, and universities like Harvard, MIT, Stanford, and the London School of Economics. Seventy-six universities feature Semco in their case studies and sixteen master's and PhD theses have been written about the company. Hundreds of newspaper stories have been written and dozens of television programs have profiled Semco.

Semler's contrarian approach to management has motivated some of the world's most respected companies to make pilgrimages to a nondescript industrial complex on the outskirts of São Paulo, Brazil, including IBM, General Motors, Ford, Kodak, Bayer, Nestlé, Goodyear, Firestone, Pirelli, Alcoa, Chase Manhattan, Siemens, Dow Chemical, Mercedes Benz, and Yashica.[14] For a while, Semco led twice-weekly tours of its facilities for groups consisting of thirty-five companies at a crack. These tours were eventually canceled because employees began feeling like animals in a zoo.[15]

CEOs have jealously eyed Semco's successes in terms of profitability, growth, sustainability, turnover, productivity, and innovation—like peering at a pot of gold on the far side of a deep chasm. Few, however, have been willing to cross what they perceived to be a wobbly, fraying rope bridge to get there. Most executives were unwilling to discard their security blankets—the sacred core precepts of traditional management—to get to Semler's pot of gold because the risks seemed to outweigh the potential benefits. This is where *Primal Management* comes in. It lays out a rock-solid business rationale for energizing the workplace based on cutting-edge science. It replaces Semler's wobbly-looking rope bridge with a sturdy four-lane highway. *Primal Management* allows you to emulate the mavericks, but without appearing soft, unbusinesslike, or unconventional.

You may have noticed that the three mavericks worked their magic inside factories dominated by blue-collar employees. The same employee-centric principles will work inside any workplace, white collar or blue collar, because they mesh with our underlying nature.

I have personally seen employee-centric ideas applied successfully inside a university hospital staffed with doctors and nurses and inside a large design firm staffed with professional architects and engineers. Authors like Peters and Waterman (*In Search of Excellence*) and Jim Collins (*Good to Great*), have found maverick-like policies at the cores of the excellent/great companies they researched—which spanned the spectrum from manufacturing to retail to professional services companies. Bottom line, these ideas will work for any company populated with human beings.

Primal Management provides a synergistic blend of theory and practice. The three mavericks and the excellent/great companies supply much of the practice (what works) while I supply the theory to explain why it works. The practice element is more powerful and convincing because of the theory, and vice versa.

I think there is an urgent need for this book because too many companies and business schools still downplay the "people factor." They focus on the tools and analytical techniques necessary to organize, coordinate, and monitor a business, but they don't emphasize the leadership skills needed to energize and empower it.[16] I think it's time for the corporate world to wise up and begin aligning itself with the emotional forces that engender passion and commitment inside organizations. *Primal Management,* and the three mavericks, show you how to morph your company into a superorganism by feeding the five social appetites that drive high performance.

CHAPTER 1

THE FIVE SOCIAL APPETITES THAT DRIVE HIGH PERFORMANCE

IS THERE A PROBLEM?

Perhaps corporate America is already optimally productive and perfectly aligned with human nature. In this case, there would be no need to muck around with a messy topic like emotion in the first place. Decades of employee engagement surveys by the Gallup Organization, Towers Perrin, and others suggest otherwise. They indicate an employee engagement crisis of mammoth proportions.

The Gallup Organization has studied employee engagement for more than forty years. Gallup defines employee engagement as "employee involvement in and enthusiasm for their work." Gallup defines its three categories of employee engagement as follows:

1. *Engaged.* Employees work with passion and feel a profound connection to their company. They drive innovation and move the company forward.

2. *Disengaged.* Employees are essentially "checked out." They're sleepwalking through their workday, putting time—but not energy or passion—into their work.

3. *Actively Disengaged.* Employees are not just unhappy about their work, they are busy acting out their unhappiness. Every day, these workers undermine what their engaged coworkers accomplish.

According to a 2005 Gallup engagement survey, the average percentages in the United States break down as follows: 31 percent engaged, 52 percent disengaged, and 17 percent actively disengaged.[1] If the Gallup survey were a college exam, what grade would we give corporate America for employee motivation? Considering that only 31 percent of employees care about their work, I'd give traditional hierarchical bureaucratic management a solid "F."

The financial fallout for failing "Employee Motivation 101" is staggering. Gallup estimates that the actively disengaged workers, alone, cost the U.S. economy $370 billion in lost productivity annually and over $1 trillion if you include indirect costs.[2] The Gallup research has identified robust statistical relationships between employee engagement and earnings per share, productivity, profitability, reduced employee turnover, and reduced on-the-job accidents.[3] The Gallup Organization concluded, "This research into earnings per share provides powerful proof that employee engagement correlates to crucial business outcomes."[4]

The engagement research demonstrates a substantial misalignment between corporate policies and human nature. If I were to give it a number, I'd say traditional management policies deviate from nature's optimal vector by around 70 degrees, resulting in major inefficiencies and lost productivity.

One Hundred Best Places to Work

Companies that work harmoniously with human nature, like the companies on *Fortune* magazine's 100 Best Companies to Work For list, would presumably harvest more energy from their workforces and therefore perform better than their less enlightened peers.

A recent study by the Wharton finance professor Alex Edmans indicates they do. Between 1998 and 2005, companies on the list posted shareholder returns averaging 14 percent compared to returns of only 6 percent per year for the overall market.[5]

What, exactly, do the 100 Best Companies to Work For do to align themselves with human nature? According to the Great Place to Work Institute, the organization that compiles the *Fortune* list, the best workplaces excel at creating bonds between employees and management, between employees and their jobs/company, and between the employees themselves. Here is how the Great Place to Work Institute describes the best companies on its list:

> [T]rust between managers and employees is the primary defining characteristic of the very best workplaces.
>
> At the heart of our definition of a great place to work—a place where employees "trust the people they work for, have pride in what they do, and enjoy the people they work with"—is the idea that a great workplace is measured by the quality of the three, interconnected relationships that exist there.[6]

I wholeheartedly agree with the Great Place to Work Institute—trust-based relationships are vitally important. They are the sinew of a corporate superorganism. Creating these relationships is step one on the road to organizational greatness. Fostering pride is also hugely important. According to my social appetite theory, it is step two on the road to sustained excellence. Policies that promote relationships and pride feed, by themselves, two important social appetites—the cooperation appetite (Chapter 4) and the competency appetite (Chapter 5).

The companies on the 100 Best Companies to Work For list do a great job of aligning themselves with human nature and harvesting the potential energy of their employees. This is not to say, however, that they align perfectly. If a typical corporate hierarchy harvests, say, 30 percent of the available energy of its workforce, a company on the 100 Best Companies list might harvest 60 percent. If I'm right, this leaves substantial room for improvement. Imagine what would happen if companies could align perfectly with human nature and capture 100 percent of the energy of their workforces! This may seem like an unrealistic goal, but it is precisely what I am aiming at in *Primal Management.*

Corporate America Is Due for a Lifestyle Change

All the hyperrational business strategies and tactics in the world will not alter employee engagement scores. In fact, hyperrational business policies are the *cause* of the employee engagement crisis, not the solution. The ceaseless quest for the next increment of efficiency has produced machinelike workplaces that stifle human nature instead of empowering it.

The solution to the employee engagement problem is not another layer or hyperrational business strategy. The solution to the engagement crisis resides deep within the realm of interpersonal relationships, commitment, and leadership. Corporations will not make a dent in the engagement problem until they undergo a fundamental lifestyle shift—until they are born again. Twenty-first-century corporations need to reject pure rationalism and learn to work synergistically with the motivational mechanism that energizes human behavior. Cool, emotionless, machinelike workplaces are yesterday's news because they throw ice water on nature's elegant motivational mechanism. In addition, such workplaces are not fit for the turbulent global marketplace where innovation and flexibility are top priorities.

Emotion's Bad Rap

The business community is partly justified in viewing emotions with disdain and trepidation. Emotions are often extreme and lead to unfortunate outcomes. I'm sure you've had emotional meltdowns or have witnessed friends or loved ones "lose it." Emotions can also be extreme and overpowering in emergency situations. These flareups can send us careening uncontrollably into an emotional pileup. When businesspeople refer to emotions as irrational, this is what they are talking about—pure passion without rational control.

Emotional pileups are just the highly visible tip of the emotional iceberg. They are memorable for their intensity and the damage they can cause to our careers and relationships. This does not diminish, however, the vital role of the larger, submerged part of the iceberg—the subtle, background feelings that ensure our survival by getting us out of bed in the morning and by imperceptibly influencing every decision and every move we make during the course of our workday.

We are not interested in the visible part of the iceberg in this book. Our target is the larger, but poorly explored, mass of ice below the waterline. We are going to strap on scuba tanks, so to speak, and explore this uncharted territory—the subtle emotional incentives that operate on the edge of conscious awareness to motivate day-to-day achievement.

Did You Hear About the Revolution?

We are not alone in our quest to explore nature's subtle incentives. The scientific community, armed with improved brain-imaging technologies and other advanced tools, is energetically exploring the same uncharted territory. The study of emotion has gone from the back burner to the front burner over the past twenty-five years and it is now one of the hottest fields in science. Recent discoveries in biology and neuroeconomics will greatly assist us in our quest to reverse engineer the motivational mechanism.

The scientific community gave the study of emotion the "cold shoulder" for most of the twentieth century and the business community looked at emotions as soft, irrational, and unbusinesslike.[7] I personally experienced this anti-emotion bias as recently as 1985 when I entered a PhD program in educational psychology at the University of Wisconsin, Madison. When I informed my adviser that I wanted to do my thesis on the relationship between emotional incentives and academic achievement, he said, "No way, that's impossible here." The Ed-Psych Department, he explained, was dominated by cognitive psychologists, some of whom denied that emotions even existed. Most cognitive psychologists in the mideighties viewed the brain as a computer-like mechanism based on pure logic and rational thought. There was no room for emotions in their Spockian formulation. These guys, I thought to myself, epitomized what was wrong with modern education. It denied the very existence of the motivational engine.

The status of emotions changed dramatically in the late 1980s with the development of PET scanners and other advanced brain-imaging technologies. Scientists finally had the quantitative tools necessary to peer into the brain and see emotions in action. The revolution in brain-scanning technology sparked a scientific revolution in neurobiology, especially the neurobiology of emotion. Major universities have institutes full of expensive technology dedicated to unraveling the biologic underpinnings of emotion. The resurgence in interest in emotions is not a fad, but a tectonic shift that is going to shake our world. The latest research demonstrates that emotions are intertwined with every thought and every decision we make.

The neurobiologic revolution has, in turn, sparked a revolution in economics. Economists, working in close cooperation with neurobiologists, have designed brain-imaging experiments based upon game theory to explore the brain's decision-making apparatus. These experiments indicate that all forms of reward, monetary or otherwise, depend upon feelings.[8] When players in an economic game plan their monetary strategy, the dopamine reward system in the basal striatum—the same brain area that processes food, sexual, and drug-related rewards—lights up on the brain scans. These experiments indicate that there is only one reward metric for human beings—sensations of pleasure and pain emanating from the basal striatum. Neuroeconomic research is putting feelings and emotions where they belong—at the core of economic decision making.

In another set of neuroeconomic experiments, the neuropeptide oxytocin, the relationship hormone, was administered by nasal spray to subjects playing the ultimatum game—an economic game where players can share a monetary reward if they cooperate with one another. Players who received the oxytocin spray were far more generous with their partners than those who received a placebo spray.[9] It is postulated that oxytocin produces pleasurable, trusting feelings by stimulating the basal striatum. These positive feelings, in turn, are thought to motivate the generous behavior—another example of feelings affecting economic decision making.[10]

The bottom line is that you no longer need to whisper when you talk about emotion in a business setting because it has finally been proven that feelings and emotions inhabit the very core of economic decision making. I will demonstrate in this book that emotions rule in business and in life because they encapsulate the fundamental survival needs of our species. In the future, managers will embrace emotions and put them front and center on the management dashboard because they are the fundamental forces that make human beings go!

THE FIVE SOCIAL APPETITES THAT DRIVE HUMAN ACHIEVEMENT

The goal of this book is to describe the best way to motivate human beings. We want to align perfectly with human nature and thereby foster optimally productive and engaged employees. Aligning with human nature, I will demonstrate, means aligning with the motivational mechanism and the five social appetites that power it. Employees at firms that align with human nature will feel good at the end of the day—better, perhaps, than when they arrived in the morning. Pleasure is nature's way of informing us that our actions are aligned with survival—which is what human nature is all about.

The social appetites, as described in the introduction, are simple survival mechanisms that obey rules and logic. The remainder of this chapter will describe these orderly mechanisms in a way that even an engineer, CFO, COO, or mathematician could love.

It would seem, at first glance, that *logic* and *emotions* are incompatible terms. One signifies clarity and the other implies subtlety and complexity. If this is your view, then it may need some revising. Appetites, drives, and emotions are based on a hard and immutable logic—the logic of survival. Illogical or unproductive systems don't ultimately survive nature's evolutionary test track.

Hunger is certainly a useful component of the motivational mechanism. The survival logic for this familiar biologic appetite is simply "eat or die." Pretty clear, wouldn't you agree?

Here is another example of survival logic. Try holding your breath for two minutes. What is the survival logic for the sensation that your chest is about to implode? The logic, again, is simple—"breathe or die." Are you starting to get the picture? Everything that is absolutely crucial for survival is governed by regulatory feelings of pleasure and pain. Nature does not leave the necessities of life to chance! This is the fundamental premise of *Primal Management*, so think about it carefully before proceeding.

Regulatory feelings of pleasure and pain govern the following biologic necessities: nutrition (hunger), hydration (thirst), oxygenation of the blood (pain of not breathing), protection from physical damage (sensory pain), energy conservation (pleasure of relaxation), and reproduction (sexual and romantic pleasures).[11]

What about social regulation? Is the social domain unregulated, or do human beings possess social appetites and drives that are analogous to the traditional biologic ones? I will prove that nature's design is symmetric and that our social world is just as rigorously and comprehensively regulated as our biologic one (see Figure 1-1). Nature did not abandon the theme of regulatory sensations when faced with the challenge of producing a social, technology-driven primate. Rather, nature's theme of using pleasure and pain to regulate human behavior was turned outward to regulate group behavior, like an appetite turned inside out. Here are five social needs that are so crucial for human survival that they are regulated by feelings of pleasure and pain.

Social Appetite #1: The Cooperation Appetite

A lone human being wandering the Serengeti Plain is just lion bait. A group of human beings, however, working as a tightly coordinated team, are a force to be reckoned with. Cooperation is vital for our species, and

Figure 1-1.   The biologic and social appetites.

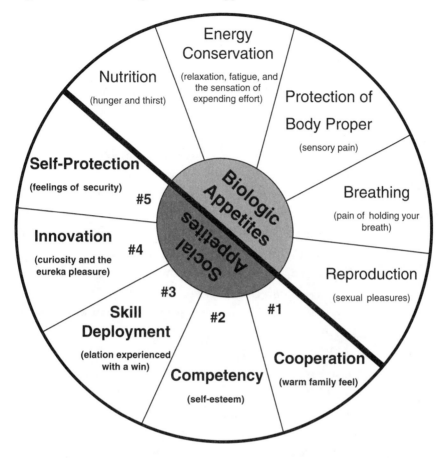

nature did not leave it to chance. Nature incorporated a bonding circuit into our psyches that I call the cooperation appetite.

The cooperation appetite is the most important social appetite in the motivational mechanism. It supplies the emotional glue that holds groups together. I will refer to it as the gateway appetite because we cannot ignite the other social appetites without first creating a tightly bonded social group, a tribe.

Cooperation is partly regulated by an area at the front of the brain, the ventromedial prefrontal cortex, which tracks our social investments.[12] In subsequent chapters I refer to this brain area as "the vault." Everything into which we freely invest energy becomes merged into our sense of self, our personal identity, our vault. Consider, for a moment, the tremendous investment parents make in their children. This investment incorporates the invested child into the parents' psychic vault. The parent subsequently protects the child as part of self. If the child is threatened, the parent feels the threat. If the child has success, the parent feels the success.

This simple example illustrates a more general truth—that the brain tracks all of our investments in children, friends, and co-workers. It even tracks our emotional investments in hobbies, pets, career, sports, and conventional assets like money and property. The totality of the investment portfolio creates our sense of self, which is something we own and protect.

Psychiatrists call this identity-merging process *cathexis*. Cathexis is the almost magical process that underlies all relationships and it is the single most important idea in this book. Chapter 4 explores this stealthy and mysterious process in more detail because it lies at the core of the motivational mechanism.

This identity-merging process may explain why the CEOs profiled in Jim Collins's best seller *Good to Great* put the well-being of their organizations ahead of their personal well-being.[13] These CEOs valued their organizations and honestly invested in them and thereby brought their organizations inside of themselves. After that, the CEO and the company were one and the same.

The neuropeptides oxytocin and vasopressin are also involved in the bonding process. When people show interest in us, or assist us in some way, oxytocin and vasopressin are released and we experience warm, friendly feelings for that person.[14] In subsequent encounters we are likely to work cooperatively with someone who has been generous toward us. We also experience these warm feelings when we contemplate the people, places, or things we have invested in, be it a child, workmate, or family pet.[15] Vasopressin and oxytocin are probably also involved in creating the warm family feeling reported inside great companies.[16]

Two percent of the population does not respond normally to oxytocin and does not experience warm feelings for the important people in their lives. Not surprisingly, these individuals have personality traits similar to sociopaths and generally lack empathy for their fellow human beings.[17]

Any workplace that encourages commitment and investment can

achieve something miraculous: a united tribe in which each person is psychologically bonded to the group and one another. The extreme opposite is a hierarchical workplace, dominated by fear, where no voluntary investment occurs. This sort of workplace will be inhabited by warring clans who battle one another for resources. Chapter 4 suggests a two-step process for helping your employees, and you, merge into a psychologically bonded superorganism.

Social Appetite #2: The Competency Appetite

Human beings are primarily skill-based creatures as opposed to instinctual creatures. We must master the survival skills of our tribe in order to survive. Nature uses pleasant feelings of high self-esteem to reward us when we are competent and painful feelings of low self-esteem to punish us when we are incompetent. These feelings are regulated by the neurotransmitter serotonin and serotonin 2 receptors in the medial prefrontal cortex and amygdala. Antidepressant drugs, like Prozac, artificially increase serotonin levels in the brain and thereby boost the patient's confidence and self-esteem.[18] The illegal drug *ecstasy* also stimulates the serotonin system and boosts feelings of self-esteem and confidence.[19]

Self-esteem is the highest denomination of emotional currency because it represents an ongoing annuity of good feelings about ourselves as opposed to a one-time payment. Companies that tap into this vital form of emotional currency will have happier and more productive employees because employees will receive a much larger emotional paycheck at the end of the day, the paycheck that ultimately matters to them the most. The competency appetite does more than encourage competence. I demonstrate in Chapter 5 that it provides the propulsive forces that make culture possible in the first place.

Social Appetite #3: The Skill-Deployment Appetite

Nature not only rewards human beings for mastering skills, but also for deploying them over and over again to achieve goals.[20] Whenever we deploy a skill successfully, we get a brief euphoric high, like the feeling of hitting a long drive down the middle of the fairway.[21] This feeling quickly fades, which is nature's signal to do it again—deploy another skill! The neurotransmitter dopamine, and dopamine 1 and dopamine 2 receptors in the basal striatum, help regulate these brief achievement-related highs. The dopamine reward system is the same brain system targeted by addictive drugs like cocaine and methamphetamine.

Type-A high achievers live for this feeling. It's their "neurotransmitter of choice." Human beings participate in sports, play Monopoly, solve math problems, and pull the one-armed bandit at the casino for one reason—we love dopamine. If a laboratory rat is allowed to self-administer cocaine, which increases dopamine concentrations in the basal striatum, the rat will generally self-administer until it dies from starvation.[22] Cocaine is an addictive drug for human beings because it pulls the dopamine lever—hard.

Imagine a world without the dopamine incentive. It would be a different world—a lazy world! If your workplace seems lethargic, then perhaps your tribe isn't being stimulated enough to get its requisite dose of dopamine. Chapter 6 is a how-to guide for developing a dopamine-rich workplace environment where everyone values the corporate game and plays to win. The alternative is a workplace full of disengaged underachievers who don't value the game and who view work as a dreadful chore.

Social Appetite #4: The Innovation Appetite

Human beings are, relatively speaking, slow, weak, and poorly armed. If we didn't compensate for these physical shortcomings with technology, we would certainly be extinct. Innovation is therefore a vital necessity for Homo sapiens, and nature allocated several important pleasures to make sure we innovate.

Curiosity is a major innovation-related pleasure and most human beings love it. Curiosity (the pleasure of novelty) encourages human beings to explore, learn, and innovate. Curiosity motivates human beings to go hiking in the wilderness, watch nature shows on TV, conduct research, visit zoos, and go on exotic vacations. The neurotransmitter dopamine, and dopamine 4 receptors in the ascending dopamine projections, have been implicated in regulating the pleasurable sensations associated with curiosity.[23]

There is another pleasure associated with innovation—the eureka moment experienced when we get an idea. I, for one, live for the eureka pleasure. It appears to be created by mu-opioid receptors in the association cortices in conjunction with the dopamine reward system in the basal striatum.[24] Creative employees crave the pleasures emanating from the innovation appetite and will not stay around long if they don't get them. Chapter 7 pops the hood on the innovation appetite and explores its component parts.

Social Appetite #5: The Self-Protection Appetite

The self-protection appetite, as its name implies, is designed to keep us safe and secure. The self-protection appetite's key component is the amygdala, a brain area that scans the environment for impending threats. If threats are detected, the amygdala reflexively triggers anxiety and fear by releasing the neurotransmitters norepinephrine and serotonin, the corticosteroid hormone cortisol, and corticotropin-releasing factor (CRF).[25] When threats are absent in the environment, a different brain area, the dorsal striatum, makes us feel safe and secure.

The self-protection appetite is the one that dispassionate, hierarchical companies rely on most. These companies, I will argue, motivate their employees using a simplistic carrot (money) and stick (fear) approach. This approach is outmoded and harmful, and creates companies that sputter instead of roar.

The stick—the fear of being fired—is easy to use. Even novices, with little understanding of human nature, can get people moving by threatening them with a stick. Overuse of the stick, however, triggers the brain's defensive systems via the amygdala and spawns a workforce composed of enemies who work against a company's interests rather than for it— hardly a prescription for improved productivity.

Employees bring major investments in education and career experience into the workplace, and these social assets are automatically at risk because of the ever-present fear of being fired. Investments in family and property are also at risk because loss of a paycheck would threaten these investments too. Investments in friends are at risk because being fired might tarnish one's reputation and therefore one's social desirability. It is not very sporting to take advantage of employees by threatening their core investments with a stick. This Neanderthal-like approach has got to go.

Chapter 8 describes a more humane, pleasure-based alternative to using the stick. This approach respects employees' core investments and strives to keep employees on the safe and secure side of nature's pleasure-pain spectrum. Instead of threatening employees' core investments, great leaders help employees protect and expand their key investments—and thereby build trust instead of distrust.

I am not suggesting that these five social appetites *might* exist; rather, I'm saying they *do* exist. The logic of survival demands them. Once nature started down the path of using pleasure and pain to guide human behavior and decision making, there was no turning back because behaviors lacking emotional incentives simply wouldn't occur. In other words, why would the rational mind choose an option with no reward over an option with emotional reward? It wouldn't. Feelings are ubiquitous. We swim though a sea of them every day. Every thought and every action is, in reality, emotional.

IMPLICATIONS OF THE FIVE SOCIAL APPETITES

Please review Figure 1-1 carefully. It represents the distillation of thirty years of pondering emotions. Figure 1-1 depicts the guts of nature's motivational mechanism! If the social and biologic appetites depicted in Figure 1-1 were somehow turned off, human beings would drop to the ground and remain there because they would have no incentive to get back up.

In the Introduction I suggested that companies should align themselves with human nature in order to achieve optimum performance from their workforces. Now we can see what that direction looks like—a set of five social appetites that regulate human survival and motivate every action occurring in the workplace. Companies that align with human nature by feeding these vital appetites will harvest more motivational energy than those that don't. It's as simple as that.

Like it or not, people focus their energies where they get the most emotional satisfaction, the most pleasure. The scientific term for pleasure seeking is *hedodynamy*—the universal human motivation to avoid painful or distressing feelings and to search for pleasant and agreeable ones.[26] If business leaders want their employees to focus their energies at work, they must understand how to ignite these natural productive pleasures in the workplace. In other words, they must craft a workplace game that human beings will instinctively enjoy playing.

Companies that ignore the motivational mechanism and its productive pleasures will get what they deserve, actively disengaged rather than engaged employees. Companies that ignore the social appetites will have a hard time competing with companies full of passionate, well-fed employees.

Components of Employee Satisfaction

When employees fill out a conventional satisfaction survey, they are essentially reporting how they feel. Figure 1-1 refines the concept of employee satisfaction by subdividing workplace emotions into five dimensions of feeling.

Companies could conceivably improve employee satisfaction by feeding just the biologic appetites depicted in Figure 1-1. They could, for example, provide employees with gourmet meals served by attractive waiters and waitresses. This would satisfy two biologic appetites simultaneously and thereby contribute to employee satisfaction, but it might also distract employees from the business tasks at hand. Feeding the biologic appetites is possible, but perhaps an ill-advised and inefficient route to improving employee satisfaction and performance.

Feeding the social appetites, on the other hand, is highly desirable because these appetites, unlike the biologic appetites, are tied directly to productive behaviors that corporations covet: innovation, skill mastery, goal attainment, and teamwork. Instead of feeding employees gourmet meals, I suggest that managers create a tribal ecosystem that satisfies the primal human desires to belong, develop skills, achieve group goals, invent, and feel protected.

Money Is a Feeling-Based Concept

The default tools to motivate employees are (1) money: "do it because I pay you" and (2) fear: "do it or I will fire you." This Neanderthal-like, carrot-and-stick approach to motivation is crude and inefficient because it fails to fully engage the motivational mechanism.

My MBA course in compensation suggested using wages, options, profit-sharing, bonuses, and vesting to motivate employees. This book takes a wider view of monetary compensation by proposing that all compensation, monetary or otherwise, is inherently emotional or feeling-based. What's more, monetary compensation can be broken down into constituent emotional components: (1) money in the bank lessens anxiety and thus reduces pain—a feeling; (2) a large paycheck is a symbol of achievement that boosts self-esteem, which is an ongoing pleasurable state; and (3) money can be converted into a myriad of emotionally satisfying goods and services, like a great meal or an exciting vacation.

In Chapter 9 I argue that the concept of *economic utility*—a measure of the relative happiness or satisfaction (gratification) gained by consuming different bundles of goods and services—is a feeling-based concept, as are the concepts of employee satisfaction and employee engagement. Economic utility, I propose, can be subdivided into the ten component feelings depicted in Figure 1-1—all of which are tied directly to human survival.[27]

I demonstrate that the only true way to rouse a human being from his or her slumber is with emotional incentives, and the true paycheck recognized by the human brain is the emotional one. In other words, emotions and feelings are the fundamental currency of the human mind and this currency comes in five denominations that correspond to the productive feelings emanating from the five social appetites.

Flawed Accounting System

The business community has traditionally used a flawed accounting system to measure employee incentives. It accounts for every penny of the traditional paycheck and benefits (extrinsic rewards) but has utterly failed to account for the intrinsic, but equally important, incentives that accrue whenever human beings interact productively with one another. It makes neuroeconomic sense to consider extrinsic and intrinsic rewards as equivalent and additive because intrinsic rewards activate precisely the same reward center, the basal striatum, as monetary rewards.[28] Since both extrinsic and intrinsic rewards are ultimately based on a common feeling metric, why hasn't the business community come up with a mechanism to measure both intrinsic and extrinsic rewards with equal fidelity and thereby capture the overall emotional paycheck?

In Chapter 2, I describe a more nuanced and accurate accounting system that tallies the whole paycheck, both extrinsic (monetary pay) and intrinsic (the five productive pleasures that drive human achievement). The improved accounting system involves an emotional health survey (Horsepower Survey™) to collect reward data and two metrics to analyze the results. This improved accounting system will hopefully lead to more informed and productive decision making on the part of management.

Pleasure-Based Management

As described above, the social appetites, just like the biologic appetites, are powered by feelings of pleasure and pain. Whenever these biologic or social appetites are fed, we feel good. In other words, we are meant to feel good every time we act in a way that serves survival, or as neurobiologist Antonio Damasio artfully put it, nature "seduces us into good behavior."[29] If the social appetites are not fed, we experience the painful side of the pleasure/pain spectrum in the form of frustration, depression, boredom, fear, and stress.

I suggest that human beings not only crave nature's productive pleasures; we are addicted to them. People who can't experience these pleasures naturally often obtain them unnaturally though the use of illicit drugs like cocaine and methamphetamine.[30] People who don't experience nature's productive pleasures at work will seek them outside the workplace in activities like sports and hobbies.

Companies basically have two choices for motivating employees— motivate with the carrot (the five productive pleasures) or motivate with the stick (fear). I argue in Chapter 8 that carrot-based management is generally the way to go.

IMPLEMENTATION WITHIN
A LARGE ORGANIZATION

I sincerely hope that CEOs and other top executives will resonate with the ideas in *Primal Management* and want to implement them throughout their organizations. Perhaps the easiest way to implement these ideas is to introduce them under a marketing banner: an approach called internal branding or employee branding. Even the most traditional, risk-averse organization should respond positively to this approach.

I assume that your organization is already proficient in marketing its products and services to external customers. Internal branding takes the concepts of external marketing and turns them inward on the organization itself. Instead of satisfying the needs of your external customers, internal branding focuses on satisfying the needs of your internal customers, your employees. Just as external marketing determines customer needs through surveys and customer focus groups, internal branding uses the very same marketing tools on employees. The last step in the traditional marketing process is to devise a product or service that satisfies the customer's needs. Similarly, the final step in the internal branding process is to design a work environment that satisfies the basic needs of your employees.

Managers understand marketing and will immediately latch on to the internal branding concept. The internal branding approach provides a brilliant, businesslike, nonthreatening format for discussing subtle employee needs. You can justify the internal branding discussions as either an employee engagement initiative to improve productivity or as a talent-retention and recruiting initiative to reduce employee turnover. All of the ideas in this book can be packaged neatly within the ensuing internal branding discussions.

The discussions of employee needs provide a perfect segue into discussing the five social appetites that are the focus of this book. While your organization is sorting out employee needs, you will already know most of the answers. Employee needs will inevitably revolve around the primal appetites to invent, master skills, achieve goals, work as a tightly bonded team, and feel protected. You will therefore have some of the answers to the exam before the test even starts!

You can start the internal branding process by administering the emotional health survey (needs survey) discussed in Chapter 2. The survey results can be used as a starting point for ensuing discussions (focus groups) with your employees.

The internal branding process will allow your employees to design their own dream workplace. Let them decide upon the tribal priorities, norms of behavior, and shared goals that support this dream workplace. Make this dream your brand image: the shared ideal against which all behavior inside the company is compared. The internal brand represents the core values of the tribe, its culture, its ten commandments.

The internal branding approach encourages employees to invest in and connect with one another simply by forcing them to confront tough issues—like what constitutes an ideal workplace and what values do we truly hold in common. Investing in the internal branding process may, paradoxically, create the invested bonds that make this approach so effective. The internal brand will have emotional power because it is agreed upon, not imposed. If someone falls short of the group's vision, he or she will not only have to answer to the tribe but also to the brain's internal disciplinarian—the competency appetite.

You, the leader, will need to embrace and model the shared values of the organization, so you had better involve yourself in the process. Internal branding is not something you can take lightly or delegate to Human Resources.

Now build your recruiting process around the internal brand image. When prospects interview, let your employees sell the group's value system and explain why your company is such a fabulous place to work.

IMPLEMENTATION WITHIN A WORK GROUP

If you are a manager or supervisor within a large, traditional bureaucracy, the internal branding idea might not work for you. In this case I recommend creating a productive, employee-centric ecosystem within your own department.

If you personally apply the ideas in *Primal Management* by wrapping your arms around your employees and taking personal responsibility for their health and well-being, I predict that your group will become markedly more productive and successful. Your colleagues may even ask for help in creating superorganisms of their own. Over time, your entire organization may follow this prescription and metamorphose into a superorganism, possibly with you as the tribal leader.

SUMMARY

We have logically derived something *very* important in this chapter. Human beings possess five social appetites that reward cooperation, competency, skill deployment, self-protection, and innovation with productive pleasures. These appetites function as an integrated system to propel human ingenuity, achievement, and survival. The productive pleasures associated with the five appetites motivate commitment, passion, and hard work, or, as Aristotle pronounced, "Pleasure in the job puts perfection in the work." Nature and business essentially want the same thing. They both want human beings to be active, to be productive, and to survive. Without this system of productive pleasures we would all be dead! Extinct! It's time for companies to align themselves with nature's productive pleasures and thereby tune their motivational mechanisms to peak efficiency.

Companies that understand the social appetites, and feed them, will have an important competitive edge in selling their products and motivating their workforces. Their businesses will resonate with confidence, creativity, enthusiasm, and commitment, precisely the attributes customers are looking for. This innovation may change how you view yourself and your world, and how you run your business. If you decide to opt in and switch to a more pleasure-based management style, you will not be alone. This is precisely how great companies become great!

If you work with human beings, you ought to understand nature's social appetites and the productive pleasures associated with them. They make the difference between a good company and a great company. The methodology I endorse creates a rare win-win scenario for employees, management, customers, and shareholders. Employees win because their emotional take-home pay increases. They're also more secure because the company becomes a superproductive superorganism that dominates the marketplace. Management wins because the company is more productive, efficient, innovative, and profitable. Managers also win because they develop authentic relationships with fired-up employees. Customers win because they get faster, better service from people who radiate good feelings. Shareholders win because they make money. Who wouldn't want this?

If you learn only one thing from this book, I hope it is a realization that *emotions rule* in every aspect of human behavior. The rational mind serves the emotions by figuring out how to fulfill our survival needs. Managers need to be clever, organized, and logical, but equally important, they need to understand the emotional "calculus" that runs the show.

I have wandered in an intellectual "wilderness" for thirty years in an attempt to unravel the underlying architecture of the social emotions. I believe I have made an important discovery—a set of social appetites that control human behavior in the workplace. I believe this discovery can help you, my tribe, survive and thrive in the unnatural environment you have built for yourselves. I think my discovery can help you convert the sterile enclosures of the modern workplace into productive, people-friendly ecosystems. If you applaud this discovery, it will magically become a thing of value that will spread organically through the corporate tribe.

The intent of this book is to reprogram your perspective, your worldview. Western culture has been hyperrational ever since the industrial revolution. You and I were brainwashed with an unrealistic worldview and we are tainted by it. Once you are recalibrated and heading in the right direction, you will naturally make decisions that are consistent with your new, more realistic view of human nature. You will not need a detailed laundry list of specific instructions, because once I get you on the right path, the steps forward will be more-or-less self-evident.

CHAPTER 2

MONITORING THE STATE OF REPAIR OF YOUR HUMAN CAPITAL

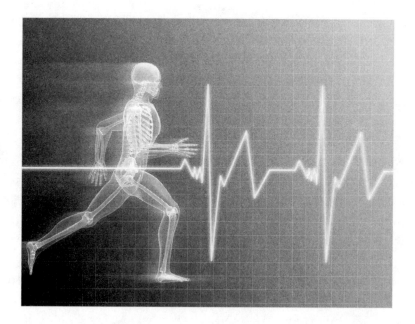

In Chapter 1 we learned that nature rewards us with pleasure when we master skills, deploy skills to achieve goals, innovate, work as a team, and protect ourselves from physical and psychological harm. If managers create work environments that feed the social appetites, then employees will feel great at the end of the day—better than when they arrived in the morning. Nature wants us to feel good as we leave work, just as it wants us to feel blissfully satiated after a wonderful meal. If your employees don't leave work with smiles on their faces, then something is wrong with your workplace! If employees feel bad when they leave work, then nature is saying, "These human beings are malfunctioning, and maintenance is needed." I describe a survey in this chapter that captures the output signals—the pleasurable and painful feelings—emanating from nature's motivational mechanism and metrics to help us visualize them.

Think of your workforce as an elaborate machine or engine for a moment. If you have 100 employees making $50,000 a year, then the annual rent for your human capital is $5 million. An actual machine of this value would be pampered and hovered over by trained technicians and monitored with elaborate sensors to make sure that it operated at its rated capacity. Its output would be measured and it would get regular tune-ups. Key parameters would be recorded and charted, minute-by-minute, in order to anticipate malfunctions before they occurred.

Human beings also come equipped with sophisticated sensors woven deeply into our brains. The outputs of these sensors are feelings of pleasure and pain. The emotional health survey captures the output from these "sensors" and the metrics—The Horsepower Metric™ and The Tune-Up Metric™—plot the data. The Horsepower Metric is essentially a control chart, just like the ones factory managers use to monitor the operational condition of their manufacturing equipment. If the Horsepower Metric reveals a problem, the Tune-Up Metric can be used to diagnose which social appetites are misfiring.

MEASURING THE EMOTIONAL PAYCHECK

The intrinsic rewards that employees experience when their social appetites are fed are nonverbal and feeling-based. The feelings that contribute to the emotional paycheck and are either positive or negative, pleasurable or painful. Some companies measure intrinsic rewards indirectly through annual employee satisfaction surveys, employee engagement surveys, or employee morale surveys. These surveys are helpful, but expensive and unnecessarily complex. They measure left-brain interpretations of feelings rather than the raw feelings themselves.

Annual surveys are too infrequent to supply real-time operational feedback. I suggest something radically different—an ongoing control chart, based on a simple monthly survey, to monitor intrinsic rewards in the workplace. This is Step 1 on the path to becoming a superorganism filled with engaged employees.

The question of how employees feel is deeply personal. Employees will not reveal this proprietary information unless they are certain it won't be used against them. The monthly survey is therefore anonymous and strictly confidential. I recommend that employers hire an outside consultant to collect and plot the data in order to protect anonymity. Transparency is also important, so I recommend posting the results.

I have developed a simple survey tool to measure the intrinsic rewards that contribute to the emotional paycheck. Employees are instructed to place a mark on seven scales that range from minus ten (painful) to plus ten (pleasurable). The first five scales measure the five emotions related to the five social appetites discussed in Chapter 1. Each social appetite contributes its own denomination of emotional currency to the overall emotional paycheck. The sixth scale measures stress: the employee's overall ability to cope with the workload. The seventh and final scale measures the overall emotional paycheck—how rewarded the employee feels overall.

Employees complete the emotional paycheck scale by mentally adding up all of their positive experiences for the month and then deducting all of their negative experiences (Note: This is more of a gut feel than a conscious accounting). The emotional paycheck scores are used to calculate the Horsepower Metric, which is then plotted as a function of time (see Figure 2-1 for a sample horsepower plot [weekly] for an actual work group). This metric is typically calculated monthly to track the fluctuating motivational horsepower, or intrinsic reward level, of the organization.

Figure 2-1. Horsepower metric, company XYZ.

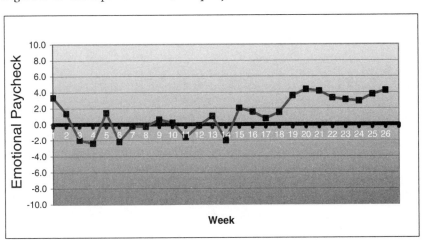

The Horsepower Metric

I chose the name the Horsepower Metric for obvious reasons. First of all, most male managers like talking about cars and engines far more than they like talking about emotions and feelings. Second, emotions propel human beings just like an automotive engine propels a car. We can go a step further by relating the five social appetites to the cylinders of an internal combustion engine. If you want a high-performance, high-horsepower workplace, the reasoning goes, then you should tune your work environment until employees run on all five motivational "cylinders" and experience all five variations of intrinsic reward. Chapters 4 through 8 explore the five cylinders in the engine, one by one. These chapters are like a "maintenance guide" for tuning the motivational engine.

On a more technical level, the Horsepower Metric measures intrinsic rewards. If the Horsepower Metric is negative, it means employees find it painful coming to work. If the metric is positive, it means employees derive intrinsic pleasure from their work. The Horsepower Metric lies at the core of our improved payroll accounting system. As I mentioned in Chapter 1, all rewards, monetary and otherwise, are registered as pleasurable or painful feelings in a brain structure called the basal striatum. Feelings, in other words, constitute the underlying currency in human affairs. By properly accounting for subtle intrinsic rewards, we gain a more accurate tally of the true paycheck that drives human productivity—the emotional paycheck.

In the following example, we are going to convert both monetary pay and intrinsic rewards into emotional reward units (ERUs). Let's consider the case of an employee who earns a monetary paycheck plus benefits that add up to ten ERUs of extrinsic reward that register as pleasurable feelings in the basal striatum. If this same employee is unable to innovate, develop and deploy skills, cooperate as part of a tightly bonded work group, or protect herself, then she will feel bad at the end of the pay cycle because her social appetites are being frustrated. These frustrations will register as painful feelings in the insula and anterior cingulate cortex[1] and translate into a deduction of, say, seven ERUs from the emotional paycheck. This employee's total paycheck is therefore only three ERUs (ten ERUs of extrinsic reward for salary and benefits minus a seven ERU deduction for unpleasant working conditions). The employee's motivation and productivity will reflect not her monetary wages but her overall emotional paycheck of just three ERUs.

This is a simple, but powerful, idea—an improved accounting system for incorporating intrinsic rewards into the overall paycheck. The only way to improve on this metric would be to monitor the neurotransmitters and neuropeptides that regulate feelings of reward in the basal striatum. If the trend line for the Horsepower Metric shows a downward deviation, management can diagnose the problem with the Tune-Up Metric and take action to remediate the problem before it affects the bottom line. The Tune-Up Metric is a diagnostic tool that looks at each of the social appetites individually to determine which cylinders are firing and which aren't. This metric allows managers to determine at a glance where they should focus their tune-up efforts. (Figure 2-4 on p. 55 shows an example of the Tune-Up Metric.)

The Horsepower Metric has many potential uses. If a company has just installed new leadership or has instituted a new policy, the Horsepower Metric allows management to assess the impact of the change on motivation. If Plant A has a high score and Plant B has a low score, management can investigate how Plant A is feeding the social appetites and copy it. If the Horsepower Metric takes an unexpected plunge, leadership can diagnose and address the cause of the malfunction using the Tune-Up Metric and authentic discussions with employees. This Horsepower Metric should be part of every company's management toolbox because *it is the master metric that drives everything else!* It also has a direct cause-and-effect relationship with hard business parameters such as customer satisfaction, profitability, innovation, and growth.[2]

When I interviewed a prominent executive in 1986, I wanted to ask him about his approach to people management, but he had something else in mind. He wanted to talk about his state-of-the-art information technology (IT) system. He explained how the IT system monitored every facet of production. The IT system generated a set of graphs at the end of the day that tracked key operational parameters for the factory. These graphs tracked things like daily production, waste, goods shipped, and the like. He explained that up-to-date information was the key to running a successful business. He said, "If I know what happened today, I will not have to worry about the company's performance at the end of the year. If I know what happened today, I can take care of any problems tomorrow so they don't affect the bottom line at the end of the year."

I wish I had invented the Horsepower Metric in 1986. I would have told him, "That makes sense, but it doesn't take the people into account. I don't see the Horsepower Metric anywhere on your management dashboard. How can you tell whether your human beings are malfunctioning?" Tracking motivational horsepower is clearly the logical thing to do. Managers should keep track of *all* the key parameters, including the motivational horsepower of the people who run the show.

GETTING THE HORSEPOWER TO GO UP

Monitoring the horsepower of the motivational engine is not for the faint of heart. It's a fickle parameter that is difficult to change. It will take four months, at a minimum, to get it to go up because this is how long it takes for human beings to develop trust.[3]

I received an e-mail some years ago from a gentleman named Bob Carpenter who had found an early version of *Primal Management* on my website and decided to contact me. I subsequently spoke with him about his fascinating experiences turning around struggling companies all over the world. Here is my recollection of our first conversation:

> *Paul, I've been a corporate turnaround artist for twenty-five years in thir-teen countries and I've always been successful. I used a formula similar to the one you recommend in* Primal Management. *Most of my assignments were in Third World countries where employees had been terribly mis-treated. The employees hated their managers, and they initially hated me. It took four months, on average, but I always turned things around by showing respect for the local culture, by attending their ceremonies, and by developing the human potential of each and every employee.*
>
> *At first they would resist and try to provoke me. They figured I was just another gringo trying to take advantage of them. If I stayed on course, however, things would eventually change and change suddenly. One day, out of the blue, instead of addressing me as Mr. Carpenter, they began calling me "Don Roberto." The prefix "Don" followed by one's given name is a sign of respect reserved for village elders. As soon as they started calling me Don Roberto, productivity improved rapidly. It was an all-or-nothing sort of thing.*[4]

Bob Carpenter's observations make perfect sense because human be-ings are guided by the group consensus. Carpenter won over converts, one by one, until the consensus of the tribe tipped in his favor. At this point, the remainder quickly followed suit. Bob's story illustrates some important truths: The horsepower of the motivational engine is hard to change, and you will not be successful unless you are in it for the long haul. When the horsepower finally changes, it will happen suddenly after months of effort.

If you manage to get your motivational horsepower into the positive five-to-eight range, congratulations! You've earned a black belt in leader-ship, one of the most difficult skills a human being can master! Your company is now equipped with an efficient, well-tuned engine and is ready to prosper in the twenty-first-century marketplace.

Value, Commit, Invest

The first step toward getting the motivational horsepower to go up, as the Bob Carpenter story illustrated, involves commitment. Motivational horsepower is not going to change, I suggest, unless managers: (1) value their employees, (2) commit to their employees, (3) invest in their employees, and (4) are willing to go to bat for their employees. In other words, managers and owners need to take personal responsibility for the health and welfare of their tribes. These four steps are absolutely necessary to becoming a consensus leader and creating a positive dynamic in the workplace. If managers aren't willing to do these things, then I cannot help them. They are stuck with what they've got—a motivational engine firing on only a few cylinders. If managers cannot commit, then they shouldn't expect their employees to commit either.

Something almost magical happens when managers overcome their inherent fear of commitment and sincerely invest in their employees. Employees subconsciously detect this commitment and investment and begin to commit and invest in return. This is the first step to becoming a consensus leader and creating a workplace full of engaged employees.

Commitment and Fear

Commitment is the key to creating a corporate superorganism, but human beings instinctively fear it. The brain automatically steers us away from commitments where the investment is large and the benefits are uncertain. The human brain is a powerful device but can track only 150 to 200 deeply bonded relationships. This processing limitation makes each relationship precious. Considering that we spend half of our working lives at work, however, it makes sense to allocate half of our relationships to the workplace.

When managers commit and invest, employees become merged with the manager's personal sense of identity. The manager's life becomes richer because the accomplishments of employees are experienced as the manager's personal accomplishments. Instead of experiencing cool detachment in the workplace, managers experience the warmth that comes with honest and meaningful relationships. Such managers would not deceive, manipulate, or otherwise harm employees, because it would feel like they were harming themselves.

CEOs and managers should routinely go beyond the call of duty for their employees. This is the quickest and most efficient path to creating a superorganism. When an employee has a serious problem, the CEO should be the first to respond. This is the fastest route to reaching the tipping point and creating a workplace full of engaged employees. Just think about the people in your life who have taken risks for you. How do you feel about these people today? If you simply cannot find the strength to commit, don't expect your employees to, either. If you want to run your company like a computer program, then don't be surprised if your crew sails left when you steer right, because human beings are not computers.

Commitment in Action

My good friend, Scott Ransom, has patiently endured my social appetite theory for the past thirteen years. In 2001, when Scott became the president and CEO of Marshall Erdman and Associates, a national designer, builder, and developer of health-care facilities, I became an adviser and confidant. Scott bounced many of his key people management ideas off of me, which I then analyzed according to my theory.

One day, while working out at a local health club, I suggested that Scott take his employee-centric management style to the next level. He responded, "What do you mean?" I said, "If an employee needs a kidney transplant, I want you to be the donor. If an employee has a house fire, I want you to save the family pet." Scott looked back at me with wide-eyed disbelief. I exaggerated my suggestion to make a point—you can't expect your employees to go beyond the call of duty for you if you are not prepared to do the same for them.

This one simple recommendation, if implemented with sincerity and authenticity by the CEO, can radiate throughout an organization and have far-reaching motivational consequences. Scott and I had many such discussions. They helped Scott to gradually distance himself from the conventional, impersonal approach to management he had been taught and take personal responsibility for the health and welfare of his employees—his tribe. In Scott's words, "If employees know you care, they will go through a wall for you." Scott's employees detected his sincere commitment and investment and reciprocated in return.

So what was the bottom-line outcome of Scott's experiment in employee-centric management? Honestly speaking, it was nothing short of amazing. Revenues almost doubled in a four-year period, profits increased 300 percent, employee engagement went from slightly below average to the top tenth percentile. Scott led a buyout of this fifty-seven-year-old family-held company, which included participation from forty managers and two outside investors in 2004. In 2008 the company merged with a publicly held health-care real estate company at a value of almost ten times the initial equity investment. One of the investors, a large, international, private equity firm, said it was one of the best returns on investment the company had realized in its twenty-three years in the private equity arena. The improved results resulted in generous bonuses, 15 percent annual retirement funding, and a sparkling new headquarters complete with an employee health club and Internet café.

Scott is a spectacular leader who balances business acumen with superb people skills. His success illustrates the benefits of balancing cool, analytical rationality with respect for the emotional and interpersonal sides of human nature.

IMPLEMENTATION

I hope I've made a compelling case for surveying the emotional health, or state of repair, of your human capital. I truly believe that every company, private or public, profit or nonprofit, should survey the emotional health of their employees on an ongoing basis. My survey and metrics provide a simple, logical mechanism for accomplishing this.

If you believe in the saying, "out of sight, out of mind," what could be more out of sight than the internal motivation of our employees. Motivation is one of the easiest things to ignore in the day-to-day rush to get projects and products out the door. It will be much harder to ignore when the Horsepower Metric appears on your desk, or computer screen, each month. Once managers get accustomed to the Horsepower and Tune-Up Metrics, I think they will come to rely upon these simple but powerful diagnostics and eagerly await their monthly results.

Survey Providers

The emotional health survey and metrics described in *Primal Management* can be procured from a number of certified technology partners. These partners can train your employees in the use of the survey, administer the surveys by e-mail, process the data, report the results, and provide benchmarking data to compare your horsepower to industry averages. These technology partners can be contacted by visiting thehorsepowermetric.com. I recommend using an outside, independent consultant for the survey in order to ensure employee anonymity and confidentiality. Employees will not divulge their intimate core feelings if anonymity cannot be guaranteed.

The emotional health survey I've developed is easy to implement on a large scale because it is short and simple. The survey itself consists of just seven pleasure/pain scales and takes less than two minutes to complete. The first five scales probe the feelings associated with the five social appetites. The sixth scale measures stress levels, and the final scale measures the emotional paycheck—the sum total of positive and negative intrinsic incentives experienced during the survey period.

Employees should receive training *before* taking the survey so they are familiar with the five social appetites and the feelings the survey is intended to measure. Feelings are often subtle and exist on the edge of conscious awareness. It may take a few survey cycles, therefore, before employees become consciously aware of these subtle motivating forces.

If you are a manager within a large traditional organization, you might want to consult with your human resources department before implementing the survey. Surveys are typically considered a human resources function, so you risk alienating your human resources director and causing problems down the road if you go it alone. Human resources departments should be interested in the survey and metrics, especially if the company is having problems attracting or retaining key talent or if there are employee engagement, productivity, or interpersonal-conflict issues.

Creating Your Own Survey

If you have a trusting workforce that isn't concerned about confidentiality, you may prefer to design and administer your own feeling survey. The first step is to develop a series of questions to probe the five dimensions of feeling that are the subject of this book. You might provide scales ranging from positive (pleasurable) to negative (painful) to record the answers to your questions as shown in Figure 2-2 (this figure is a simple paper version of the survey I used for an early beta test).

If your organization prohibits you from implementing a survey, for

Figure 2-2. Simple version of the survey from an early beta test.

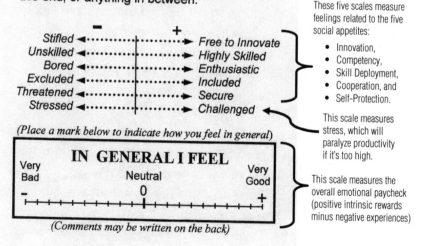

budgetary or other reasons, you can always do an informal survey on your own. Position yourself inconspicuously near the main entrance to your office and observe the facial expressions and body language of your employees as they file in to work. If you discern more apathy than enthusiasm, your motivational engine probably needs some tuning. Even without a survey and metrics, you can still implement the tune-up suggestions in *Primal Management*. In this case, let improved performance be your metric.

Assessing Employee Needs

In Chapter 1 I introduced internal branding as a businesslike way to incorporate employee needs into day-to-day management discussions without causing derisive snickers or suggestions that you are "going soft." If anyone tries to mock the internal-branding approach, remind them that corporate America generally earns a failing grade for employee motivation (Gallup statistics), and that companies that get the motivation part right, like the "100 Best Companies to Work For," perform far better financially (14 percent average shareholder returns according to the Wharton study cited earlier as opposed to just 6 percent for a typical company).[5]

Internal branding, as you may recall from Chapter 1, is a businesslike marketing-based approach to employee motivation that treats employees as internal customers. Just as with external marketing, internal branding assesses the needs of the internal customers and then designs a product—the workplace environment—that satisfies those needs. Satisfying the needs of your internal customers ought to translate into improved productivity, talent retention, and employee engagement.

Once your executive team has accepted the internal branding concept, the emotional health survey (needs survey) is a natural first step. We have already determined that all human beings hunger to innovate, to feel competent, to achieve goals, to work as part of a bonded team, and to feel protected. These are the basic needs that drive human achievement, and the emotional health survey is designed to accurately measure whether or not they are being satisfied.

Announcing the Survey to Your Employees

Announcing the emotional health survey to your employees should be a snap. After all, you are pointing them in a direction that leads directly to increased success and fulfillment. It shouldn't take long for your employees to catch on and realize that they should take the emotional health survey very seriously. You may hear comments like, "Nobody has ever bothered to ask me how I feel before."

Figure 2-3 is a sample letter that you can modify to announce the survey to your employees. Better yet, announce it with passion and in person. You should announce the survey confidently and in good conscience. Human beings need to innovate, master skills, achieve goals, and work as part of a tightly bonded team to remain mentally healthy. Leadership done right, in other words, provides a vital public service because human beings are built to be active and productive in the service of the tribe. Failure to be active and productive has serious psychological consequences, as we explore in Chapter 5.

Tuning the Engine

If the Horsepower Metric (see Figure 2-1) plots in the positive 4 to 8 range, congratulations: You have a well-tuned motivational engine and your employees enjoy their work. If the Horsepower Metric is negative, however, your workforce is malfunctioning, or emotionally malnourished, and corrective action is indicated. In this case, the Tune-Up Metric will tell you at a glance which social appetites are being fed and which are being starved (see Figure 2-4).

The Tune-Up Metric is a spider plot consisting of six axes radiating outward from a central point like the spokes on a wheel. The six axes present data from the first six pleasure/pain scales on the emotional health survey. If a social appetite is being fed, its corresponding axis on the Tune-Up Metric will plot outside the heavy black hexagon on the spider plot. If a social appetite is being starved, the corresponding axis on the Tune-Up Metric will plot inside the heavy black hexagon.

The Tune-Up Metric shown in Figure 2-4 indicates a reasonably well-tuned motivational engine because all of the social appetites plot in the

Figure 2-3. Example letter introducing survey.

Dear Employee,

I am respectfully asking all employees to participate in a monthly emotional-health monitoring program. I believe that a properly structured workplace should resonate with positive feelings, confidence, creativity, enthusiasm, and commitment. The monitoring program will help us determine if our motivational engine is well-tuned or sputtering.

You will receive a monthly e-mail from a technology provider containing a link to the online survey form. This monitoring program is anonymous, so please express your honest feelings on the survey form. The monitoring process is simple. Take a quiet moment to: (1) reflect on how you feel about your work experience and (2) document your feelings on the online "Emotional Health Survey Form."

Please use the following simple procedure to document your feelings.

- The form contains seven emotion scales, six to measure various components of workplace reward and a seventh scale at the bottom to measure overall reward.

- Click on each of the scales to indicate how you feel. You may select the positive end of the scale (I feel good), negative end (I feel bad), or anything in-between.

- Do not attempt to interpret how or why you feel a certain way, just report how you feel. Try to focus on your workplace experiences as opposed to feelings related to events outside of work.

- The scale at the bottom is meant to measure your overall emotional paycheck—your positive experiences over the past month minus your negative experiences. In other words, how rewarded did you feel over the past month?

- This is an anonymous survey, so DO NOT provide your name. Comments and suggestions may be written at the bottom of the online survey form. The surveys will be processed by an independent technology provider so management will not see the individual forms (just the aggregate results).

The survey data will be used to determine whether our motivational engine is humming or malfunctioning. The results will be posted on the employee bulletin board.

This innovative program will be used to: (1) determine whether our workplace satisfies the deep needs of our employees and provides a rewarding overall experience, (2) alert management to motivational issues within our workforce before they impact business success, and (3) evaluate our programs, policies, and procedures to ensure that they foster a rewarding and emotionally healthy workplace.

It's in everyone's interest to cooperate in this monitoring program—including management. The intention is to improve work satisfaction and performance. If you don't leave work with a smile on your face, there is a problem and I want to hear about it. I believe this program will provide a win-win outcome for everyone involved.

Sincerely,

Figure 2-4. The Tune-Up Metric.

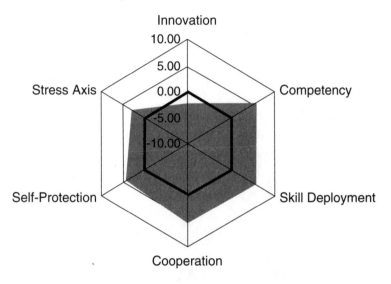

positive, or pleasurable, zone—except for the innovation appetite, which falls inside the heavy black hexagon. In this case the manager in question would refer to the tune-up suggestions listed in Chapter 7—the chapter dedicated to the innovation appetite.

A Note of Caution

An internal branding program is a leadership initiative that belongs in the lap of the CEO. It cannot be delegated to the human resources department or anyone else. It is an executive responsibility to motivate and inspire the troops. This is what leadership is all about. The internal branding approach provides an opportunity for the CEO to wrap his/her arms around, and take responsibility for, the health and well-being of the corporate tribe.

Don't be surprised if your horsepower is initially negative. Dispassionate bureaucracy and impersonal management systems slowly squeeze the energy out of an organization, and managers have not been taught to value employee feelings. Don't blame yourself for the initial score, but focus instead on getting the score to go up by energizing and reinvigorating your organization. The Horsepower Metric will hopefully lead you and your employees into the most interesting, rewarding, and successful parts of your careers. If it didn't provide an emotional win for all parties, including management, I wouldn't even suggest it.

As I mentioned earlier, it is very difficult to alter how your employees feel about their work. Changing how employees feel will require management to change the way it feels too. Changes at the emotional level are conceptually simple, like treating people with respect, but very difficult to implement. Getting the horsepower to go up will require transparency, sincerity, authenticity, and a deep commitment to the tribe. Employee motivation will not respond to propaganda, manipulation, or other forms of self-serving behavior. If you are successful at making deep changes at the emotional level, they will radiate throughout your organization and empower it.

SUMMARY

The emotional health survey described in this chapter captures the five productive pleasures emanating from nature's motivational mechanism and summarizes them in the form of a Horsepower Metric. This survey and metric can be used to monitor the intrinsic rewards that drive workplace productivity and excellence.

I sincerely believe that every workplace should administer a monthly or quarterly emotional health survey and track the results religiously using the Horsepower Metric. No parameter, I suggest, is more important for the long-term success of a business than the motivational horsepower of our employees.

If the Horsepower Metric is negative, it means that our employees are malfunctioning and that corrective action is needed. The malfunction can be diagnosed using the Tune-Up Metric, which will indicate which of the five social appetites are not being satisfied in the workplace. Managers can use this diagnostic information, along with the tune-up suggestions in Chapters 4 through 8 of *Primal Management*, to tune the motivational engine and thereby achieve optimal employee motivation.

CHAPTER 3

EMOTIONS:
SOFT OR HARD?

DEPROGRAMMING MANAGERS FROM HYPERRATIONAL TO BALANCED

I suspect that many managers view the complex (soft) world of emotions, motivation, and interpersonal relationships as a dark and dangerous room that they would rather not enter. They would rather hold employees at arm's length and treat them in a detached, professional manner.

The hyperrational, emotionless approach to management is unnatural, inefficient, counterproductive, and downright unbusinesslike. A more productive approach is to treat emotional management as a vital business skill that can differentiate you from the competition. Companies like W. L. Gore, Whole Foods Market, Southwest Airlines, Google, Nucor Steel, Herman Miller, Enterprise Rent-A-Car, Quad/Graphics, and 3M are examples of companies that became dominant forces in their industries by paying attention to the subtle, people side of management.

I hope that, by the end of this book, you will subscribe to this view. The task of converting emotions from soft to hard is challenging because we've all been exposed to a lifetime of hyperrational brainwashing. One option would be to send the entire business community to deprogramming centers like the ones used to rehabilitate cult members. If you don't have time in your schedule to be systematically deprogrammed from hyperrational to balanced, this chapter should serve as a workable substitute!

It's okay if you currently view emotions in the workplace as soft or irrational. It's okay if you currently prefer cool, professional relationships with your employees. I hope to convince you in this chapter, however, that your life, and the lives of your employees, will be richer, more rewarding, and more successful if you stop looking at emotions as soft and start seeing them for what they are: hard, but subtle, phenomena that are vital to the success of your business.

SUBTLE AND VEXING EMOTIONS

Human beings function best (in terms of survival) when they are externally focused because this is where dangers and opportunities lie. If we think about the conscious mind as a theater, the main actors on the stage are our vivid senses of sight, hearing, touch, and smell. Senses hit the mind hard. Their signals are far stronger than the feelings that occur simultaneously in the background. Our feelings are like shadows projected on a backdrop behind the actors. These shadows are barely noticeable to us, the audience. Background feelings are subtle, but they serve a vital purpose. They remind the audience, you and me, that the show is about survival and that the show will close unless we take care of our survival needs.

Not surprisingly, the concept of behaviorism—which ignores the inner theater of subjective experience—held sway in the business community for much of the last century. Behaviorists like Pavlov, B. F. Skinner, Thorndike, and Watson naturally chose to focus on the hard, observable, and quantifiable aspects of human behavior instead of the hazy and subjective world of thoughts and feelings.[1] The behaviorist approach made sense as long as emotions and motivations were inaccessible, but it does not make sense today. Advances in technology have allowed neurobiologists to peer inside the brain and see emotions in action. In other words, neurobiologists have made the inaccessible accessible and have helped turn the study of emotions from a soft science into a hard one.

THE LAWS OF EMOTIONAL PHYSICS

I claim in *Primal Management* that emotions are hard, not soft, and that my approach to studying them is also hard and engineering based. The hardest of the hard sciences is physics. The laws of physics govern everything from the movements of galaxies to the movement of electrons around an atom. I propose that emotions, as forces, also obey their own immutable laws. Here's my attempt at developing some basic laws of emotional physics.

Let's start this discussion by considering the evolutionary purpose of effort. Why isn't everything *effortless*? If we look at effort as a mild to severe form of pain,[2] it must carry some message and warn us of some danger. Effort, the discomfort that accompanies intentional movement and thought, I propose, protects us from wasting energy. The sensation of expending effort presumably evolved as part of the body's energy-conservation strategy. This is why lions spend much of the day lounging between kills. There is no sense using energy when you don't have to.

Looking at effort as an emotional cost makes survival sense. Nature doesn't want us to squander energy if there is no pressing survival reason to do so. Our Ice Age ancestors evolved in an environment of periodic scarcity and often faced the specter of starvation. You certainly would not want to waste your precious energy stores under such conditions; hence, nature evolved the sensation of effort to put a cost on activity and the sensation of relaxation to put a premium on inactivity. This is an important idea: The sensations of effort and relaxation keep us from squandering precious energy resources.

Even thinking uses energy. This is probably why thinking also takes mental effort. The human brain is a very energy-hungry device. It makes up 2 percent of the body's weight but uses 20 percent of the body's energy. The developing brain of an infant uses 60 percent of the body's energy output. The brain uses more energy when it is actively engaged in solving a problem than when it's not. This is how PET scanners work. PET scanners use radioactively tagged glucose to identify which parts of the brain are actively working and metabolizing. The parts of the brain using the most sugar light up on the PET scan image.

If effort and relaxation were designed to keep us in "park," what force puts us in "gear"? Newton's first law of motion states that an object at rest will remain at rest unless acted upon by some force. I propose a similar law of emotional inertia: Human beings at rest will remain at rest unless acted upon by an emotional force—a feeling. I propose in *Primal Management* that there are five sources of positive motivational energy—the productive pleasures associated with the five social appetites—that leaders can use as carrots to put employees in "gear." Great leaders, I suggest, learn how to draw on all five of the productive pleasures to maximize motivational energy (horsepower).

Fear and anxiety, unfortunately, are the primary motivational forces that most companies use to get employees out of park. These forces are easy to create because all you need is a sharp stick to use as a prod. Fear is a pervasive, ever-present motivator in modern life. Its overuse in the workplace, however, creates needless stress and causes employees to become resentful and angry. Fear is a quick-fix motivator with lots of unpleasant side effects. If it's the only tool in a manager's motivational arsenal, he or she has a serious problem.

Do you understand how the five social appetites and their associated pleasures move your employees? Without these emotional forces, employees would remain stuck in perpetual park and would complete zero work. This aspect of my theory implies that feelings are the true incentive system of the human brain because they alone qualify as forces that can get things moving. This idea is very, very important. Emotions are the incentive system of the human brain and influence *everything* we do— and without them we would remain in perpetual park.

Before I leave the topic of effort, I'd like to pose a question. Does it make sense for the human brain to automatically track where we invest our efforts and for what purpose? I suggest that it is vitally important for the brain to track energy investments (effort) and to create a sense of ownership over the physical or psychic objects resulting from those investments. This investment-tracking mechanism, I propose, resides mainly in the brain's ventromedial prefrontal region, and I refer to it as "the vault" in this and subsequent chapters. This investment tracking mechanism is hugely important because it's responsible for the cathexis bonding process discussed in Chapters 4 and 5.

OVERVIEW OF NATURE'S HARD DESIGN

Nature's motivational design is powerful and elegant, like the designs of the human hand, the human eye, or the human circulatory system. To help you understand and appreciate the overall design I continue my discussion of emotional physics, but this time I incorporate all of the social and biologic appetites and the regulatory feelings (emotional/ forces) they create.

Here is the set-up. Imagine, first of all, an emotional landscape that is constantly moving and undulating, like a stretchy rubber membrane that is being raised and lowered from below by pneumatic pistons. One moment the emotional landscape is flat and in the next moment part of the surface rises up and another portion sinks down in response to the pistons underneath. At any given moment, the entire landscape is in a state of movement. The pistons, as you may have guessed from our previous discussion of emotional physics, are the ten biologic and social appetites shown in Figure 1-1 in Chapter 1 that regulate human survival.

Now imagine that your conscious mind is a marble rolling around on this dynamic emotional landscape. You, the marble, do not control the appetites. Rather, they generally control you. Emotions and feelings arise in the limbic system. They are triggered by events and circumstances and the conscious mind, the marble, is subjected to them. The individual pistons can rise and fall, deforming the stretchy surface above them. If the hunger piston is activated, for example, it will pull on the membrane from below and create a cone-like depression in the motivational landscape. You, the marble, will spiral into this depression by the force of emotional gravity (hunger)—unless you consciously resist the pull. You might think to yourself, "No, I'm going to finish this report before I eat." You can consciously resist the pull of emotional gravity and move away from the hunger depression by expending mental energy, but the depression will continue to deepen and its attraction will increase. You will need to expend more and more mental effort to resist the pull of emotional gravity. Eventually the cost of resisting gravity becomes prohibitive so you do what you are told. You put down your report and devise a logical, rational strategy for finding food and thereby move to the center of the hunger depression.

Once your body is refueled, the hunger depression disappears and other regulatory depressions appear on the landscape. These depressions then propel you in new directions that depend on your current biologic and social needs. If an attractive man or woman happens by, you might take off in hot pursuit under the gravitational influence of another important appetite. Your ability to manage these competing, and sometimes contradictory, emotional forces is called emotional intelligence.

Who's in charge here—you or the appetite? I would say the appetite usually calls the shots because, one way or another, we all need to address our basic survival needs. How soft can emotions and feelings be if they force us to march to their beat? In this case, emotions are hard and we are soft.

A professor once asked me to explain the emotional forces that roll him out of bed in the morning. I told him that the self-protection appetite is normally the social appetite that rolls us out of bed. When the alarm clock rings, we are nestled comfortably in the bioregulatory depression created by the energy-conservation appetite. If you're like me, you wake up in the middle of that depression in a blissful state of relaxation. My immediate inclination is to press the snooze button for five more minutes of rest. Then the self-protection appetite is activated and anxiety sets in. I start thinking about the repercussions that will ensue if I hit the snooze button again. I become aware that some of my key investments in career and family will be at risk if I don't get up. My answer was, therefore, that asset-protective anxiety (self-protection appetite) causes him to get out of bed in the morning, unless it's Saturday, in which case it might be hunger, the bathroom, or a game of golf (skill-deployment appetite).

In Chapter 1 I spoke about extreme emotions as just the tip of the emotional iceberg. The motivational landscape metaphor we just explored explains the rest of the iceberg: the massive part below the water-line that consists of subtle feelings of pleasure and pain that motivate everyday human behavior. At any point during the course of an average day, one or more of these gravitational forces guides us to develop relationships, strive, invent, hone skills, and protect ourselves from harm. Life, as you can see, revolves around feelings because feelings are proxies for the fundamental requirements for survival. They steer our every move and influence every decision. In other words, emotions rule!

The emotional health survey described in Chapter 2 is designed to capture and quantify the motive forces that get your marbles out of park. The Horsepower Metric tallies these forces and provides a simple visual display to track the fluctuating power of your motivational engine.

NATURE'S PROGRAMMABLE APPETITE

Not all of the biologic and social appetites are fixed and automatic. There is one special appetite, the competency appetite, that is programmable via the group consensus. This special appetite allows a group of human beings to sculpt their own emotional landscape by creating regulatory depressions wherever they see fit. Without the competency appetite, the phenomenon of culture would not exist because social norms and expectations would lack emotional force. The competency appetite may be a bit confusing, so here is a simple example to explain how it works.

Imagine a tribe of Ice Age mammoth hunters. One of the hunters, after months of trial-and-error experimentation, develops a new type of stone spear tip, a Clovis point, that can easily penetrate the thick hides of wooly mammoths. As the tribe feasts on roasted mammoth meat, it honors the hunter who invented the new technology. The tribe members applaud the inventor and his invention. By applauding the new skill, the tribe unwittingly activates the competency appetite. The applauded technology automatically becomes an emotionally valued social asset that is desirable and worth acquiring. In terms of the landscape metaphor, the group, by applauding the technology, creates a regulatory depression on the emotional landscape that causes members of the tribe to spiral in like moths to a flame. Members of the tribe are subsequently motivated to invest weeks or months of concerted effort to acquire the valuable technology and thereby boost their self-esteem.

The competency appetite is hugely important because it is under group control and gives group-based decisions a powerful emotional bite. Without this sophisticated, programmable appetite, we would be at the mercy of our biologic appetites. The competency appetite gives the group veto power over the biologic appetites by giving group decisions emotional force. Without the competency appetite, the phenomenon of culture would not exist because social norms and cultural expectations would simply be ignored.

Group approbation works like magic—it turns skills, ideas, relationships, and conventional assets like property and money into metaphorical gold. Once the group has defined value, the individual members of the group work vigorously to acquire it and thereby boost their self-esteem. This, by the way, is precisely how Nike uses Michael Jordan to sell sportswear. Michael Jordan was applauded by the global tribe and was thereby bestowed with an aura of value. Now, everything Jordan "touches" feels valuable and worth acquiring. If managers are esteemed and applauded by their corporate tribes, they can acquire this "magical" power too. I talk more about this approbation phenomenon in Chapter 5 because it provides the psychological basis for leadership.

In summary, it's a bit deflating to the human ego to think of the conscious mind as a marble being rolled to and fro across an emotional landscape by the whims of social and biologic regulation; however, this arrangement makes survival sense. If emotions are proxies for our biologic and social survival needs, then it is logical for the conscious mind to serve these vital needs. Free will, according to this metaphor, is a design feature that allows for some flexibility for juggling, prioritizing, and sometimes resisting emotion forces, especially when two or more regulatory needs arise simultaneously. The conscious mind also has the ability to dampen or mute incoming emotional signals by turning attention away from them. The life challenge for the conscious mind, the marble, is to chart a course into the future that maximizes emotional gain on a fluctuating surface of social and biologic regulation. In a nutshell, this is what life is all about, and if human beings did not possess this sophisticated emotional mechanism we would not survive as a species.

MEET ELLIOT, A REAL-LIFE MR. SPOCK

I imagine that many managers will stubbornly cling to their hyperrational ways, despite my best arguments. These individuals will be unmoved because hyperrationalism is their reality. It is what they were taught and what they are comfortable with—it's their worldview.

For the hard-core hyperrational manager, I suggest a real-world experiment to settle this matter once and for all. If emotions are truly soft, irrelevant, and primitive and do more harm than good, then why not turn them off for real? Hyperrational managers could, for example, volunteer to have their ventromedial prefrontal lobes disconnected. This procedure would leave them unable to experience normal social emotions, but their intelligence and biologic appetites would be unaffected. This operation would also disengage the five social appetites and irrevocably alter the emotional landscape.

Before anyone signs up for this surgical procedure, here are some hard facts from the medical community that may cause volunteers to reconsider. Many human beings have had their ventromedial prefrontal lobes disconnected so we know for a fact that it doesn't make one better. Tens of thousands of mental patients had their frontal lobes mutilated in just such operations. The operation, as you might have guessed, was called lobotomy. Lobotomy operations calmed frantic extreme emotions, but they also eliminated the normal, productive emotions that coax human beings to cooperate, master skills, achieve, and invent. This operation damaged or destroyed all five social appetites in the motivational mechanism.

Turning off emotions does not, in fact, turn us into the rational and competent Mr. Spock depicted in the TV show *Star Trek*. Rather, it creates dysfunctional human beings, with severely compromised motivation mechanisms and horrible decision-making abilities. Antonio Damasio, in his book *Descartes' Error*, described how a normal, hardworking individual named Elliot behaved after suffering damage to his ventromedial prefrontal region because of a tumor.[3] His story vividly demonstrates how you and I would likely behave without intact social emotions.

The story begins after Elliot underwent a sudden personality change that left him incapable of holding a job. The new Elliot differed remarkably from the old one. Elliot had been a solid citizen, a role model for his colleagues and family. As his condition worsened, Elliot became irresponsible and lazy. Elliot's physician suspected a brain tumor, and he was right.

A brain tumor, a meningioma the size of a small orange, was found in Elliot's ventromedial prefrontal region—a vital brain area involved in processing social emotions. The tumor was removed, but the damage was permanent. Despite Elliot's obvious brain damage, he was denied disability benefits because his intelligence, as measured with standardized tests, was normal. As far as the government was concerned, Elliot was perfectly fine and not eligible for disability benefits. At this point, Elliot's physician referred him to Dr. Damasio for further testing.

Damasio suspected that Elliot had a serious disability, but one that was difficult to detect with standard tests. Like many patients with frontal lobe damage, Elliot was charming, pleasant, but emotionally constrained.

Damasio also noticed that Elliot was not threatened or embarrassed by probing personal questions. One researcher described patients like Elliot as "unnaturally natural."[4] Others describe them as detached because they respond to personal questions like a third-party observer rather than as someone describing his or her own life experiences.[5]

Dr. Damasio ran Elliot through battery after battery of tests. Despite his real-world difficulties, he scored normal to superior on all of them. Damasio eventually found a test that yielded a strange result. Elliot did not react emotionally to images of human suffering. Elliot commented after one session that he felt no reaction to the disturbing photos, positive or negative. Dr. Damasio summarized Elliot's predicament as "to know but not to feel."[6] In other words, he had become a true Mr. Spock.

Elliot's work behavior was also abnormal. Typical of frontal lobe patients, he was not a self-starter. He needed prompting to get up and prepare for work. Using the terminology introduced in this chapter, Elliot could not get himself out of emotional "park" because he did not experience the anxiety that gets normal human beings moving in the morning.

Once up and going, Elliot often drifted off-task. Patients like Elliot are sometimes referred to as *vacillating* because they pursue one goal, lose interest, and then pursue a completely different goal before completing the first. They may also persist in tasks well beyond what is required or reasonable. Neurologist Walter Freeman commented, "They rarely throw themselves wholeheartedly into any activity."[7]

Elliot's supervisors and colleagues tried to convince Elliot to change his work habits, but to no avail. Elliot's life, as Dr. Damasio put it, was "now beating to a different drum."[8] In terms of emotional physics, he had different emotional forces acting on him compared to the rest of us. Elliot was fired from a series of jobs because he no longer experienced the vital emotions that propel striving and achievement. In other words, his emotional landscape was simplified to the point that it lacked the fundamental propulsive forces that make normal human beings self-managing and self-directed.

Elliot's decision-making skills were also profoundly abnormal. He lost his family's savings in questionable business deals, got divorced, remarried, and got divorced again. Compromised decision making is another common symptom of frontal lobe damage. Dr. Damasio noticed something unusual after Elliot had been asked to come up with options for dealing with a real-world problem. Elliot, as usual, breezed through this test. However, afterwards, Elliot commented, "And after all of this, I still wouldn't know what to do!"[9]

Damasio eventually concluded that emotions were fundamentally intertwined in decision making because they represent the value proposition in the mind's cost-benefit analysis. Without intact emotions, in other words, all options feel the same, so there is no basis for choosing one option over another. Here is how Damasio put it:

> I began to think that the cold-bloodedness of Elliot's reasoning prevented him from assigning values to different options, and made his decision-making landscape hopelessly flat.[10]

Emotions, as you can see, represent the value system of the human mind and provide both the cost and the benefit terms in any "rational" cost-benefit analysis. Pure rationality is a myth because emotions are a necessary accompaniment to any decision. If we remove them from the calculation, our decision-making becomes deeply flawed, like Elliot's.[11]

Professor Nigel Nicholson of the London Business School makes this point eloquently in *Managing the Human Animal*. Here is how he describes how feelings affect supposedly rational decision making:

> [E]verything that goes on in the mind is inflected by emotion, even when we are unaware of it. When we make what looks like a dispassionate choice based upon limited information—Shall I buy A or B?—invisible feelings tug at our preferences, whether they are brands of pasta in the supermarket or equities on a stock market. Distant emotional impressions from images and memory traces that are beyond conscious recall steer our final choice.[12]

Elliot degenerated into a lazy malingerer because his cost-benefit decisions at work had been fundamentally altered. Work still involved emotional costs in the form of effort, but without compensating benefits in the form of nature's five productive pleasures. Every workplace decision therefore had a negative emotional return on investment, and Elliot did the rational thing—almost nothing unless prompted by others.

In light of these sobering medical facts, I doubt that any sane manager would ever volunteer to have his or her social emotions turned off! Elliot proves that Spock's TV persona was a fallacy. A truly emotionless Mr. Spock would have been lazy, indecisive, and a burden to the starship *Enterprise. Emotions, as you can see, are not an option. We would not* be better off without them. Emotions are hard regulators of survival and we'd be dead or irreparably disabled if we turned them off.

MEET DR. MILLER: A "BORN-AGAIN" CONVERT FROM THE HYPERRATIONAL CAMP

Our Western culture is, like the mythical Mr. Spock, hyperrational. We have been programmed by our educational system to disregard and disrespect emotions. Does this mean, however, that we are condemned to a life of hyperrationalism, or can we be rehabilitated?

Here is the story of a hyperrational individual who attempted to deny his emotions until he was thirty-seven years old, but then became a "born-again" believer in emotions after reading Daniel Goleman's book, *Emotional Intelligence*. If you are on the verge of rejecting pure rationality, and becoming a born-again believer in emotions, perhaps this story will push you over the edge.

This case features Dr. Kenneth Miller, a physician who tried to emulate Mr. Spock's character from age seven onward. He, like Spock, tried to bottle up and deny his emotions. The following quotation describes Dr. Miller's valiant attempt to live by reason and logic alone and how this strategy was ultimately dysfunctional. The quotation comes from Dr. Miller's review of Daniel Goleman's book *Emotional Intelligence* on Amazon.com:

> *I placed my original order for Dan Goleman's book* Emotional Intelligence *about one month before its release in 1995 after reading the* Time *magazine cover story "What Is Your E.Q.?"*

At the time I was going through a very difficult divorce, and I was asking myself the question "What did I do to deserve this terrible mess?" I was a 37-year-old medical internist then who, in seventh grade, modeled my emotional style after Mr. Spock (from Star Trek) to avoid emotional issues I faced then.

I accepted the messages from my parents and teachers who taught me that if I earned good grades, went to college, received an undergraduate and hopefully a graduate degree, then I shall expect to become happy and successful in life. Well, I DID that. I got the T-shirt. I graduated from high school as class valedictorian, winning the science award, I was awarded by my classmates "most likely to succeed," and I won a very handsome scholarship which paid all my undergraduate tuition for four years and offered me a summer job. In college I won more scholarships and graduated Phi Beta Kappa in the top 3 percent of my class. In medical school and residency I did well, but this was more difficult for me as I had to learn to deal with many emotionally and socially challenging issues I was poorly prepared to deal with. I got through them, but initially I was not very adept at dealing with them.

When I entered professional life I started to ponder more the emotional issues in the lives of my patients, and in my own life, and I was slowly coming to terms with the importance of these issues. In 1995, as I reflected upon the failure of my marriage and the miserable circumstances in which I found myself, I realized my biggest contribution to the failure of that marriage was the rational "Spockish" persona I brought to that relationship and my lack of attunement to my inner emotional life. I was ready for a new paradigm of how intellect should relate to feeling.

Goleman's insights on emotional intelligence revolutionized the way I relate to my intellectual and emotional life. Where formerly I was of the belief that the mind was the key to happiness and success in life (and the emotions merely got in the way of clear-headed reasoning), I have now come to view that the true formula for success and happiness is the development of an intelligent mind surrendered to an intelligent heart. In my practice in internal medicine, I have come to realize that issues of emotional intelligence (or rather, lack of it) either cause or drive numerous medical problems, and I regularly strive to teach my patients about emotional intelligence, and I often share Goleman's book, Emotional Intelligence, *(or abridged audiocassettes) with them. The book has made a very profound contribution to my practice, to my life, and to the lives of many of my patients. I have given talks at educational conferences to encourage educators to teach emotional intelligence. I have written articles in magazines and books regarding a model of education which integrates intellectual, emotional, moral, and spiritual intelligences (I see emotional intelligence as a gateway to moral and spiritual intelligence).*

Especially to those of you who are stuck in the "mind is everything (and ignore your emotions)" paradigm of happiness and success in life, I urge you to read this book. The same goes for educators, physicians, and corporate leaders. I rate Goleman's book, Emotional Intelligence, *among the top five most life altering books of my life, and that deserves five stars (if not ten).*

Dr. Miller's story vividly demonstrates the fallacy of the hyperrational approach to life. Emotions are not evil or bad. They are essential regulatory systems built deeply into our brains. Spockish attempts to completely stifle emotions are folly. Emotions should be artfully managed and channeled toward useful purposes, but not stifled. They remind us to invent, develop strong and meaningful relationships, master skills, and protect ourselves. These are good things, so there is no need to stifle these productive and necessary emotions.

Perhaps Aristotle had it right when he stated that a virtuous person is one who experiences emotions at the right times and on the right occasions and toward the right persons and for the right causes and in the right manner.[13] Aristotle's suggestion mirrors Daniel Goleman's recommendations in *Emotional Intelligence*.[14] They both agree that managing emotions is a crucial skill for human beings to master, especially leaders. Aristotle, by the way, tutored Alexander the Great, one of the most phenomenal leaders of all time.

Are you ready for your own, born-again experience, or are you already a believer? If you're a manager and you want to be truly successful in your work, I suggest you become a convert to the view that emotions are vitally important in business and in life because they are the fundamental forces that move the marbles (people) around inside your office.

SUMMARY

This chapter's message to business leaders is, "Ignore emotions at your peril!" Making the transition from good to great will require managers to accept the notion that emotions are hard, vital, and more important for sustained financial success than any other single factor. There is simply no way around this conclusion because emotions and feelings drive behavior. It would be irrational and unbusinesslike to ignore a factor that is so crucial to an organization's success.

A manager's first step toward aligning with human nature, and giving emotions their rightful respect, is to track them in the workplace by measuring the horsepower of the motivational engine. If the Horsepower Metric described in Chapter 2 indicates that the engine is misfiring, the next rational step is to diagnose which of the social appetites are malfunctioning with the Tune-Up Metric. The final step is to tune the workplace environment and thereby improve motivational horsepower. Chapters 4 through 8 provide specific tune-up suggestions in the event that one or more of the social appetites are misfiring.

It's not easy to change old habits, especially when you've lived in a culture that has historically devalued emotions as irrational. I hope to change your worldview and get you moving in a completely new direction based on science, logic, and respect for the emotional forces that ensure our survival. This direction will require you to invest effort, but I promise that the effort will be amply compensated with emotional rewards. In other words, the direction I propose has a positive emotional return on investment and is well worth the effort.

SOCIAL APPETITE #1: THE COOPERATION APPETITE

How to Merge Individual Employees into a Coordinated Superorganism

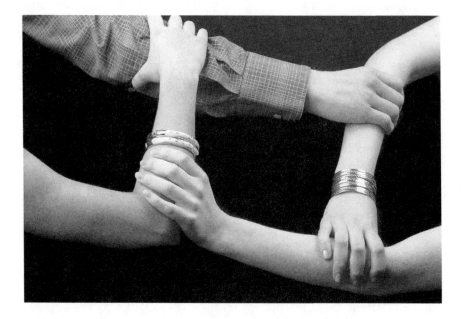

INTRODUCTION TO HUMAN BONDING

Chapter 4 is a how-to guide for building a tribal superorganism. Corporations are not superorganisms or tribes merely because a group of employees work in the same building. Similarly, sports teams are not superorganisms merely because they wear the same color jerseys. Most workplaces are neither united nor tribal. Rather, they are composed of a loose aggregation of disconnected individuals who battle one another for resources and the next rung in the hierarchy. This is why management is such an exasperating profession and why managers are forced to spend an inordinate amount of time brokering border disputes and quelling interpersonal warfare.

Interpersonal conflict is like friction in the corporate machine. It burns up precious energy and money. It creates wasted heat—energy expended for no productive purpose. The object of this chapter is to show managers how to lubricate the corporate gears by reducing backbiting, malicious gossip, simmering jealousies, and childish turf wars. The goal is to focus employees' energy on getting the job done instead of plotting revenge, fuming, and endlessly ruminating on real or perceived slights. I show managers how to take warring factions and bond them together into a coherent tribe where the unit of thought becomes "we" not "me." This may seem impossible, but it's not. We are going to achieve these wonders through the miracle of cathexis.

Cathexis is a psychiatric term. It refers to a mysterious process by which the things we value and invest effort into become merged with our personal sense of self, our identity. If you want to create a tribal superorganism that is optimally motivated, then you *absolutely and positively must understand cathexis!*

I mentioned this mysterious phenomenon in Chapter 1 in relation to parents and children. Parents invest mightily in their children, and the child gradually becomes merged with the parent's identity. If the child is hurt, the parent feels the hurt. If the child succeeds, the parent feels the success. This investment and bonding process lies at the heart of employee loyalty, at the heart of teamwork, and at the heart of employee engagement. It supplies the emotional glue that holds societies together.

Without this identity-merging process, human beings wouldn't care about one another. We'd scatter.

Anything can be captured, brought inside, and appended to our sense of self through the miracle of cathexis. If you can activate this process inside your organization, the thought process will gradually change from me (self-interest) to we (group interest). I will henceforth refer to cathected relationships as invested relationships because this is how they are created—through investment.[1]

I don't think the brain makes any distinction between investing in people; investing in things, like a garden or home-improvement project; or investing in skills. Each and every investment is tracked, appended to self, and subsequently protected and nurtured as part of self. A threat to any asset in the investment portfolio automatically triggers territorial anger by way of the amygdala—the brain's version of an early-warning radar.

How can we tell if we have truly connected with something and brought it inside? The things we bring inside give us a warm and friendly feeling when we contemplate them. If we have lovingly restored a classic car, we feel this glow when we admire or drive the car. If we have connected with our home by completing innumerable home-improvement projects, then we get a warm feeling when we return home after work. The same thing goes for investments in friends, family, and workmates. These warm feelings are produced by two closely related neuropeptides called oxytocin and vasopressin. When these neuropeptides are turned off in animals by deleting them from the genome, then females don't care for their pups, males and females don't bond, and males don't defend their territories.[2] These are very important molecules for regulating bonding behavior in animals and in human beings. These rewarding feelings can be turned on in the workplace by encouraging interpersonal investment.

Bonding is based on *consensual* investment. If you want to build a superorganism, you've got to convince employees to *opt in*. If employees and managers opt in and freely invest in one another and the organization, they will gradually begin to think and act as one. They will also experience warm, rewarding feelings in the workplace; the same esprit de corps our ancestors felt when hunting parties ventured into the wilderness to stalk large game. These positive feelings will boost their emotional paycheck and improve efficiency and coordination. Truly great companies have this feel! In fact, it is the starting point for becoming great.

PERSONAL EXAMPLES OF BONDING

In Chapter 3 I stated that it makes survival sense for the brain to track the body's precious energy investments and the assets resulting from those investments. Beyond pure logic, however, it's hard to conceptualize bonding because it is completely subconscious and not intuitively obvious. Since bonding is so obscure, I will now provide some personal examples of bonding in action.

Bonding with a Skill

Here is a personal example of bonding. My wife and I started taking karate after several years of watching our children take lessons at a top-notch studio in Madison, Wisconsin, called Kicks Unlimited. Two of our instructors, Mr. Welch and Mr. Spridco, were world champions who appeared on a Discovery Channel extreme martial arts special.

I'm now a brown belt, which is one belt away from black belt. Every time I advance a belt level I feel a little more competent and confident *all the time*. I now feel confident in situations where I didn't feel confident before because I know I can protect myself. This is the main benefit of karate, improved self-esteem and the annuity of positive feelings that comes with it.

My karate skill has become a valuable addition to my social-asset vault. I now own this skill. I have emotionally bonded with karate by virtue of the effort I freely invested in it. My amygdala is tracking and protecting this investment. Karate is now part of my core, my sense of self, my identity. I take pride in it and it boosts my feeling of self-worth. I now classify myself as a martial artist, and if someone criticizes my karate asset, I will get angry.

This is just one simple example of how human beings bond with skills, ideas, property, relationships—really just about anything—by investing energy and thereby bringing the object of our investment inside. In a healthy workplace, I argue, we want to bring our managers, co-workers, and the enterprise as a whole inside by willingly investing in them.

Bonding with a Place

Here is another example of bonding. It involves my move from Madison, Wisconsin, to Houston, Texas, in 1980 when I graduated from the University of Wisconsin with a master's degree in geology and took a job with a major oil company. I loved Madison. It was my dream city: progressive, offbeat, thoughtful, and exciting. It was the state capital and home to a major university. It was the Berkeley of the Midwest, a hothouse of ideas and energy. I never knew what to expect on my way to classes. One day I might encounter political protesters and the next a group of Moonies looking for converts.

During my later years, a professional clown ran the student government and his vice president was a puppet. The Pail and Shovel Party, as they were called, promised to rename the university from the University of Wisconsin to the University of New York, which is where the ringleaders were from. They even built a full-scale Styrofoam replica of the Statue of Liberty's head and torch on frozen Lake Mendota to perpetuate the ruse. Madison was a hoot!

Madison had a small-town feel with big-city amenities. Madison was also picturesque. The downtown was situated on a narrow strip of land bordered by Lake Mendota on the north and Lake Monona on the south. Madison consistently ranks among the top places to live in the United States.

Houston was a boomtown in the early 1980s. The 1979 Iranian revolution had shut down most of Iran's oil production, thereby causing prices to peak at $39.50 per barrel. These record high prices stimulated the oil industry into a feeding frenzy. Moving there gave me culture shock. It was a sprawling city of endless strip malls built over a former swamp. It was a sweltering place, more fit for insects than human beings. Only Detroit and New Orleans had higher murder rates at this time. Giant cockroaches the size of your thumb and stinging fire ants were endemic. I was sometimes awoken by an early morning clang—the result of an armadillo colliding with the metal railing surrounding my patio.

Houston had a somewhat lawless, boomtown atmosphere. Whenever there was a traffic jam on the I-10 freeway, cars and trucks would make their own makeshift exit ramps wherever they felt like. Discarded beer bottles littered the landscape. The locals sometimes referred to northerners like me as "damn Yankees." Bottom line, Houston was on the opposite end of the spectrum from Madison, and I wanted out. I had no intention of living in Houston long term, so I never got comfortable. I felt as though I was on an extended business trip and living out of a hotel room.

In 1983, everything changed. Oil prices crashed, and the Houston economy was thrown into a tailspin. Workers who had never experienced unemployment were suddenly jobless. Houston had gone "bust." The minister at my church asked me to represent the congregation on a steering committee to set up a food pantry in downtown Houston. He explained that five of the largest churches in Houston were pooling their resources to deal with the crisis. Each church, he explained, could nominate one representative for the steering committee, and he wanted to nominate me.

I was literally speechless. I was trying to think of ways to get out of this unwelcomed opportunity as he spoke. I was too busy at work, I thought to myself, to take on a major commitment. My knee-jerk, self-protective instinct was to say "No!" Something strange happened, however. I admired the minister and didn't want to disappoint him. I also felt a desire to pitch in during the emergency. I nodded yes, even though my instincts were screaming, "No!" I believe that all forms of commitment include this fearful stage. If employees and managers push through the fear and opt in anyway, authentic bonding can occur.

The first meeting of the Emergency Aid Coalition was a simple affair. It consisted of one geologist (me), a dentist, and three female retirees. The initial conversations focused on the scope of our mission. One of the retirees suggested we hand out bag lunches at a central location. I looked at her with amazement. I said, "I think we need to do more than hand out bag lunches. We are dealing with entire families in crisis. We need to give them enough breathing room to obtain help from family members or to connect with governmental agencies. We are dealing with a major crisis, and we have major resources at our disposal." I suggested that we think big and plan to hand out enough groceries to last each family one week. I suggested we collect enough food to supply fifty families per day. My plan would require the five churches to collect 1,250 bags of groceries each week. The group accepted my plan, and the Emergency Aid Coalition was off and running.

The mayor of Houston organized a rally to encourage our efforts. We stood with the mayor while newspaper reporters snapped pictures. The ministers and priests at the five churches made the relief effort a major priority. Food and volunteers streamed in. What started out as a stopgap food program evolved into much more: a counseling program, a health clinic, and a dental clinic.

Something miraculous happened as a result of my investment in the Emergency Aid Coalition. I no longer disliked Houston. I had psychologically bonded with Houston through my investment in it. Houston lived inside of me, and I suddenly cared about it. I no longer felt like a stranger in a strange land. In other words, I had connected. I had gone from disengaged mercenary to civic warrior and had surprised myself in the process. Even twenty-five years later, I still have a fond place in my heart for Houston. Such is the miracle of cathexis.

This story illustrates a general point—even the most hard-core, disengaged employee can be converted into a dedicated and engaged one. In order to accomplish this magical feat in the workplace, managers need to follow my Houston formula because the process is always the same. The first step is to develop a bond with the employee, just like the minister developed a bond with me through his own commitment and investment. Had I not admired the minister, I would have given his assignment the thumbs-down. The second step is to give employees a compelling mission and convince them to volunteer their efforts. My compelling mission was to help out in an emergency. If employees don't volunteer for the corporate mission, bonding will not occur. The brain tracks only our voluntary investments, not our forced ones. To harness the bonding process, managers should act as though employees are not being paid. The corporate mission must be engaging, compelling, and intrinsically worthy of investment because nobody is going to invest in something they don't deeply value. That's the simple beauty of emotional bonding—it requires just two steps: value and invest. These two steps, repeated across many employees, create the sinew that holds a superorganism together.

THE EVIDENCE FOR BONDING

If you think that the bonding process is spooky, you're absolutely right. Who would imagine that our intimate and personal sense of self is actually constructed, bit by bit, by an investment-tracking mechanism built deeply into our brains? Who would imagine that our sense of self grows as we incorporate skills, property, people, pets, hobbies, and groups into our frontal-lobe vaults and create a sense of ownership over them? Spooky or not, it makes perfect survival sense for our brains to keep track of and protect our precious investments.

My sense of self includes my wife and kids, my mother, other family members, friends, my karate and golf skills, Houston, my theory of social emotions, and many other assets. These owned assets are protected by my amygdala and stored in a very specific part of my brain—the ventromedial prefrontal lobe. My ventromedial prefrontal region is located just behind my eyeballs. It is the vault where my belongings are stored.

As you might recall from Chapter 3, this brain area was targeted in certain lobotomy operations designed to relieve anxiety and emotional distress in mentally ill patients. Many lobotomy operations were conducted under local anesthesia with the patient awake and alert. The surgeon knew when he had destroyed the target area when the patient suddenly relaxed. Whatever real or imagined problems the patient had been obsessing about disappeared with the flick of the scalpel.

Something else also disappeared: the patient's entire investment portfolio—the things in the vault that the patient had been obsessing over. If I were the patient, I would have gone from caring about my friends, family, and career one second to not caring the next. I would no longer care about my karate investment, and I would not react with anger if my karate skills were criticized. I would no longer value karate, and I would no longer perform the skills unless ordered to. Intellectually, I would remember the skills, but I would see no value in using them.

Within seconds, everything I had valued would have disappeared, just as though thieves had broken into my brain's vault and stolen my prized possessions. I would still remember my friends, skills, history, and possessions, but they would not belong to me anymore. I also wouldn't care about myself as a growing and developing human being because "myself" would no longer exist.[3] Without the brain's equivalent of a vault, I would experience neither pride in my accumulated victories nor sadness in my accumulated defeats. I would live in a perpetual now—caring only about my current biological needs for things like food, sex, and rest. Lobotomy, by destroying my core investments, would have converted me from a caring and responsible social being into a smart but solitary creature.

Meet Walter Freeman, the Champion of Lobotomy

One of the main lobotomy practitioners was the brilliant neurologist Walter Freeman. Freeman was personally responsible for roughly 3,500 lobotomy operations.[4] He also invented the notorious ice-pick operation. Freeman was one of the most respected scientists of his day and carefully tracked his patients, some for as many as thirty years, and thereby documented the profound changes in social behavior produced by lobotomy. Nobody, then or since, was as knowledgeable about the long-term effects of damage to the ventromedial prefrontal region.

Freeman came to realize that the changes produced by lobotomy were consistent with the nearly total obliteration of sense of self.[5] The therapeutic effect of lobotomy lay in its ability to relieve abnormal levels of anxiety. Unfortunately, it also seemed to eliminate the normal levels of asset-protective anxiety that motivate human beings to tend to their investments in spouses, friends, children, careers, education, hobbies, and skills. Lobotomy patients showed no interest in enlarging, maintaining, or protecting their portfolio of psychic investments because their machinery for cataloging and tracking social investments (their vault) had been destroyed. Keep in mind that lobotomy did not affect intelligence. Lobotomized patients, just like Elliot, could breeze through most psychometric tests just as easily as they could before the operation.

Here's a tally of the social deficits observed in lobotomy patients by

Freeman and others. These deficits vividly illustrate how badly human beings malfunction without their vault of lifelong social investments.

- According to Freeman, "Some patients have taken serious beatings—financial, occupational, even physical—and have come up smiling."[6]

- They were unconcerned with their relationships with friends or family members.[7]

- They were often irresponsible in their use of financial assets.[8]

- They were also unmotivated to tend to the chores of daily life, and simple inactivity was not at all displeasing.[9]

If prefrontal lobotomy truly destroys the patient's core sense of self, then, theoretically, lobotomized patients cannot be insulted because they don't have any psychic investments to defend—there is no self to protect. This was, in fact, one of the most peculiar and universal manifestations of lobotomy discovered by Freeman—the inability to be insulted.[10] Here is how Freeman described this peculiar trait:

> Patients lose their sensitiveness to criticism by virtue of prefrontal lobotomy, and they will accept with a smile the most insulting epithets—in fact, the more insulted they are, the better patients seem to enjoy it. They appreciate the quickness of wit on the part of their opponent, and while unable to keep up with the fertility of imagination that is used by their interlocutor will do their best to keep up the vilifications.[11]

Investments in relationships are also part of sense of self because the people we invest in are added to the vault. Lobotomy operations that destroy the vault should also destroy the patient's relationships. This prediction matches the observed social behavior of lobotomy patients. For example, the postlobotomy patients in Freeman's studies often took a certain irreverent delight in tormenting close family members without any sign of remorse. Here are two of Freeman's case studies that illustrate a disregard for former close relationships:

Case 49: When we accused one of our patients of bullying her husband, she retorted: "Why shouldn't I? I've always wanted to have my way, and I'll have it now. Of course I bully him."[12]

Case 196: "I blow up sometimes and make her (his wife) very unhappy. I'm a lot less considerate than I used to be. When I hurt her, I feel bad for a minute, but I get over it. I am ashamed that I don't feel worse, but I just don't. . . . It's difficult for me to be interested in anything, things don't make much of an impression on me . . . my wife says I have a cold personality. I sometimes take pleasure in arguing with her, and then I throw salt in the wound. I seem to take some sadistic pleasure in it. . . . When my wife says sharp things to me, I start arguing but my feelings aren't really hurt. I should make an effort to stop arguing but I don't." Though he said he felt ashamed, there was no evidence of it while he spoke.[13]

Cooperative behavior was also lacking in most of Freeman's lobotomy patients. This is not surprising, because, without an intact bonding mechanism, they'd have no way to connect with the social world and bring it inside. According to Freeman, jobs involving teamwork were generally not compatible with lobotomy patients.[14] They were also unmotivated to participate in community-involvement activities.[15] Self-sacrifice, altruism, reverence, patriotism, contemplation, and introspection no longer interested them, either.[16] Lobotomy patients, it seems, were permanently disengaged from everything and everyone, even from caring about themselves and their futures.

You can picture the investment portfolio, the vault, as the core of the motivational mechanism. The social appetites, all five of them, serve the core. Without the core, human social behavior disintegrates. Freeman's lobotomy patients ceased to function as productive social beings because their motivational cores and the productive pleasures that serve them were turned off.

The lobotomy data provide clear evidence that social investments are the stuff that the human sense of self is composed of. Sense of self is the core of the motivational mechanism. It's built from the planks of our lifelong social investments. It's the central star of human behavior, and the social appetites revolve around it like planets. If you want your employees to work as hard as you do and care about your business as much as you do, then you need to encourage consensual investment. This is the only way to create a group of human beings who think and act as one—a superorganism.

BONDING AND LEADERSHIP

In 2001 Jim Collins wrote *Good to Great*, one of the best-selling management books of all time, with over 2.5 million copies sold. Collins systematically and painstakingly compared the eleven great companies he had identified with their not-so-great counterparts in order to identify the key factors that differentiated them. Collins tried to downplay leadership as a factor, but the data kept bringing him back to it as a key characteristic of great companies. All of the eleven great companies were led by humble leaders who put the organization ahead of personal interests and glory.

Journalists who wrote about the great leaders profiled in Collins's book described them as quiet, humble, modest, reserved, shy, gracious, mild mannered, self-effacing, and understated.[17] Collins wrote that leaders like Darwin Smith (Kimberly-Clark) and Colman Mockler (Gillette) were ambitious for the company's success rather than for their "own riches and personal renown."[18] The behavior of the very best leaders, what Collins calls Level 5 leaders, makes perfect sense from a bonding perspective. These leaders valued their organizations and invested deeply in them. These investments caused the CEOs' personal identities to merge with their corporate identities until the two entities became psychologically inseparable.

If we could look deep inside Darwin Smith's vault with special glasses we'd probably discover that Kimberly-Clark made up a major portion of his core investment portfolio. Kimberly-Clark was part of Smith just as surely as his arms and legs were part of him. In other words, Kimberly-Clark was the most valuable asset in Darwin Smith's vault. Smith merged with Kimberly-Clark and brought it inside. The company's victories were subsequently experienced as Smith's personal victories. If an employee had a success, Smith experienced it as his success. Smith didn't really put the company ahead of his personal interests. Rather, the company's interests and his personal interests merged into one. Smith didn't need personal kudos because he was already receiving plenty of them through his psychic connection to his company. Such is the magic of invested bonds.

BONDING TO THE WORKPLACE

What happens when new employees enter the workplace? Do they immediately bond with their workmates and start absorbing the culture of their new tribe? I think not! Many enter the workplace warily, trying to assess whether the employer is friend or foe. Perhaps their mothers or fathers had experienced several rounds of corporate downsizing at the hands of cool, bottom line–driven, publicly held corporations. They are unlikely to invest their souls into a company that wouldn't think twice about terminating them. This would violate the rule that human behavior makes survival sense.

Most employees probably enter the workplace as mercenaries with their own agendas. They do not automatically bond with the corporate tribe nor accept true membership in it. Their true loyalties probably lie elsewhere. The employment contract is often a marriage of convenience. Most employees, according to the Gallup Organization, invest enough effort to earn a paycheck, but no more.

Sadly, many employees come to view their work as an unrewarding and thankless chore. Considering that human beings spend half their waking lives at work, this is a tragedy. When the workforce is demoralized, everyone loses: employees, employers, customers, and shareholders. The status-quo approach does not maximize emotional wealth for the overall ecosystem and is therefore dysfunctional. It produces underachievers instead of overachievers. It produces workplaces where only 31 percent of employees are committed to the corporate mission.[19]

How can companies convince new employees to commit and cathect with the tribe? Harry Quadracci, the founder of Quad/Graphics, was aggressive. He didn't dillydally. Harry Quadracci personally asked for commitment up front—before employees got on his corporate bus. I experienced Quadracci's indoctrination speech when I took a job in the training department at Quad/Graphics while earning my MBA at the University of Chicago. It went something like this:

> *"If Quad/Graphics is not your number-one choice, then don't work here. Go find your number-one choice and apply for a job there." Harry continued, "If we are your number-one choice and you are willing to commit to Quad/Graphics and freely invest your efforts here, then I will commit to you and do everything in my power to be worthy of your commitment and investment."*

Quadracci's employees did not connect with Quad/Graphics immediately because the process takes time—four months at a minimum. Quadracci did, however, put employees on a path leading to an authentic, invested relationship.

I recommend that all CEOs meet with prospective employees and make the same social contract Harry Quadracci did. Don't delegate this vital leadership function to someone else. This is the first, mandatory step for creating a workplace full of engaged employees—a superorganism.

MEASURING BONDING IN THE WORKPLACE

How does one measure the strength of interpersonal bonds and the bonds between employees and employer? Here are two available options:

1. The emotional health survey discussed in Chapter 2 is designed to measure bonding. Survey scale 1, in particular, was specifically designed to assess the degree of interpersonal bonding in the workplace with the following question, "Do you feel excluded in the workplace or included? In other words, do you experience a warm, family feel in the workplace?" The "warm, family feel" is meant to refer to the

pleasurable sensations produced by the neuropeptides oxytocin and vasopressin—the relationship hormones.

2. Employee engagement surveys also measure the degree of emotional connection within the workplace. They therefore provide a second vehicle for measuring bonding.

The term *employee engagement* was originally coined by the consulting community and each firm defined it somewhat differently. My favorite definition, which was coined by the Conference Board, an industry-funded, human resources think tank based in New York, is: "A heightened emotional connection that an employee feels for his or her organization, that influences him or her to exert greater discretionary effort to his or her work."[20] This definition resonates nicely with the invested bonds and family feel discussed in this chapter.

The concept of cathexis goes beyond a mere bond, however. Rather, it involves the merging of identities. An engaged employee not only connects with the workplace but brings it inside by voluntarily investing in it. This investment creates an asset in the employee's frontal lobe vault that contributes to the employee's core sense of self and produces feelings of ownership over the asset. Assets in the vault are guarded and protected by the amygdala and threats to these assets instinctively trigger an emotional, fight-or-flight reaction.

If engaged employees truly bring their employer inside themselves, then they should react angrily and emotionally to any threat directed against the employer because such a threat would also be experienced as a personal threat to themselves. This instinctive emotional reaction, I propose, would be the purest and truest measure of employee engagement.

I am not suggesting that employers should actually connect their employees to a polygraph machine and then instruct the polygraph operator to hurl insults at the employee's CEO, supervisor, and workmates. Trying to measure engagement in this way would obviously destroy it—just as the Heisenberg Uncertainty Principle states that you cannot observe quantum events without disturbing the very thing you want to measure!

FORMAL APPROACH TO DEVELOPING A CONNECTED (TRIBAL) WORKFORCE

Bonding is an important part of a dynamic, high-performance workplace. Nothing, in my opinion, is more important. We now turn our attention from the theoretical to the practical: How, exactly, does one create a connected workplace?

Bonding is a slow and subtle process, but it is an actionable goal in most organizations. The process can be either informal or formal. Both methods will work, so pick the approach that best suits your personal style and organizational constraints. Developing invested relationships can be natural and organic or systematic and planned, as described below. Perhaps bonding is simply too important and urgent to be allowed to grow on its own. Here is a prescription for intensive cultivation of bonding: a procedure for rigorously sowing the seeds of bonding and tending the crop. This may be the fastest way to grow a tribal superorganism.

In order to develop a formal approach to bonding we will need to think of the tribe as a highly integrated network—like a computer network or the Internet. This idea is consistent with the latest trend in sociology: social network theory. According to one version of this theory, there are two ways that employees can bring value to an enterprise:

1. Employees can be "competency nodes," which means they are extremely good at what they do. Competency nodes don't need to be networked to bring value to the organization. Competency nodes can obtain cooperation from other employees simply by bartering their extraordinary skills.

2. Employees can also be "trust nodes." Trust nodes are emotionally intelligent instead of technically talented. They bring value to the organization by virtue of their social capital, their network of deep interpersonal relationships. Trust nodes can draw on their network to solve difficult problems. Trust nodes are connected to one another with links produced by invested bonds.

The ideal situation is a network in which each individual is both a competency node (expert) and a bonded trust node. This type of people network can mobilize communal resources most efficiently. This is how companies can turn themselves into highly competent and interconnected superorganisms.

The OPO Demonstration Test

Building a human trust network is a slow but straightforward process. This process is based on the cathexis bonding phenomenon we have been discussing. I recently worked with the Organ Procurement Office (OPO) at a major hospital to build a real-life connected workgroup. The executive director of the OPO, let's call him Dr. T, is a transplant surgeon. I worked with the OPO for six months in 2007 to build an interconnected trust network and thereby improve integration and coordination. The OPO, according to Dr. T, was a superorganism early on, but lost its superorganism qualities during a period of rapid growth. Dr. T wanted to recapture the earlier dynamic because it was the most exciting and productive period in his organization's history.

Every person in the OPO was a potential competency node and every invested relationship was a potential link in the network. Our goal was to double the number of interpersonal links in six months. We hoped to build the equivalent of a human Internet, one relationship at a time, until we had created a richly interconnected network, a superorganism. Just as with the Internet, employees who were plugged into the OPO "people net" would be able to draw on its far-flung expertise and resources.

Here is a simple example of the bonding process in action. Let's start with two hypothetical employees, "A" and "B." Now let's encourage employee A to:

- Value and admire B

- Invest in and mentor B by helping B solve problems

- Go to bat for B if he or she has a crisis

If we can convince B to do the same with A, then, gradually, through the miracle of cathexis, A and B will psychologically merge until they become AB. Now, if A has a success, B will feel that success, and if A has a problem, B will come to the rescue. A doesn't have to be jealous of B because B's victories are also A's victories. A won't sabotage B's efforts because that would be like A hurting him- or herself. Interpersonal warfare no longer makes emotional sense for AB because it would have a negative emotional return on investment (EROI). A and B are now a link in the interpersonal network, and this link increases the power and efficiency of the overall network.

The OPO's trust network, just like the Internet, is a means of sharing resources. In the example I gave above, employee A connected with employee B and thereby gained access to B's skills and knowledge. If employee B had a pre-existing network, A would have gained access to that too. For example, if B had already connected with employees J, R, and Q, then A would also have access to these resources by virtue of his or her connected relationship with B.

People with more network connections are considered to have greater amounts of social capital (more resources they can draw on). Social network theory is a booming area of research and is quickly becoming the core concept in sociology and political science. The people with the most interpersonal links are considered most crucial to the efficient operation of the network. If a highly linked person is fired, for example, information flow, group coordination, and productivity are seriously jeopardized. A highly linked individual is like the server or router in a computer network. If you shut down the office server, all hell breaks loose. Interpersonal links that bridge separate departments are considered particularly valuable to overall coordination and information flow.

Steps in the Formal Bonding Process

Our first step toward building a trust network at the OPO was to randomly pair up the staff. The goal for each pairing was to develop a connected bond within six months. After six months, we planned to randomize the pairings and start again. Each pair advanced through the following four-step bonding process during the first six-month period:

- *Step 1: Looking for Value.* The first step in the bonding process is to learn to value and admire one's partner by listening to his or her bio. This is a fun, nonthreatening, ice-breaking step because human beings love to tell their personal stories. The partners tell their stories and then they look for things they have in common or things they admire in one another. Human beings will no sooner invest in a relationship they don't value as in an underperforming stock or mutual fund.

• *Step 2: Learning About One Another's Core Investments.* The second step is to discover partners' core investments. Human beings spend most of their time defending or developing the core investments in their vaults. If the partners share their key investments with one another, the things they are most proud of, then they learn two things:

  • Where they can step without threatening or endangering their partner's turf and thereby damaging the relationship, and

  • How they can most effectively help their partner enhance and protect the key assets in his or her vault.

By examining the assets in each other's vaults, the partners learn about each other's strengths and capabilities—information that may be useful down the road.

• *Step 3: Mutual Mentoring.* The next step in the bonding process is designed to encourage partners to invest in one another and thereby bond with one another. I call this step mutual mentoring. If employee A has a problem, it becomes B's problem, and vice versa. I recommended that the partners meet once each week to help one another solve workplace or personal problems. Mutual mentoring is the foundation of the bonding process. It's the human equivalent of the grooming process that glues primate societies together.

• *Step 4: Mutual Therapy.* The final step in the bonding process is mutual therapy. We have each suffered defeats in life that make us feel incompetent in certain areas. These psychic wounds weigh down our self-esteem and stifle our performance. They are continually present in the background, saying, "Don't forget about me!" These wounds can be healed by developing the missing skills. Some of the pairings, I hoped, would reach this deep and meaningful level of bonding. This step came last in the OPO's formal bonding process because it is the most personal and invasive. It is also the most threatening because it entails exposing one's core weaknesses—the assets missing from the vault. If employee A exposes a psychic wound, it's employee B's job to help remove the psychic "splinters."

For the employee pairings within the OPO to reach Level 4, they needed to act and feel like therapists. This required a depth of commitment seldom found in the workplace.

Psychiatrist Scott Peck described the therapeutic level of commitment in his best-selling book *The Road Less Traveled*. According to Peck, the therapist must lay him- or herself on the line and be prepared to suffer along with the patient. He compares the level of commitment to that between a parent and child.[21] Peck cited the case of a wealthy female patient named Rachel to illustrate the level of trust required to gain access to inner psychic wounds. Peck had treated Rachel for twelve months with little success. One day the woman announced that she could no longer afford to pay the fee for her sessions. Peck agreed to cut his fee in half for the woman, which deeply affected her. Coming from a wealthy family, Rachel had never been offered a break before.[22] It was Peck's willingness to sacrifice his normal fee, to suffer with her so that she could heal, that gave him access to the inner sanctum where Rachel's deepest wounds were hidden. Her therapy was ultimately successful and she was reborn as a healthier human being.

You might think this four-step bonding-building process sounds wasteful and irrelevant to the task of running a profitable business. The Gallup Organization has eight million employee surveys in its worldwide database that say otherwise. Each survey in the database consists of numerous individual questions. The Gallup Organization continuously mines this vast database looking for meaningful correlations between survey responses and hard business outcomes, like improved profitability. What question do you think best correlates with tangible organizational outcomes? The answer is startling from a traditional management perspective, but predictable from the bonding and social networking perspectives. The best predictor of organizational success is an affirmative answer to the following question:

"Do you have a vital friend at work?"

Human beings are designed to form intimate tribal groups where each individual is bonded to the tribe and to one another. This is our natural habitat and where we operate most efficiently. The Gallup statistics strongly support this view.

Having close relationships in the workplace releases oxytocin and vasopressin and thereby contributes to the emotional paycheck and makes employees feel more rewarded at work. Developing tight bonds in the workplace is doubly powerful because it not only improves employee incentives, but simultaneously improves coordination and information flow by expanding the social network.

Outcome of the OPO Beta Test

Dr. T and I eventually combined both the informal and formal relationship-building approaches at the OPO. Dr. T pursued the informal approach to bonding by hosting monthly cookouts at his home and by spending time listening to his employees and acting on their concerns. The formal relationship-building process was eventually deemed too intrusive and embarrassing for this particular group, so we switched to the more businesslike, internal branding approach discussed in Chapter 1. After four months, the typical timeframe reported by Bob Carpenter to reach a motivational tipping point,[23] the OPO's emotional health score jumped four points from neutral to moderately positive. It has stayed at this position ever since. Dr. T reports that he has reclaimed the exciting dynamic of the OPO's early days. The most tangible result has been decreased employee turnover. Turnover is a big deal at the OPO because the doctors and nurses who work there are highly skilled and specialized and it can cost upward of $250,000 to train an organ procurement specialist.

The bonds we developed at the OPO will hopefully be permanent. If an employee leaves the OPO for some reason, the bonds will stretch, but not break. If employee B moves to California for personal reasons, for example, then employee A's network will simply become expanded into a new geographic region.

EAST MEETS WEST, AND THEN EATS WEST

Many Westerners think of Chinese companies as either brutal sweatshops or as outdated and inefficient state-run enterprises. Both of these types of businesses exist in China, but there are also superorganisms—family-owned companies that left China during the Communist revolution, but that are now returning in force. Chinese family-owned companies, we will find, have many of the characteristics of a superorganism.

Not only does China have many family-owned companies that resemble superorganisms, but the Chinese government has embarked on an aggressive economic, military, and political expansion program. Yan Xuetong, a Chinese foreign affairs specialist in Beijing, recently claimed in a scholarly journal that China has already surpassed Japan, Russia, Britain, France, Germany, and India in measures of economic, military, and political power. That leaves it second only to the United States. If you own or run a company in the United States, you should be afraid, very afraid!

China's dizzying rise should not be underestimated. The Chinese have been talented entrepreneurs and merchants for thousands of years. Chinese culture is based on a networking system called *guanxi* (gwahn-shee) that is similar, in many ways, to the formal bonding approach described in this chapter. Chinese society as a whole has a deep tribal character that harmonizes with nature's emotional architecture. Chinese entrepreneurs have successfully used their *guanxi* system in business for over a thousand years. Wherever you look in Southeast Asia, the ethnic Chinese diaspora makes up a small percentage of the population but dominates the local economies. Examples include Thailand (3 percent ethnic Chinese control 60 percent of trade), the Philippines (3 percent control 70 percent of trade), and Indonesia (4 percent control 70 percent). The total assets of the Chinese diaspora have been estimated to be between $2 trillion and $3 trillion. In national terms, this group constitutes the third-largest economy in the world after the United States and Japan. The Chinese economic juggernaut is growing rapidly, not just because of Western investment, but, more important, because of investment by the Chinese diaspora.

Many successful Chinese companies that fled China after the Communist revolution are moving back home. Some of these wealthy expatriate companies are adapting the best practices of Western rational management to their homegrown trust-based system. The result is a potent hybrid that feeds all five social appetites. I am concerned that the Chinese family-owned conglomerates may dismantle Western multinationals the way Nucor bested Bethlehem in the steel industry. The Communist government hopes to tame its entrepreneurial beast and use it to dominate the West. One way to defend against the Chinese economic juggernaut is to become more like them. Become a superorganism yourself.

Dr. Ming-Jer Chen, in his book *Inside Chinese Business*, describes how Chinese companies are combining the best aspects of Western rational management with their homegrown networking approach. According to a prominent Chinese businessman quoted in Dr. Chen's book:

> *The goal of this integration is to keep the best of Asian business practices— the emphasis on entrepreneurship and a sense of family—while adapting the most successful of Western practices: formal strategic planning, clear and consistent accounting, and a focus on innovation, customer service, and quality.*[24]

Dr. Chen suggests that this combination of Eastern and Western traditions will be a powerful force to be reckoned with in the years ahead.

If you want to resist China's march toward economic domination, you need to create a superorganism by striking a harmonious balance between emotion and intellect. This will give you a fighting chance against the Chinese juggernaut. The Chinese don't make a sharp distinction between business relationships and family relationships. Business partners, in other words, are family. Subordinates often refer to supervisors and managers as "big brother," "big sister," or "good uncle."

Perhaps Western companies can learn something from the Chinese *guanxi* system. After all, it lies at the core of a culture that has thrived for thousands of years. *Guanxi* loosely translates as "connections" or "personal relationships."[25] *Guanxi* implies reciprocity—if I help you, you will eventually reciprocate the favor. Ideally it includes a warm, personal connection as well. It is the commitment of time to build deep durable relationships that best defines *guanxi*. The strongest *guanxi* exists between family members, but the *guanxi* network typically extends beyond family to include people who have shared meaningful experiences together like old friends, college classmates, former colleagues, and buddies who served in the military together. Chinese seek to establish *guanxi* relationships with people they find respectable and who are referred by someone else in the network.

Japanese management is based upon *wa*, a concept similar to *guanxi*. It involves committing to a group and then forging consensus goals and selflessly committing to them—all within the context of warm mutual friendships. Harmony is the byword within *wa*-based companies. Japanese *wa* applies mainly to group relations, while Chinese *guanxi* refers primarily to one-on-one personal relationships irrespective of group membership and where gift-giving and reciprocity are mandatory. *Guanxi* tends to be a bit more utilitarian and less based upon deep emotional bonds than *wa*.[26]

Both *guanxi* and *wa*, I propose, are made possible by the cathexis-bonding phenomenon discussed in this chapter whereby the things we invest in are automatically brought inside and help define who we are as persons—our sense of self. We-based Chinese and Japanese companies based on trust networks have a number of important advantages over traditional me-based Western firms founded on individual achievement and internal competition. Following are some of those advantages.

Self-Regulation Benefit of a Connected Trust Network

A major source of tension between Western and Chinese business cultures pertains to the concept of formal, written contracts. The Chinese view written contracts as redundant, at best, and insulting, at worst. According to the Chinese way of thinking, relationships make written contracts unnecessary. From the traditional Chinese trust-based perspective, it is unthinkable that a business partner would renege on a verbal agreement because such behavior would not only damage one relationship, but would ripple through the network like a string of exploding firecrackers and damage business opportunities far and wide. The Chinese are sensitive to being humiliated, or losing face, for the same reason; bad behavior or good behavior gets magnified by its radiation through the network. A trust network is self-regulating because one selfish act could wipe out a lifetime of careful relationship building, a lifetime of investment. This is why the Chinese play by the *guanxi* rules and why saving face is so important to them.

The *guanxi* trust-based system is self-regulating just as human beings in general are self-regulating when they belong to intimate tribal groups. Ming-Jer Chen points out that a trust-based system is, in many ways, more efficient than the standard Western model because it "dramatically cuts both paperwork and the need for external institutions such as lawyers and banks."[27] I would extend this thought. A trust-based system can eliminate entire levels of management hierarchy and dramatically reduce oversight and record-keeping expenses. A trust-based organization is therefore inherently lean, flat, and efficient.

Peters and Waterman noted that the excellent companies they studied were, invariably, lean and flat. In other words, they were self-regulating superorganisms with a shared culture:

> *Without exception, the dominance and coherence of culture proved to be an essential quality of the excellent companies. Moreover, the stronger the culture . . . the less need was there for policy manuals, organizational charts, or detailed procedures or rules. In these companies people way down the line know what they are supposed to do in most situations because the handful of guiding values is crystal clear.*[28]

Harry Quadracci built a deep *guanxi*-like network in his printing plants and enjoyed the economic benefits because of it. Quadracci invested in his workers and treated them as partners. He trusted them to fulfill their part of the bargain without an elaborate system of oversight. Quadracci's relationship with his workforce made detailed rules and regulations redundant, just as contracts are redundant in the *guanxi* system.

Quad/Graphics also lacked formal job descriptions. Quadracci wanted his employees to take personal responsibility for any problem that needed solving. His attitude was, "If you see a problem, fix it."[29] Supervisors at Quad/Graphics were not overseers who issued orders; rather, they were resources to help employees solve problems.

Most U.S. employees, as the Gallup engagement survey revealed, are disengaged employees who don't really care about their employer or its goals. Western publicly traded companies have earned this situation by stressing "hitting the numbers" above all else. Many Western companies are oversight intensive, because trust networks don't exist.

Nucor Steel is a trust-based superorganism in the steel industry. Nucor, like Quad/Graphics and Semco SA, is lean, flat, and self-managing. Ken Iverson, Nucor's former chairman, described Nucor's trust-based approach in his book *Plain Talk* as follows:

> *[T]he truth is, simplicity is what makes Nucor successful. At least, it's a big part of it. We've consciously tried to push aside the complexity, hierarchy, bureaucracy, and much of the other nonsense that characterizes life inside so many large corporations.*[30]

Self-management greatly simplifies the Herculean task of managing a large, complex company and focuses attention on what really matters—customers and getting the work done. If your company is drowning in structure, complexity, and paper pushing, perhaps you should metamorphose into a superorganism too.

Insurance Policy Benefit of a Connected Trust Network

Trust networks are especially valuable in times of crisis. The *guanxi* trust-based system evolved in an environment of uncertainty and insecurity. The ethnic Chinese diaspora in Southeast Asia, for example, often consisted of persecuted minorities within their host nations. *Guanxi* networks were like insurance policies that the Chinese could draw on in times of crisis. Not surprisingly, the Chinese view adversity as the true test of a relationship: an opportunity to prove its depth.

Like the Chinese, Harry Quadracci was able to draw on his trust network in times of need. Quadracci's workers went beyond the call of duty when they drove off union organizers outside the Pewaukee, Wisconsin, plant in the late seventies. They also went beyond the call of duty on July 12, 2002, when Quad/Graphics suffered a devastating fire at its sprawling, 2.2 million-square-foot Lomira, Wisconsin, printing plant. Twenty-five thousand pallets of printed material went up in smoke during the fire. Firefighters poured fifteen million gallons of water on the ensuing blaze.[31] Quadracci's employees instinctively came to the rescue like warrior ants defending the nest. Within two weeks all of the work had been reprinted or scheduled for printing. The printing industry was astonished and Quadracci was ecstatic![32]

Quadracci's employees responded vigorously to the emergency because of the *guanxi*-like relationships he had painstakingly established beforehand. When a superorganism is in danger, everyone instinctively feels the pain and responds immediately. Employees in a typical workplace are unlikely to respond in this way. Disengaged employees are more likely to fan the flames during an emergency than extinguish them.

The employees inside a superorganism simply *care* more than the average employee. They have taken their employers inside themselves and locked them into their vaults. Employees working for the three superorganisms, Quad/Graphics, Nucor, and Semco SA, cared enough about their employers to drive off union organizers who wanted to sow seeds of discontent.

Emotional Paycheck Benefit of a Connected Trust Network

In many ways, Dr. Chen concludes, Chinese and Western worldviews are philosophically opposed. He characterizes Western culture as analytical, linear, individualistic, quantitative, and task oriented. Chinese have a more holistic view. *Guanxi* networks strive to maximize gain for the network as a whole. Western culture is me-oriented and Chinese culture is we-oriented. Here is how Dr. Chen describes the difference:

> *In evaluating its business, a Chinese company is likely to ask, "Is there harmony among employees? Is everyone growing and developing along with the business? Do the members of the company see rewards being shared equally?"*

*By contrast, Western companies focus upon individual achievement
and tend to stress hard indicators—net income or sales, profit margins,
and earnings per share—when assessing performance.*[33]

Dr. Chen concludes that the Western me-based approach can "reduce
motivation for group harmony and cooperation." In other words, you
cannot build a superorganism using pure rationality because it will lack a
heart and its moving parts will not be securely connected.

I have argued in this book that all rewards are emotional in nature.
Monetary reward represents just one component of an individual's overall emotional paycheck. The Chinese system seeks to maximize the overall
emotional gain of the group and therefore makes sense from a macroeco-
nomic perspective. It generates the greatest amount of emotional wealth
for the greatest number of people.

Humans are supposed to be embedded within a tribal trust network
in order to feel valuable and valued. The *guanxi* system accomplishes this.
Human beings in a *guanxi* network therefore *feel better* because they get
their daily dose of oxytocin or vasopressin, that warm "family feel." They
also have a clear target to shoot for to build self-esteem and release serotonin. Employees therefore receive a pleasure bonus on top of their monetary paycheck, and this bonus contributes to their commitment and
productivity.

SURVIVAL OF THE FITTEST?

If I say the name Charles Darwin, what is the first thing that jumps to
mind? How about, "survival of the fittest"? The industrialists and robber
barons of the nineteenth century thought Darwin meant survival of the
fittest *individual*. They figured that they were the fittest and therefore
destined to survive at the expense of their workers. The robber barons
used Darwin's famous proclamation to justify an abusive form of sweatshop capitalism. Sweatshop capitalism triggered violent riots and the rise
of unions. It also gave birth to communism.

The robber barons misread Darwin. He actually stated that human survival is based on the survival of the fittest *group*, not the fittest individual.

> *There can be no doubt that a tribe including many members who, from possessing in a high degree the spirit of patriotism, fidelity, obedience, courage, and sympathy, were always ready to give aid to each other and to sacrifice themselves for the common good, would be victorious over most other tribes; and this would be natural selection.*[34]

This quote puts an entirely different spin on survival of the fittest. If Darwin is right, then companies that are we-based will triumph over companies in the marketplace jungle that are me-based.

The nineteenth century was the era of cutthroat dog-eat-dog capitalism. The twentieth century was the era of cool and calculating hyperrational capitalism. Perhaps the business community will get Darwin right this time around and make the twenty-first century the era of corporate superorganisms, where companies' structures reflect the elegant motivational mechanism incorporated into our design. Until scientists can reengineer human nature, this seems like the intelligent thing to do.

PERSONAL IMPLEMENTATION

The implementation suggestions in *Primal Management* will seem pretty basic. This is because a few deep changes at the emotional level will unleash far-reaching changes at the behavioral level throughout an organization as energizing feelings take hold. The steps to turn on the cooperation appetite, for example, and thereby activate cooperative, coordinated behavior among your employees, are disarmingly simple: (1) value your employees and (2) invest in your employees. If you do these two things, then your employees will feel included as opposed to excluded and will experience a warm, family feel in the workplace that will translate into a positive (pleasurable) score on the Tune-Up Metric.

Both of these steps sound easy, but they are anything but. They require effort, commitment, and an entirely new management mind-set. We are immersed in a competitive me-based culture from birth onward, so we-based thinking is largely foreign to us. We are taught to compete in sports, at school, and in the workplace. It is therefore far easier to find managers who think they are better than their employees, and who feel vaguely threatened by them, than it is to find a manager who truly treats employees as equals and sincerely invests in their development and thereby takes them inside.

I recently had this discussion with a friend at an open-air rooftop bar in Chicago. My friend, who I hadn't seen in twelve years, was recently promoted to an executive position with a professional-services firm. I told him about my book project and was surprised by his combative and condescending remarks: "Paul, the professional-services world is a dog-eat-dog jungle. It's survival of the fittest. I can't tell you how many times I've been cheated or manipulated by management. It's the guys at the top who hold all the cards and who manipulate the system to reap the biggest rewards. Now I'm one of those guys and I'm going to protect my position from all comers—including my employees. I deserve the rewards and perks of management because of all the abuse I've put up with over the years."

My friend's attitude, though somewhat shocking, probably represents a fairly typical experience inside large, hierarchical corporations. It's like a dysfunctional family where abuse perpetuates abuse. How can we blame my friend, and people like him, for being self-interested and aggressive toward their colleagues and employees considering that our economic system is based upon a philosophy of competition and rational self-interest?

I sympathized with my friend and shared my own war stories of petty abuse at the hands of the corporate hierarchy. Then I tried to convince him that there's a dramatically better way—a win-win scenario where everybody prospers. Employees in this win-win world, I explained, are highly motivated, highly collaborative, and highly innovative. The employees within a win-win organization act as a coordinated, synergistic whole, and one employee's weaknesses are compensated for by another employee's strengths. This type of corporate superorganism, I explained, wins big in the marketplace so, in the final analysis, there are more rewards to divvy up. It also feels good to live inside a superorganism because you feel like part of a big family—you feel like blood and you care about its future. My friend was unconvinced so I decided to outline both the costs and benefits of my employee-centric approach to management. What follows is roughly how our conversation proceeded.

The Costs

In order to activate the cooperation appetite within your work group, I told him, and turn it into a flat, trust-based superorganism, you will need to go though a period of adjustment and investment that will not feel like a win. In fact, it may feel like you are losing status and perks and investing a great deal of effort. You will need to bite the bullet and tough it out during this adjustment period. If it weren't for this difficult hurdle, there would be lots of superorganisms running around in the corporate ecosystem. Fortunately for him, I explained, superorganisms are still quite rare.

Cost 1: Overcoming Various Forms of Prejudice

Step 1 in the two-step bonding process is to value your employees, I said. This step is crucial because we are not going to sincerely invest in a person, place, or thing that we don't find valuable and worthy of our investment—and without investment, bonding will not occur. Valuing employees sounds easy, but it is definitely not. There are many forms of subtle prejudice that interfere with it. It is more common, I suggested, for managers to view employees as lazy, uncooperative, and, for various reasons, unworthy of commitment and investment.

Here are some of the prejudices managers need to overcome to reach superorganism status:

* Employee went to the wrong school

* Employee comes from the wrong socioeconomic background (blue collar versus white collar)

* Employee is of the wrong gender

* Employee is not attractive or is too attractive

- Employee was born into the wrong race or in the wrong country

- Employee belongs to the wrong religion, or no religion

The list of possible prejudices is endless, and the reasons for devaluing the people around us are infinite. The sad truth is, if someone isn't exactly like us, our brains will happily identify subtle differences that can then be used as a springboard for devaluing and discriminating against that person. This sensitivity to differences is probably a legacy of our Ice Age heritage where "different" often equated to "dangerous" (a hostile tribe looking to acquire one's territory and resources).

If we don't confront these primitive defensive impulses up front, I suggested, they will result in employees feeling devalued and then acting that way. Managers need to take pride in confronting these dark instincts and make equality and respect in the workplace a top priority.

My favorite example of corporate prejudice-busting pertains to Ken Iverson, the social architect of Nucor Steel, a $14-billion-a-year dynamo in the steel industry.[35] Hierarchy, Iverson wrote, is simply a form of prejudice. Iverson likened management's treatment of workers in a hierarchy to the South's treatment of blacks in the early 1960s before desegregation. When Iverson took over Nucor's Vulcraft division in Florence, South Carolina, in 1962, the plant still had segregated black and white dressing rooms. The plant, in his words, was divided into "we" versus "they." A week after Iverson arrived, he knocked down the wall separating the black and white dressing rooms as a hierarchy- and prejudice-destroying gesture. Iverson and his colleagues at Nucor recommended that corporate America do the same, by knocking down executive parking spaces, corporate jets, meetings at posh resorts, company cars, first-class travel, corner offices, executive dining rooms, and anything else that puts a barrier between employees and management.

Life within a hierarchy quite literally hurts for the many low-pay, low-status employees at the broad base of the pyramid. Hierarchies are like the feudal systems of the Middle Ages where kings and nobles ruled over serfs. The trappings of hierarchy create class divisions that make it hard for both managers and employees to break out of the "me" mentality. The solution, I proposed to my friend, was to flatten the hierarchy by treating everyone as valuable to the organization. In this corporate flat-land, managers are not better than anybody else. As Ken Iverson liked to say, they simply have a different job to do.[36] Managers can even take this flattening process a step further by putting the interests of employees ahead of their own—a growing trend called servant leadership.

Enlightened managers who respect and value employees at the base of the pyramid (who, by the way, perform most of the actual work) create an enormous increase in the emotional paycheck of those employees. They also cause employees to feel empowered and confident instead of meek and incompetent. Managers who serve their employees instead of bullying, intimidating, or lording over them provide an emotional boost that translates into superior productivity, superior decision making, superior innovation, and superior economic performance. Structural flatness is crucial to the emotional calculus of creating a high-performance, egalitarian organization.

I counseled my Chicago friend that the very act of psychologically climbing down from his roost in the hierarchy would provide a motivational boost to his work group that would more than compensate for his temporary reduction in perceived status. The impact of a manager stepping down a notch gets multiplied when all of his or her employees emotionally step up a notch. This translates into an energy gain (or emotional payroll increase) for the organization as a whole that translates into improved performance.

Cost 2: Investing Four Months of Up-Front Investment

Once we value our employees, I told my friend, and respect them as equals, and commit ourselves to serving them, we are ready for Step 2 of the two-step relationship-building process—investment. The goal of this step is to bring our employees inside until their interests become synonymous with our interests. Success in the investment step creates a profound sense of connection that will make interacting with our employees a pleasure for both parties. Not many managers are willing to proactively make this up-front investment, which is another reason why tribal super-organisms are so rare. They may try something like this for a week or two but then give up when they don't see immediate results. The trick to making this two-step process work is to *not* expect immediate results.

The traditional term for this investment process in a corporate setting is *mentoring*. A traditional mentor takes an employee under his or her wing and shows the employee the ropes, shares insights, listens patiently to problems, and helps him or her in any way possible. Traditional mentoring provides a brilliant vehicle for fostering investment. It leads in the right direction, but creates one-way investments and one-way relationships. I therefore suggest that managers and employees engage in two-way, or mutual, mentoring. If the manager has a problem, it becomes the employee's problem, and vice versa. Mentoring was an important part of my job satisfaction in the oil industry and environmental-consulting business. One of the main reasons I worked hard in these jobs was to please and impress the mentors who had generously encouraged me and invested in me.

Investment, I told my friend, can take many forms. One simple suggestion is to keep notes on your direct reports just as you would with a client. Then explore your employees' lives deeply, like Jacques Cousteau exploring a coral reef. Explore their life histories, their hopes and dreams, successes and failures, and the key assets in their social-asset vaults. Get to know them so well that you could almost write a biography about them. Listen to your employees empathically and objectively, without projecting too much of yourself into their stories. Make sure to look for things you admire in the employees you are mentoring—especially the deep values you hold in common that can form the basis of a lifelong friendship. Your employees will initially wonder "what's up." If you are consistent and authentic, however, disbelief will gradually morph into trust and commitment and your employees will begin investing in return.

It typically takes a substantial four-month investment to create a meaningful trust bond because human beings are instinctively cautious and trust must be earned though consistency, integrity, and investment—you need to ante up. The investment will automatically pull your employees inside your social-asset vault and create a sense of protective ownership over them. There is one shortcut to building trust bonds that supersedes the four-month rule—put yourself at risk for your employees, or go beyond the call of duty for them. The most durable bonds I have studied occur between soldiers in battle. Deep, lifelong bonds are created when soldiers risk their lives for their comrades. These bonds can be created quickly and persist for many decades. You can create similar bonds by being the first person to respond when an employee experiences a personal crisis. A few acts like this will ripple through your growing trust network and strengthen all of the bonds.

In middle school I had a run-in with the class bully that illustrates this bonding principle. It involved a kid who had been held back twice and who actually belonged in high school. I was heading to a friend's house after school in seventh grade when I encountered the bully on the school's football field. There we stood in the middle of the field with nobody else in sight. In typical bully fashion he knocked the books out of my hand and proceeded to shove me backward, itching for a fight. I was speechless, because nothing like this had ever happened to me before. Then, out of nowhere, Mike, one of my classmates, appeared and wrestled the bully to the ground and quickly subdued him. I thanked Mike profusely and he responded with a casual, "No problem—that guy's a jerk." To this day I would gladly jump to Mike's rescue should the need ever arise. The moral—if you want your employees to jump through fire for you, you'd better be willing to do the same for them. Think of the people in your life who have gone beyond the call of duty for you. How do you feel about these people today?

After I finished describing the many investments involved in developing bonded relationships, my Chicago buddy, now looking a bit exasperated, asked, "Do I have to give up my paycheck too?" "Actually, no," I responded, "wages are largely set by the marketplace based upon education, experience, and performance so you don't need to take a pay cut. Your employees will not balk at traditional pay disparities because they reflect the economic realities of an open marketplace." Then he asked, "What if my mentee quits and joins a competing firm? My investment would be wasted or perhaps turned against me." The bonds we are talking about, I replied, are meant to be lifelong. The employee may leave for some reason, but he or she will remain in your vault. Your mentee may return some day with new skills or send leads or recruits your way. Who knows, he or she might even offer you a job at some point. No matter what happens, you will still have an ally willing to come to your aid.

The bonds managers forge through the mutual-mentoring process are the single most important factor in reducing employee turnover. It's the mutual investment in relationships that creates employee loyalty and motivates hard work with minimal supervision. Once someone has sincerely invested in us, and we in them, we don't want to endanger the invested relationship by letting our mentor down—and this includes letting the mentor down by quitting.

I told my friend that there are infinite ways for him to invest in his employees. If he needed more detailed guidance, I suggested that he read books dealing with trust, servant leadership, mentoring, community building, and loyalty. These books contain many excellent ideas that you can experiment with, I told him. You will know that you have reached the goal—an authentic, invested relationship—when your employees' successes start feeling like your own personal successes. At this point you will naturally act in the best interests of your employees because their interests and your interests have become one and the same.

The Benefits

I next described the powerful benefits of creating a superorganism that, in my opinion, vastly outweigh the up-front costs. One important benefit, I explained, is the pleasure a mentor feels when interacting with his or her employees. It feels good to spend time with your mentees. It feels like spending time with good friends thanks to the relationship hormones oxytocin and vasopressin. These warm, friendly feelings create a deposit to the emotional paychecks of both parties in the mentoring relationship. These positive feelings therefore constitute a major benefit in our emotional cost-benefit analysis.

Employees who bond with their managers, and who feel valued on account of it, work extremely hard to maintain this feeling, just as the Chinese work hard to protect their *guanxi* relationships. Invested employees work harder, respond quicker, and require less supervision because the manager's needs are experienced as the employee's needs. You are able to trust employees more and delegate more difficult assignments to them with full confidence that your employees will perform.

These benefits are not subtle. According to Bob Carpenter, the corporate turnaround artist mentioned in Chapter 2, you could easily double the productivity of your work group by investing just four months of effort into the mutual-mentoring process. Bonded relationships should be encouraged not just between managers and employees, I told my friend, but between employees themselves. The more relationships created inside the superorganism, the better it will hold together in times of trouble and the better information and skills flow to where they are most needed. The bottom line is that a we-based superorganism is going to function in a more coordinated and competent fashion and thrive in the marketplace because everyone cares about the tribe and pulls in the same direction. Superior financial performance is therefore another major benefit of we-based superorganisms. Other benefits are less fear and stress, less absenteeism, less turnover, and improved strategy execution.

After I reviewed the costs and benefits involved in creating a we-based superorganism I asked my friend to contemplate the lifestyle differences between the "me road" and the "we road." The differences we discussed are summarized in Table 4-1.

"Well, what do you think?" I asked my friend. "Is it worth paying the four-month up-front 'toll' to enter the 'we road' or to simply continue down the 'me road'?" My friend, thankfully, agreed to give the two-step bonding process a try. This was only a month ago, so it is too soon to report the outcome of our rooftop meeting in Chicago.

I think deep collaboration is the trend of the future. I see me-based hierarchies stumbling in the face of spirited competition from we-based superorganisms. Japanese companies, as I already mentioned, are founded on the concept of *wa*. To achieve *wa*, Japanese are expected to deeply commit themselves to group goals and suppress their individual selfish goals.[37] They take their company inside themselves and it helps define who they are—exactly what I am proposing with the two-step bonding process.

Everyone needs to make their own, independent cost-benefit analysis to decide which road to take. If you decide to head merrily down the me-road, the ideas in this book will not help you. As a geologist I was trained to see the big picture. The earth is 4.5 billion years old and the granite countertop in your kitchen is probably a hundred million years old. From

TABLE 4-1. COMPARISON OF A ME-BASED MANAGER TO A WE-BASED MANAGER

Attitudes of a Me-Based Manager	Attitudes of a We-Based Manager
Employees are inherently lazy and untrustworthy and must be carefully watched. I need detailed rules, regulations, and systems to keep them in line.	Human beings, when embedded in a tightly bonded group, instinctively want to be productive and to serve the group. My employees don't need constant supervision because they care about me and their co-workers and eagerly pursue our shared goals.
It's all about me. Employees who don't cater to my needs are history.	I value and serve my employees and thereby motivate them to volunteer their best efforts.
I make all the decisions and complete most of the work because my employees are either incompetent or untrustworthy.	I trust my employees to do the right thing and make good decisions so I delegate freely. My employees seldom disappoint me.
I don't really care about my employees. They are like pawns on a chessboard to me. I just want to make a killing and retire early. They can fend for themselves.	My employees matter to me and we have an exciting and productive work group. We enjoy tackling difficult challenges and achieving success as a team. We also enjoy getting together outside the workplace. In essence, it hardly feels like work.
When employees screw up I make public examples of them, sort of like a public hanging.	When employees make mistakes I correct them in private in a positive way to make them stronger. They never take offense because they know I have their best interests at heart.
I feel nothing for my employees. They are units of production, nothing more. If an employee is smarter than me, he or she is a potential competitor so I get rid of him or her.	I enjoy my employees and feel good when they succeed. Their success feels like my success.

a geologic perspective, human beings don't live very long. In just the snap of a finger, we are gone. How do you want to spend your brief moment in the sun and how do you want to be remembered when you are gone?

If you take the me-road through life you may, or may not, end up with a barrel full of money, but your legacy will be nil. The we-road creates a lasting legacy—because we leave part of ourselves inside the employees we mentor. We also create a healthy ecosystem that will continue to provide tremendous value in our absence. Paradoxically, by focusing on your employees' well-being instead of making a fortune for yourself, you are more likely to end up with a barrel full of money than if you had taken the me-road in the first place. From the big-picture perspective, the we-road adds more value to the corporate ecosystem than the me-road, so logically, it's the best way to go.

One parting word of caution about the we-road. Trust is difficult to create, but easy to destroy. The Chinese are very careful not to betray anyone within their *guanxi* trust network because any infraction is magnified as it propagates through the network, destroying carefully built relationships along the way. The same goes for the we-road. It requires rigorous consistency in dealing fairly with others.

ORGANIZATIONAL IMPLEMENTATION

I am now switching focus from managers inside large organizations to address the CEO or owner of the organization. A CEO can create a tribal superorganism much faster than an individual manager can. I suggest, furthermore, that CEOs should make the creation of a we-based superorganism their number-one goal.

We-based superorganisms, I suggest, are gaining momentum in the marketplace and are quietly gestating inside many organizations—particularly in the "100 Best Companies to Work For." CEOs across the country are already thinking in terms of "we" instead of "me"—even in the face of relentless short-term pressures from me-based analysts and investors on Wall Street.[38]

Advice for CEOs

I described a businesslike, marketing-based approach for creating a super-organism in Chapter 1. This process, as you may recall, is called internal branding. Internal branding treats employees like internal customers and aims at creating a workplace environment that satisfies employee needs. Internal branding can help you, the CEO, create a forum and methodology for addressing the touchy subject of employee needs. You should bless and support the internal branding process and be its biggest cheerleader.

Chapter 2 introduced an emotional health survey to measure whether or not employees' needs to innovate, master skills, deploy skills to achieve group goals, belong to a tightly bonded team, and feel protected are being satisfied, along with two metrics to visualize the results. The Horsepower Metric provides a safe and businesslike way to track employee needs without appearing soft—after all, every manager should desire a powerful, high-horsepower workplace.

If the CEO blesses the Horsepower Metric and focuses on it in meetings, managers throughout the company will pay attention to it and begin experimenting with ways to get the horsepower to go up. I do not recommend pinning promotions or bonuses to the metric because this creates motivation to game the system and thereby subvert its purpose. Simply encourage managers to use the metric and to implement the tune-up suggestions discussed in *Primal Management* and let the ensuing results speak for themselves. Share your success stories widely and consistently encourage managers and employees who take the we-road instead of the me-road.

Let's assume that you, the CEO, have already conducted the survey and the results, as depicted using the Horsepower Metric, are sitting in front of you. If your horsepower is in the positive 4 to 8 range, congratulations, your motivational engine is already well tuned and you probably have the superior financial results and customer satisfaction to prove it. A positive score also means that your employees experience intrinsic pleasure from their work, which contributes to their emotional paycheck and motivates high performance.

Now let's assume the opposite—that your company has negative horsepower. This means that your employees, for a variety of potential reasons, find it painful to come to work. In other words, their social appetites are not being satisfied and they are, in a sense, starving. This should not be a shock considering the competitive me-based management culture we are all immersed in. A negative score can be seen as a good thing because it means that improved financial performance is just a few simple, but challenging, steps away.

A quick glance at the Tune-Up Metric will reveal which social appetites are causing pain in the workforce. If the cooperation appetite shows a negative score, it should be your first priority because, as I said before, it is the linchpin for maximizing the horsepower of the motivational engine. If the cooperation appetite isn't being fed, then the other social appetites probably aren't being fed either. The monthly review of the Horsepower and Tune-Up Metrics provides managers with an ideal venue for uncovering the causes of emotional pain and dissatisfaction and taking actions, as a group, to eliminate them.

If, for whatever reason, you choose not to use the emotional health survey and related metrics to track your motivational progress, you can still follow the internal branding methodology described in Chapter 1. For example, you can ask managers to conduct monthly focus groups with employees to identify their key needs and then work toward satisfying those needs. You can also apply the ideas in *Primal Management* to help you tune the motivational engine. In regard to a metric for measuring employee motivation, your improved success and positive work climate should suffice.

The ultimate goal of the methodology proposed in *Primal Management* is to create a human-friendly ecosystem where everyone can thrive. You should therefore proceed boldly and forcefully with confidence that you are serving everybody's interests. If anyone (think Wall Street analysts and short-term investors) gives you grief regarding this employee-centric approach, use the facts, statistics, and logic in *Primal Management* as your heavy artillery to strike back.

If you lose focus or courage on your quest, try rereading the following quote from Ken Iverson, the chairman of Nucor Steel:

> *What we did was push aside the notion that managers and employees have inherently separate interests. We've joined with our employees to pursue a*

goal we can all believe in: long-term survival. We run Nucor first and foremost to ensure that, a decade or two from now, there will still be a place for our children and grandchildren to work without being laid off. That is our higher cause.[39]

CEOs who succeed in forging a we-based superorganism, like Ken Iverson did, will notice a change in the feel of the workplace. Employees will begin cheering the organization's successes, much like football fans bond to, and support, their favorite sports teams.

CEO Suggestion 1: Embrace and Model the Two-Step Bonding Process

This chapter deals with the cooperation appetite, so let's explore some ideas for feeding this crucial appetite and getting the score to go up. First and foremost, it is crucial for CEOs to embrace and personally implement the two-step bonding process discussed in this chapter. Let your actions be an example for the rest of the organization regarding how employees should be treated. If you, the CEO, engage in mutual mentoring, for example, this will trigger a top-down cascade of mentoring behaviors as managers seek to emulate your actions. This cascade will accelerate as the organization's performance ramps up and as managers experience, firsthand, the power of a properly tuned engine.

CEO Suggestion 2: Implement Hierarchy-and-Bureaucracy-Busting Policies

A superorganism is self-managing, self-motivated, and self-organizing, with minimal need for external structures and controls. A trust-based superorganism will do the right thing naturally and organically without such external systems. You can therefore have fun engaging in hierarchy and bureaucracy busting as you create a we-based organization.

Vanguard's CEO, Jack Brennan, regularly honored employees who identified outmoded or abusive systems with a bureaucracy-busting sticker they could proudly display in their offices.[40] Your focus as the leader of a superorganism should be to dismantle redundant, disrespectful, or burdensome systems that reduce motivational horsepower and waste time and energy. If the system in question serves a vital business purpose, let your employees redesign it so it is more internal-customer friendly. This way systems serve people instead of the other way around.

Hierarchy busting is another CEO imperative for creating a we-based organization. The Japanese saying—"the nail that sticks up gets hit"— comes to mind as a good motto for a hierarchy-busting campaign. Anybody who tries to put him- or herself above others by building a castle on a hill, or a personal gilded silo to commemorate his or her perceived greatness, should have their ramparts pulled down. Hardcore me-based managers will inevitably seek preferential treatment, will brutally defend and fortify their hilltop edifices, and will arrogantly and coldly subjugate and terrorize the people around them. We-based CEOs must quickly recognize the signs of egotistical empire building and toss hand grenades through the castle windows.

The theme of hierarchy busting arose repeatedly during my research into we-based companies. Ken Iverson devoted an entire chapter to the subject in his wonderful book *Plain Talk*. Ricardo Semler, the social architect of Semco SA, was similarly antihierarchy in his book *Maverick*.

In conclusion, the CEO of a we-based superorganism should delegate confidently, flatten the hierarchy firmly, simplify the bureaucracy rigorously, and empower and serve the folks who actually do the work. This is the formula that the three mavericks used to achieve long-term financial and organizational success.

CEO Suggestion 3: Encourage Mutual Investment

Tom Rath, of the Gallup Organization, describes policies to encourage bonding in the workplace in his book *Vital Friends*. Rath's suggestions are simple and easy to implement. The Gallup Organization's statistics indicate that only 20 percent of employees invest in relationships at work. This means that only 20 percent of employees are connected with their managers and workmates. Rath's statistics suggest that the other 80 percent of employees don't really care. They are unbonded, disconnected, and probably feel excluded from the corporate tribe.

Tom Rath suggests that building bonds in the workplace can be as simple as signaling to employees that relationships at work are okay by sponsoring activities outside work such as volunteer events, sports leagues, company cruises, trips, and parties. The CEO can point out that relationships are crucial for the harmonious and efficient operation of the workplace. If your company has a rule against managers socializing with employees outside of work, get rid of it immediately.

I have already mentioned the importance of mutual mentoring. Mentors take workmates under their wings and share their wisdom and knowledge. This automatically results in bonding because bonding occurs wherever there is consensual investment. According to Rath, only 17 percent of employees report that their managers have made an investment in their relationships with employees in the past three months. This implies that only 17 percent of employees have anything resembling a mentor. Rath bemoans this statistic:

> We want and need managers who care about our lives beyond the workplace. Gallup has asked more than 8 million people to respond to the statement "My supervisor, or someone at work, seems to care about me as a person" and has found that people who agree with this statement:
>
> • Are more likely to stay with the organization
>
> • Have more engaged customers
>
> • Are more productive
>
> If you're fortunate enough to have had a manager who treated you like a friend and cared about your personal life, you probably understand the difference this type of genuine friendship can make. The best managers in the world are not only experts in systems, processes, and technical competencies—they are experts in your life. And because of this, they increase your engagement and productivity at work.[41]

Here are additional straightforward suggestions for encouraging relationships in the workplace from Tom Rath's books *Vital Friends* and *How Full Is Your Bucket?*[42]

• Try to learn something new about the people you regularly interact with.

- Share personal stories in order to encourage others to share theirs.

- Compliment when you see progress or strength.

- Make regular appointments with your employees to discuss problems or set goals.

- Don't be afraid to ask for help. Asking employees for help encourages them to invest in the relationship.

- Design a social area into your workplace where employees are encouraged to congregate and socialize outside their cubicles.

Tom Rath's list is certainly not exhaustive. There are infinite ways to encourage investment and mutual mentoring inside your organization. If you need more guidance, read books dealing with topics like mentoring, trust building, loyalty, or servant management. They will contain excellent suggestions for building invested, authentic relationships. If you'd prefer a more structured approach to bonding, try the formal four-step process discussed earlier in this chapter.

CEO Suggestion 4: Promote Accountability

It may appear as though I've gone soft in this chapter on my promise to deliver a hard solution to employee motivation. Nothing could be further from the truth. Nature's motivational mechanism is extremely hard, is designed around human survival, and demands two important forms of accountability. The primary form of accountability inside a superorganism is the approval or disapproval of the group. The consensus of a tightly bonded group has direct control over feelings of high and low self-esteem. These pleasurable and painful feelings are, in my opinion, the ultimate drivers of high performance and the ultimate system of accountability. In a superorganism it hurts more to lose one's respect in the eyes of the group than it does to take a financial hit.

Financial accountability is also important for a superorganism. Money is, in essence, the lifeblood, or sustenance, of the superorganism, so financial incentives should reflect the financial reality of the group's performance in the marketplace. If the superorganism is floundering in the corporate jungle, then financial compensation should communicate the severity of the dysfunction, just as pain receptors transmit the state-of-repair of the body. If human beings lacked pain receptors, we'd be unable to detect whether we are hurt or not and unable to avoid hazards in the environment. The same goes for a financial incentive system that fails to provide accurate survival feedback.

Ken Iverson developed a simple and straightforward compensation scheme to reflect the financial reality of his enterprise. He offered his steelworkers a low base pay, so lackadaisical performance would hurt, and production bonuses based upon how much steel was produced.[43] This simple group-incentive plan focused everyone's attention on cooperating to maximize productivity and surviving over the long haul. Most of his employees responded enthusiastically and earned far more than industry average wages after factoring in their substantial performance bonuses.

Ricardo Semler instituted a similar compensation plan at Semco SA. He paid base salaries commensurate with industry averages and then shared operating unit profits according to the following formula:

- Taxes: 40 percent

- Reinvestment: 12 percent

- Shareholders: 25 percent

- Employees: 23 percent

Semler, as the main shareholder, wasn't thrilled with the 23 percent profit-sharing arrangement, especially considering that profit sharing at most companies runs between 8 and 12 percent. In his words, "But I kept telling myself I stood to make at least as much money in partnership with a motivated workforce as I would as the sole beneficiary of the fruits of less-inspired workers."[44]

Semler cautions that profit-sharing plans don't result in greater productivity at companies populated with disengaged, unmotivated employees. It works only when it "crowns a broad and comprehensive program of (employee) participation."[45] Semco employees were allowed to distribute their 23 percent share of the profits any way they chose. Most of the time, factory committees distributed profits evenly, with managers, supervisors, and workers receiving an equal share. This was perceived as far more equitable than having senior management shell out the money according to an ad hoc, mysterious formula.

Shareholders are another important constituency that deserve their share of the harvest. Iverson spoke lovingly about long-term value investors but was openly hostile toward short-term speculative investors. He compared short-term investors to drug addicts looking for a quick fix, but ignoring the inevitable withdrawal symptoms the short-term fix imposes on future prospects and long-term shareholders. Iverson counseled CEOs to steel themselves against these jackals of the corporate ecosystem and focus instead on creating a long-term win-win scenario for managers, shareholders, employees, and customers.[46]

There are infinite ways to subdivide a superorganism's harvest. Not sharing profits equitably, however, will trigger defensive and angry feelings that can kill your superorganism and ruin the win-win dynamic it is based upon. In a standard me-based organization there is a natural tendency for shareholders and managers to take most of the harvest and minimize the employees' share. This type of selfish behavior is unwise. Neuroeconomists, for example, have noticed that a pain-sensing part of the brain, the anterior insula, lights up in brain scans when unfair monetary offers are made in game-theory games like the prisoner's dilemma.[47] Another neuroeconomic study showed that the brain's pleasure center, the basal striatum, is activated in social-dilemma games when a wronged party retaliates against another player for unfair behavior, like failure to reciprocate a previous financial payout.[48] This research suggests that employees who feel wronged in the workplace will experience pleasure—the sweet taste of revenge—when they retaliate, even in the face of financial penalties, like getting fired.

Researchers have discovered that they can combat angry feelings in these economic game-playing scenarios by administering the neuropeptide oxytocin via nasal spray before the game play begins.[49] Oxytocin, as you may recall, is the relationship hormone we are trying to administer naturally through the relationship-building suggestions in this chapter. This research suggests that we-based management, by naturally stimulating the release of oxytocin, can reduce the likelihood of destructive, interpersonal warfare in the workplace.

Whatever the compensation scheme the CEO ultimately selects, it should be something that the majority of employees agrees is fair. Failure to follow this simple rule risks triggering harmful and divisive feelings that can severely reduce the horsepower of the motivational engine and harm everyone in the long run.

SUMMARY

Nature expects human beings to cathect with one another and thereby become bonded together as a coherent, coordinated tribe. In other words, nature expects us to be part of a networked superorganism with a shared identity and shared purpose. The people we cathect with become welded into our personal identity. Their experiences become our experiences and their victories become our victories. Cathexis binds us together and allows us to participate in the lives of the people around us. It allows us to live multiple lives within one lifetime.

The Chinese network-based culture has persisted for thousands of years, I believe, because it conforms to nature's deep emotional architecture. The Chinese culture, as described by Ming-Jer Chen, has all the qualities of a superorganism. The Chinese are also highly entrepreneurial and eager to learn from the West. The Chinese entrepreneurial "beast" also has a tough and crafty Communist "taskmaster" that has little love for the West. What will transpire in the years ahead? Will the Chinese *guanxi*-based family conglomerates dismember the Western multinationals like Harry Quadracci dismembered his competitors in the printing industry, or will Western corporations rise to the occasion and perhaps become superorganisms themselves? According to my theory of social appetites, Chinese *guanxi*-based businesses run on more motivational cylinders than their Western counterparts. This, I believe, gives the Chinese a significant motivational advantage.

The Chinese trust-based system is certainly adaptable to Western societies because Harry Quadracci proved it at Quad/Graphics, Ken Iverson proved it at Nucor Steel, and Ricardo Semler proved it at Semco SA. The superorganisms built by the three mavericks were as dedicated and committed as any Asian company. Like a *guanxi* network, they were also harmonious, self-regulated, and responded vigorously to unforeseen emergencies.

The formal cathexis-building process discussed in this chapter is very similar to Ming-Jer Chen's recommendations for building a *guanxi* network. It's quite remarkable that my thirty-year quest to unravel nature's emotional architecture has led me to an ancient culture based on Confucian philosophy.

CHAPTER 5

SOCIAL APPETITE #2: THE COMPETENCY APPETITE

How to Develop a Workplace Populated with Confident Experts

INTRODUCTION TO THE COMPETENCY APPETITE

The cooperation appetite described in Chapter 4 ensures that human beings work together as highly coordinated teams. The competency appetite, the subject of this chapter, plays an equally vital survival role—it makes sure that we master the survival skills (technology) of our group.

Unlike instinct-driven animals, human beings must master difficult and complex skills in order to survive. This is why we are equipped with a powerful competency appetite that rewards mastery and punishes incompetence.

The basic idea behind the competency appetite is quite simple—if we master the survival skills of our group, our self-esteem ratchets upward and we feel more capable and confident. If we fail to master the necessary skills and acquire the necessary survival assets, our self-esteem ratchets downward, and we feel incompetent.

The competency appetite is vitally important for creating a high-performance workplace because it motivates hard work, persistence, mastery, and pride in one's profession. Our goal in this chapter is to activate the competency appetite and thereby create a workplace filled with confident and skilled experts.

Without the competency appetite, human beings would lose their ability to act with a shared purpose and a shared technology and would cease to be human beings at all. Without the competency appetite, we would all resemble Dr. Damasio's lazy and unfocused patient, Elliot, described in Chapter 3, who didn't care about his career or what others thought of him. The competency appetite needs to be thoroughly disassembled because it is just as subtle and inscrutable as the cooperation appetite described in Chapter 4.[1]

SEROTONIN AND THE COMPETENCY APPETITE

The competency appetite, as mentioned in Chapter 1, is partly regulated by the neurotransmitter serotonin and serotonin 2 receptors in the ventromedial prefrontal lobes and the amygdala. When our skills match the consensus expectations of the tribe (the target), serotonin is released in the ventromedial prefrontal lobes, which causes us to experience high self-esteem. Antidepressant drugs, like Prozac, operate by increasing the concentration of serotonin in the brain's synapses artificially. Prozac creates a false sense of competency by making people feel like they are competent, even if they aren't.

Peter Kramer, in his best-selling book, *Listening to Prozac*, agonized over Prozac's ability to create a false sense of competency.[2] He was disturbed by the drug's reach—its ability to fundamentally alter personality and life priorities. I think his concern was justified because the drug interferes with nature's vital cultural autopilot—the competency appetite.

PROGRAMMING THE COMPETENCY APPETITE

The competency appetite, as I already mentioned in Chapter 3, is programmable via the group consensus. The group determines which skills are valuable and worth acquiring, and which are not. This powerful social appetite imparts emotional bite to group edicts and allows the group to sculpt ridges and valleys into the emotional landscape and to thereby channel human behavior in socially desirable directions (think back to our discussion of emotional physics in Chapter 3). Without this crucial appetite, we (the marbles) would be entirely at the mercy of our basic biological drives because group priorities would lack the emotional force necessary to counteract them on the undulating emotional landscape.

The programming aspect of the competency appetite is stealthy. It seeps into us from the groups we affiliate with. The term commonly used to describe this stealthy programming is "culture." Culture, we will discover, does not just happen. It is made to happen by the competency appetite and the emotions that empower it. Once the cultural target is programmed into the competency appetite, we are forced to acquire the group's target by powerful feelings of high and low self-esteem—the most valuable denomination of emotional currency.

I hope you can appreciate the elegance of nature's design. The cultural autopilot is disarmingly simple, like the thermostat in your house. The group consensus determines the set point, or target temperature, and self-esteem motivates us to reach the target by developing skills and acquiring desirable assets that promote survival (the social assets in our vault). As long as we maintain alignment with the target, we experience high self-worth and feel valuable and confident. If we move off-target, the competency appetite automatically detects a discrepancy and creates painful feelings of low self-esteem until we successfully reacquire the target by developing the missing skills or acquiring the missing assets.

The competency appetite is programmed by friends, parents, colleagues, and the media over the course of our lives. The group, in other words, determines what skills and assets are valuable and worth acquiring. Once programmed, we are emotionally guided by the competency appetite to home in on, and acquire, the targeted skills. Every human being has his or her unique target programmed by his or her unique network of friends, family, and other affiliations. We are not aware of this programming. It seeps in from the 100 or so people who are closest to us.

The target is not stationary. It shifts when we join new tribes with their own unique priorities. The target changes, for example, when we go to college, enter the workplace, or go into retirement. If we fail to keep pace with the shifting cultural target by mastering new skills, we fall out of alignment and experience low self-esteem. Staying happy requires constant adjustments to keep our skills and achievements in sync with society's ever shifting target.

I don't mean to imply that all our life goals are programmed by the group consensus, because each of us has our own, personal, idiosyncratic goals and values as well. These personal goals and values do not contribute to self-esteem, however, until they are applauded by our group.

Peer Pressure and the Competency Appetite

It is scary to think that the groups we affiliate with subliminally program our values and priorities and influence our life course. We recognize this consensus-driven mechanism in our children and call it "peer pressure." I've seen peer pressure in action with my son, Christopher. Several years ago I tried to interest Christopher in football so I'd have someone to play catch with. He, unfortunately, had no interest. Shortly after he entered sixth grade, however, Christopher walked into my office and asked me to throw the football with him. When I inquired about his change of heart, he explained that his classmates (school tribe) were now playing touch football at recess. From one day to the next, football went from being a chore to a socially valuable skill worth mastering. My son began pestering me to throw the football with him. Such is the ability of the group to define value and influence behavior.

Human beings are driven by the group consensus but we are loath to admit it. We use the term *peer pressure* to describe the power of the group consensus in our naïve children, but we fail to recognize the same mechanism operating pervasively in the adult world. The programming aspect of the cultural autopilot, as I mentioned earlier, is wickedly subtle.

The Competency Appetite as the Mechanism of Culture

Modern cultures are so complex that it hurts to even contemplate them. In addition, our native culture is such an integral part of our worldview and it colors our sense of reality so thoroughly that it is hard to think about it as something separate from reality. To understand the true nature of culture we need to simplify the discussion by considering a small group of human beings, with a common set of priorities, struggling to survive in the wilderness—which was precisely the sort of environment where the competency appetite evolved.

The following scenario illustrates how the competency appetite provides the emotional underpinning that makes culture possible in the first place. Imagine a tribe in the Kalahari that suddenly faces an environmental challenge, a drought. Finding water becomes a priority. Tribe members who figure out innovative ways for obtaining life-giving water, say by observing where certain plants grow and by developing tools for digging deep into the earth, become respected water-finding authorities who are applauded by the tribe. The innovators set a performance standard, or target, for the tribe because the brain has a sophisticated consensus-detector that stamps applauded skills as valuable. The members of the tribe who do not possess the new skills experience low self-esteem and a desire to acquire the new skills (the target) to restore their positive self-regard. Everyone emulates the skills of the innovators in order to reestablish their former level of self-esteem—to reestablish social homeostasis.

Now let's imagine that the tribe is attacked. Suddenly, weapon-making and fighting skills become the priority. The competency appetite then steers everyone to develop fighting and weapon-making skills. The entire skill-acquisition process is motivated by a desire to acquire and maintain high self-esteem and avoid low self-esteem. The competency appetite is the mechanism that forces tribal communities to master the business of survival—to become survival experts. I hope you agree that the competency appetite makes perfect survival sense.

Why Put the Group in Charge of Programming?

Readers may balk at the notion that they are programmed by external forces; however, the logic in favor of external programming is irrefutable. If individuals could create their own cultural programming, they could cheat the system. If I had control of my own competency appetite, for example, I could program in "idleness" as valuable. My competency appetite would then detect my idleness and reward me with feelings of high self-esteem. If I had control of the programming, I could reward myself with maximum pleasure for the least expenditure of effort. This would violate the idea that human behavior makes survival sense. Self-programming would make me happy but extinct. It is not an option.

We don't need to look far to see what happens when human beings are allowed to dispense pleasure for themselves. Drug addicts do precisely this. Cocaine and methamphetamine addicts, for example, give themselves dopamine highs that nature intended for rewarding achievement (skill deployment). The phenomenon of drug addiction vividly illustrates what happens when individuals are put in charge of rewarding themselves—namely, they cheat and give themselves undeserved rewards. This is why nature put the group in charge of setting the bar (the target) and defining which behaviors are valuable and which are not. Putting the group in charge of value creation has other important benefits, such as getting everyone moving in the same direction with a standardized technology.

The Wisdom of Crowds

There are other reasons for putting the group in charge of programming. Recent research indicates that a group will generally outperform individual experts in making complex decisions involving many variables and in predicting future events.[3] Individual experts cannot look at a complex problem from as many angles, or draw upon as much experience when making decisions, as a group.

Las Vegas casinos use the wisdom of the group in setting odds for sporting events. They begin with the opinion of expert oddsmakers, but then adjust these starting odds based upon the bets that are placed (the pooled opinions of the betting public). This time-tested system minimizes the casino's exposure to risk, just as the consensus of our ancestors reduced the tribe's exposure to risk and thereby made our existence possible. The stock market is another example of pooled wisdom, which is why it is so devilishly hard for managed stock funds to consistently beat index funds, which respond to the bets (wisdom) of the masses.

Corporations are now tapping into the opinions of their employees to make sales forecasts. Sales predictions are important for retail stores because they are used by the purchasing department to order inventory. Best Buy's employees routinely trounce the oracles (merchandising executives) in predicting holiday sales.[4]

A book titled *The Wisdom of Crowds* by James Surowiecki details many such cases of group wisdom prevailing over individual experts. One of the more interesting cases involved *Who Wants to Be a Millionaire?*, the television trivia show where the questions become progressively more difficult. If a contestant doesn't know the answer to a particular question, he or she can request a lifeline—a phone call to a knowledgeable friend or a poll of the studio audience. Friends have been correct 65 percent of the time, while the studio audience has been correct 91 percent of the time. If we assume that contestants typically phone their most intelligent and knowledgeable friends for help, Surowiecki argues that *Millionaire* is a good example of the wisdom of the crowd beating individual experts.[5]

Now lets think back to the Ice Age, when tribes needed to make life or death decisions all the time. Which tribes were more likely to survive, the ones who got the answer right 65 percent of the time by listening to individual experts, or the tribes that polled the group and then acted based upon the group consensus? I think you can see the advantages of a consensus-based brain.

The power and wisdom of the group is generally ignored in corporate America. Decisions are made by experts with advanced degrees without consulting the troops on the ground. Me-based managers and executives are not consensus leaders chosen by the tribe. They therefore lack the ability to influence the group's goals and define the group's priorities because their plans have not been blessed by the group and therefore lack emotional value. Self-centered managers rely, instead, on rules, regulations, and the coercive use of authority to get things done.

Managers can ignite the power of the group consensus by committing to their employees and creating a bonded work group with a true tribal dynamic, as discussed in Chapter 4. The group consensus will then organically define values and goals and set standards of behavior. Members of such a work group will automatically feel bad (experience low self-esteem) if they do not acquire the skills and achieve the goals that serve the group's survival. This is how human beings are designed to function—automatically and organically without a thick policy manual and cadre of overseers.

THE PENALTY FOR NOT HITTING THE TARGET

If we accept the idea that the competency appetite is programmed by the group consensus, then what happens if we consistently miss the consensus target by failing to develop the requisite skills?

Human beings are skill-based creatures. If we are not competent in the survival skills of the tribe, then we are dead. Competency, as I mentioned before, is a necessity for our species. Perhaps this is the role of depression—to make us feel incompetent and worthless if we are worthless in the eyes of the tribe. Competency-driven depression, I believe, is nature's version of tough love. It is the penalty imposed by nature for ignoring the survival priorities of the group.

Nature's uncompromising message is, "You must belong to a tribe and you must master its skills if you want to feel valuable and valued." Anything else would not make survival sense. Managers provide a valuable public service when they help employees develop skills and thereby feel capable and confident. On the flip side, me-based managers starve the competency appetite and can push their employees toward the brink of mental illness.

That said, I think there are two basic types of competency-related depression. One type has a message—clean up your act and master the survival skills of your group. This type of tough-love pain is an integral part of the competency appetite. Without it, the competency appetite would lack the emotional bite to regulate behavior. The other type of depression is more like a disease caused by the complexity of modern societies—a programming error that jams the cultural autopilot.

Depression is characterized by social retreat and endless rumination over past and present failures. Social retreat is a hiding behavior motivated by a sense of worthlessness and shame. I suspect that this retreat is a form of self-preservation. It protects the depressed individual's remaining social assets from destruction by failure and social rebuke.

When someone is depressed, the competency appetite floods the mind with images of past and present failures in order to focus the attention of the conscious mind on the problem. The message is simple and clear—corrective action is needed.

High achievers are often motivated by nature's version of tough love. Michael Jordan failed to make the varsity basketball team in high school two years in a row. This was a humiliating defeat for Jordan because skill at basketball was important to his tribe. Jordan dug deep and practiced hard to get the low self-esteem monkey off his back. The rest is history.

Each of us has suffered defeats and festering wounds, thanks to the competency appetite. The good news is that acquiring the missing skills or assets can heal these wounds. I once thought I couldn't learn a foreign language. Learning a foreign language is easy for children, but difficult for adults. I persisted, however, and I am now fluent in German. I subsequently went on a ski vacation to Austria where I met my wife, Britta, who is German. I now have a home in Germany and a home in the United States. My life is immensely richer because I faced, and healed, my foreign-language wound.

I was also once afraid of public speaking. When I taught geology classes at the University of Wisconsin, however, I decided that teaching my students was simply too important to let fear get in the way. I decided not to be afraid, and, surprisingly, I wasn't. I quickly developed into a confident and competent speaker after this experience. These two anecdotes illustrate how skill deficits that once dragged on my self-esteem now buoy it. If it were not for the competency appetite, and its painful and persistent reminders, my life path would have been completely different, probably for the worse.

Depression Caused by Programming Errors

The competency appetite works best within the context of small groups with a single value system. What happens when a guidance system designed for small, coherent groups is suddenly placed into the modern context populated by a smorgasbord of groups with indistinct boundaries? Modern humans can belong to a bewildering array of groups, all of which compete to program the set point or target of the competency appetite. In modern societies there are multiple captains fighting to program nature's autopilot: family, spouse, country clubs, service clubs, church groups, peer groups, work groups, sports groups, friends, school groups, and so forth. In such an environment, the competency appetite may be unable to parse a coherent target from all the conflicting cultural noise.

If there are multiple captains programming the autopilot, what happens if they simultaneously punch in different targets? Consider, for example, the following situation involving a teenager. The teen's peer group may applaud drug taking and binge drinking, while the adolescent's parents applaud abstinence. The teen is faced with an emotional no-win scenario. No matter what he or she does, he or she will be punished by the competency appetite and suffer a reduction in self-esteem. No matter what the teen does, he or she will hit one target, resulting in higher self-esteem, and will miss the other target, resulting in shame and painful and persistent wounds to the psyche.

Pain is only helpful when it is accompanied by a sense of where the problem lies. Imagine, for example, that someone sticks your finger with a pin. A reference point, your finger, accompanies the pain from the pinprick. Pain with a location, a referent, is helpful and adaptive. It tells you to pull your finger away, not your foot. Similarly, low self-esteem is helpful if it motivates the tribe to master crucial survival skills. In the modern context, however, conflicting programming signals can overwhelm the competency appetite. In this case, it can administer pain (low self-esteem), but without a clear referent for corrective action. This, I believe, is the cause of the most crippling type of depression—chronic pain with no idea of its source. This is the type of depression that can easily spiral out of control.

Here is a second type of programming error that can cause depression. Imagine a situation where parents do not program a child's autopilot. In this instance, the default programming entity might become the popular media, which then program the child's mind with unachievable standards for beauty, strength, and skill, thereby condemning the child to a lifelong feeling of incompetence. In this case, the target is impossible to achieve, and competency is impossible to attain. Deviant social programming can therefore sculpt a nightmarish no-win scenario. This form of depression is not as dysfunctional as the first, because the child at least has some kind of target to shoot for.

Evolutionary psychologists refer to these types of problems as genome lag. The competency appetite evolved in an environment characterized by small, coherent groups of 150 or fewer individuals. This design is not optimal in a complex social environment composed of many competing and sometimes ill-defined groups. Hence, modern societies are stricken with epidemics of depressive illness and drug abuse.

The Epidemic of Depression Is an Opportunity for Leadership

The lifetime incidence rate for depression is around 20 percent of the population. In other words, 20 percent of us are going to become clinically depressed at some point in our lives. The incidence of depression is high and getting worse. Lewis Judd, the former chief of the U.S. National

Institute of Mental Health and chair of the psychiatry department at the University of California, San Diego, said, "I see depression as the plague of the modern era."[6] The World Health Organization expects depression to be the second leading cause of disability after heart disease by 2020.

The epidemic of depression and related mental illnesses in Western societies is both a curse and an opportunity. It indicates a distinct shortage of both community and leadership. Leaders who can bring individuals together and weld them into a superorganism are doing them a great favor. Human beings desperately need to belong to such groups. If the consensus leader also has a vision for a better future and projects clear and powerful values and goals, then he or she provides the target that human beings desperately need to achieve homeostasis and self-esteem. Such leaders create a bright beacon within the cultural fog and thereby provide a valuable mental health service to society. In the future, we can either medicate our population to feel competent, or we can do it the old-fashioned way—we can place them into a bonded tribal setting and encourage them to master the survival skills of the group.

Human beings need to be embedded in a group to feel valued and valuable. We need a tribe and a target to feel good about ourselves. Human beings are not inherently lazy. We are built to be creative, to be productive, and to serve the tribe. If the workplace doesn't qualify as a committed tribe, however, nature's autopilot is inoperable and managers are left with the default solutions for motivating human beings—money and fear and a hierarchy of overseers.

Great leaders program nature's autopilot with confidence and boldly steer their groups in the direction of survival. Great leaders work with nature's consensus-driven mechanism instead of against it and thereby achieve organizational greatness. Great leaders create a workplace ecosystem that is both optimally productive and mentally healthy. Leaders should go about their work resolutely and with the confidence that they are providing a tremendous public good!

PERSONAL IMPLEMENTATION

As I said before, all the social appetites operate by simple rules. If you make a few simple but challenging changes at the emotional level, you will change the way your organization feels and hence how it performs. Our focus here is to develop a workplace full of competent experts who excel at their craft and work tirelessly to perfect it. Developing an expertise in the modern corporate context means a lifelong commitment to learning. Employees need to immerse themselves in their chosen profession and read widely to learn from other experts and stay abreast of the latest thinking.

Becoming an expert is like drawing a picture. You start out with a sketch or outline and then fill in the textures and colors, brushstroke by brushstroke, until you have a richly detailed mental image of your chosen field of expertise. When this mental image comes into clear focus, you are an expert—the go-to guy or gal inside your organization. You are the expert hunter who sets the standard of excellence for the tribe.

The motive force, or productive pleasure, I am describing how to turn on in this chapter is an energizing feeling of high self-esteem. We want to create a workplace populated with experts where employees walk tall and feel proud and confident, regardless of their function within the organization. This feeling motivates excellence and skill mastery and constitutes a major addition to the emotional paycheck that drives high performance.

Human beings desperately hunger for this feeling, and if they are unable to find it at work they will focus their energies outside of work where they can obtain it from activities like hobbies and sports. If they still can't satisfy their competency appetites, then they may satisfy it artificially with antidepressants like Prozac.

Check the Score

The obvious first step to feeding the competency appetite within your company and igniting the rewarding feelings it controls is to check the Tune-Up Metric. If the score for the competency appetite is in the positive 4 to 8 range, congratulations; your employees already feel like confident, capable, and respected experts and are already receiving substantial self-esteem bonuses on their emotional paycheck. They are ready for challenging assignments and will complete them swiftly, efficiently, and beyond your expectations. All you need to do is to continue to respect them as experts and praise them lavishly when they achieve the impossible.

What if the opposite is true? What if your employees have been beaten down by a succession of self-centered managers and by impersonal bureaucratic systems that make them feel powerless and incompetent? In this case, you may need to rehabilitate your employees using the suggestions presented below.

Implementation Step 1: Encourage Employees to Master Skills

The competency appetite is designed to reward human beings for putting in the months or years of hard work required to become truly adept in the survival skills of the group. Within a bonded group this process should occur naturally because human beings instinctively want to feel respected by their tribe.

If you want to give the process of skill mastery a kick start, you might encourage employees to take martial arts classes to show them what it feels like to become an expert at something. The martial arts, in my opinion, provide an excellent template for developing confident and competent experts in any field. Here are some of the elements of karate instruction that align beautifully with nature's competency appetite:

•   *Is a Socially Valuable Skill.* The competency appetite motivates mastery of socially valued skills. Karate is such a skill in our culture because it is generally applauded by the greater tribe, which makes it feel valuable and desirable. When we watch a martial arts demonstration we think to ourselves, "I wish I could do that." This is an important requirement to becoming an expert at anything. You need to perceive the skill as desirable—something that will make you feel better and stronger if you possessed it. The same sort of dynamic motivates people to put in years of hard work to become a doctor, lawyer, or master craftsman. This is why every position within a company must be seen as respected and valued, otherwise why would anyone want to master it?

•   *Generates Mutual Respect and Trust.* Karate instructors are not like drill sergeants. Rather, they treat students at every belt level with great respect. Instructors look for improvements to compliment more than they look for errors to correct. If they spot an error they simply demonstrate the correct skill and politely ask the student to repeat it. Corrections are given in a calm, respectful, and friendly manner so that students come to see them as helpful suggestions rather than destructive criticism. Students also treat their instructors with respect. For example, black belts are addressed as "sir," and when instructions are given, the entire group responds, "Yes, sir." Students bow-in as they enter the practice floor and bow-out when they leave to show their respect for their classmates, their instructors, and the overall instruction process.

• *Requires Measurement Against Demanding Standards.* Becoming an expert is a demanding and serious pursuit. Karate instruction is based on memorizing a form for each of the nine color-coded belt levels. Each form consists of fifty, or more, choreographed blocks, kicks, and strikes. Even small deviations from the form are corrected by the instructor and the moves repeated until they are as close as possible to perfection. As a student of karate I don't mind this strict conformance to standards. The skill would not be valuable if it were only half learned or performed in a sloppy fashion. If the need arises to use these skills in a self-defense situation, students want to be confident that they can perform the skills with speed, accuracy, and power. In a corporate setting the standards of perfection should be similarly demanding so employees not only feel like experts, but function as experts too.

• *Breaks Training in a Difficult Skill into Many Small, Doable Steps.* It takes three to five years to earn a black belt in karate—about the time it takes to earn an undergraduate degree. If you had to master the entire skill set before you got your first "attaboy" or "attagirl," few would ever attempt it. The karate skill is therefore divided into nine belt levels and four stripe levels within each belt level, for a total of thirty-six doable increments. It is possible to move up a stripe level every two or three weeks or so, and a belt level roughly every four months. Each belt level requires a group belt test, after which the next belt in the sequence is ceremoniously presented by the instructor. This system provides a sense of continuous improvement as one's self-esteem ratchets upward with each new belt level.

My experience in the martial arts has been rewarding. I quite literally felt stronger, and better about myself, as I advanced through the belt levels. Karate training, in my opinion, is a superb way to experience improved self-esteem, without the need for a serotonin reuptake inhibitor, like Prozac. The corporate community can learn important lessons regarding human motivation by studying this ancient art form.

Implementation Step 2: Treat Your Employees Like Experts

If a work group's competency appetite score on the Tune-Up Metric is negative, it means that employees feel painfully incompetent in the workplace. There are a number of potential reasons why employees might feel incompetent and unrespected. The most common reason has to do with the hierarchy issue discussed in Chapter 4—employees probably see themselves as denizens of the broad, lower-tier of the dominance hierarchy. Managers need to disabuse them of this notion by explaining how their job is important to the manager personally and to the survival of the enterprise in general. If managers value their employees as experts, within a short time, I suggest, they will begin feeling and acting like experts.

If your department or work group is just a small component of a large, dysfunctional hierarchy, then create a high self-esteem ecosystem within your corner of the bureaucratic machine, and let the outstanding performance of your integrated team of experts draw the attention of the managers around you. Your colleagues will begin to notice that your employees walk a little taller, procrastinate less, and get the job done faster and better than anyone else. At this point you might want to clue them in to your secret—you work harmoniously with human nature rather than against it.

I hope the importance of self-esteem and the competency appetite is becoming clear. Companies that develop high-performance cultures learn how to tap into this powerful emotional force. They know how to bond with employees, respect employees, and build their capabilities and self-esteem. The key to developing a high-performance culture is to treat every job as vital and respect every member of the tribe as an expert.

Implementation Step 3: Heal Psychic Wounds

There are many reasons why employees might feel like failures and then perform according to their low internal expectations. As I mentioned earlier, we have all failed at something or other during the course of our lives and we all have festering psychic wounds to prove it, thanks to the tough-love aspect of the competency appetite. These psychic wounds drag on our self-esteem and degrade our performance. Since you are already a trusted leader, your employees might be willing to expose their soft underbellies and describe the psychic wounds that secretly torment them.

Several years ago I mentored a friend's son after he confided in me that he felt learning disabled with regard to math. On an incompetency scale from 1 to 10, he felt like a perfect 10. I proceeded to question the boy about his supposed disability because I knew, from experience, that psychic wounds can be healed. I, too, had struggled at math, so I could empathize with him. I initially found math as dry as day-old toast. Gradually, however, I made friends with mathematics and learned to admire its power and precision. I ended up getting an undergraduate degree in engineering and performed admirably in my many math courses (As and Bs). I therefore challenged the boy's assumption that he sucked at math.

I said, "OK, perhaps you aren't that great in math, but maybe, just maybe, you don't suck quite as badly as you think you do. Maybe you are only a 9 out of 10 on the lousy scale. Maybe your brain is not congenitally miswired, but rather, you had lousy teachers who did not explain to you the power or beauty of mathematics, much less its many useful applications." I proceeded to describe my own, tortuous journey through the educational system and the good and bad math teachers I encountered along the way. By the end of our conversation, he agreed that maybe he wasn't quite as bad at math as he had assumed. He also agreed to give math another try. The boy never became a wiz at math, but he graduated from high school with decent math grades, attended college, and went on to a successful career in business.

Helping an employee heal a psychic wound is one way you can go beyond the call of duty for your employees and deepen your relationships with them. It is like pulling the thorn out of a tiger's paw, and your employees will be eternally grateful. Harry Quadracci had an interesting way of healing psychic wounds at Quad/Graphics. Much of Quad-racci's executive team was made up of high school graduates with little or no college education—not exactly society's image of the competent executive. Quadracci's blue-collar executives had lots of psychic wounds in need of treatment, so he pushed them beyond their comfort zones as a way of proving they were more talented, capable, and competent than they thought they were. Each assignment was an opportunity for em-ployees to prove to their boss, and to themselves, that they were just as capable and competent as executives with MBAs. By repeatedly crashing his employees into their preconceived limitations, and proving them false, he built up the self-esteem, confidence, and skills of his workforce, and his employees thrived on it. Quadracci often described the mission of Quad/Graphics as, "Helping employees become more than they ever thought they could be."[7] Quadracci, by removing the thorns from his tigers' paws, earned the undying loyalty and trust of the people around him. By boosting the self-esteem of his employees, Quadracci super-charged his motivational engine and reaped spectacular productivity as a result.

ORGANIZATIONAL IMPLEMENTATION

The competency appetite is a marvelous leadership tool for CEOs of large organizations. In fact, it is difficult to run such organizations without it. As we already learned in this chapter, the competency appetite operates like an autopilot—a cultural targeting system that is programmed by the group consensus. Once it is programmed, the group is compelled to ac-quire the target by feelings of high and low self-esteem.

This magical ability to set the group's target is transferable. Talented executives can obtain targeting authority if the consensus of the tribe deems them worthy (if they are applauded by the corporate tribe). Ob-taining targeting access to the cultural autopilot greatly simplifies the practice of leadership. Your life as CEO will be easier because you will not need to bully or cajole your employees into doing what you want. Rather, you will merely need to point in the direction you want them to go and leave the rest to the competency appetite and the feelings that empower it.

I assume, in this section, that you have already implemented the suggestions in Chapter 4 and that your company has already metamorphosed into a trust-based superorganism and you are its respected consensus leader. If not, return to Chapter 4 and implement the two-step relationship-building process described there.

It is impossible to gain programming access to the cultural autopilot until you first demonstrate your skills under fire and earn the loyalty of your employees through your devotion to them. You need to be seen as the respected elder of the tribe—a celebrity of sorts—who commands the attention of the group. Once you possess this magical status you will be like Michael Jordan, everyone will want to be like you and the things you touch will feel desirable and worth acquiring. Steering the corporate ship will then become effortless because all you will need to do is point at the target and your tribe will energetically seek to acquire it.

Set the Course

Assuming that your employees view you as their consensus leader, it's then time to set a course that everyone can agree on. Peters and Waterman observed that excellent companies program a heading for the corporate ship by defining a few, primary values that are supported by a clear and stirring imagery and metaphor.[8] Leaders must paint a picture of a better future and thereby provide a vision and shared purpose for the group. This purpose must transcend making money. It must be something your employees would volunteer to do in their spare time, even if you didn't pay them.

According to Peters and Waterman, the excellent companies they studied were rigid with respect to the direction they were sailing and expected complete employee buy-in. On the other hand, the excellent companies were loose regarding the details of running the ship. Employees could choose the duties they enjoyed most and could execute those duties creatively in any way they saw fit. Employees could choose navigation, ship maintenance, general seamanship, provisioning, and so forth, as long as they committed to their crewmates and the overall mission. This simultaneous loose-tight organization is one of the key defining characteristics of excellent organizations, according to Peters and Waterman.[9]

Harry Quadracci had a similar loose-tight approach to leadership. Regarding vision and direction, he was tight. Quadracci fought ruthlessly to maintain total control of the overall direction of Quad/Graphics. A lifetime of immersion in the printing industry had given him an intuitive understanding of the marketplace and the best direction in which to sail. If his executive team challenged his vision or direction, he got angry. Quadracci knew exactly where he was heading and would not tolerate dissention on this crucial issue. He especially would not tolerate interference regarding his egalitarian, employee-centric approach to management.

Ricardo Semler, the Brazilian maverick, had a completely different leadership approach compared to Quadracci. Whereas Quadracci capitalized on his celebrity consensus-leader status to steer Quad/Graphics to success in the printing industry, Semler demurred. He could have grabbed the emotional tiller at Semco SA, but didn't. Semler had achieved rock-star status in Brazil by the time his best-selling book, *Maverick,* was published in 1993. When he gave talks, he drew huge, admiring crowds. Semler's employees looked to their CEO/guru for guidance and direction because he seemed all-knowing and infallible. Semler, however, knew that he was just as fallible as anyone else. The true guru, he concluded, was the collective wisdom of his employees. Semler gracefully bowed out of the limelight and took his seat as just another employee with roughly the same rights and decision-making power as anyone else. He sometimes regretted this decision, however, especially when his pet projects got voted down by the tribe![10]

Semler wasn't against leadership because leaders always float to the surface within any consensus-driven group. Semler, however, wanted leadership disseminated broadly. He wanted employees to flow in and out of leadership positions as conditions warranted. The best leader under one set of circumstances, he felt, might be the worst leader under another set of circumstances.

SUMMARY

The basic message of this chapter is that human beings are built to master the survival skills of the tribe, and nature created a powerful incentive, self-esteem, to make sure we do. Put more simply, it feels good to be regarded as an expert in one's profession. Companies that encourage their employees to become skillful, and recognize them for their skill, provide them with a powerful form of emotional reward that is, in many ways, more valuable than money. Employees will work very hard to maintain this annuity of good feelings once they have tasted it.

Leaders who help employees master their professions provide a vital mental-health service because the penalty for being deemed incompetent is chronic, unremitting pain. As I said before, incompetency is not an option for skill-based creatures such as ourselves. Human beings are not designed to be lazy malingerers. Rather, we are designed to struggle, strive, and master the survival skills of the group.

We also explored the big picture of social regulation in this chapter—the cultural autopilot that is programmed by the group consensus. This mysterious, subliminal process programs which life goals are laudable and worth pursuing and which are not. Nature, as I argued earlier in this chapter, had no option but to put the group consensus in charge of determining which goals and directions in life are valuable and which are not. This group programming seeps into us from the 100 or so people we are closest to. The cultural autopilot operates only in workplaces where the individual members are emotionally bonded to one another—where they think and act as one.

Leaders can program the cultural autopilot, and thereby determine which goals are valuable and worth achieving, if the group bestows this right. Leaders who earn the right to program the autopilot obtain a powerful advantage over executives who don't. A consensus leader merely needs to point in a direction he or she wants to go and the tribe will automatically and enthusiastically comply under the influence of intrinsic emotional incentives dispensed by the competency appetite.

The competency appetite lies at the heart of cooperative and coordinated society, and we would be in serious trouble without it. If you want to become a spectacular leader who takes control of the group's social rudder, then you need to be a consensus leader. In other words, if your employees had the choice, they would vote you in as their consensus leader and follow you even if they were paid nothing.

CHAPTER 6

SOCIAL APPETITE #3: THE SKILL-DEPLOYMENT APPETITE

How to Design a Rewarding Workplace That Resonates with the Joy of Achievement

DOPAMINE AND THE THRILL OF A WIN

In the last chapter we determined that human beings desperately want to be competent in the survival skills of the tribe and that feelings of high and low self-esteem are designed to steer human beings in this direction. Mastering life skills is not enough to ensure survival, however, because human beings also need to repeatedly deploy the skills they've already mastered to achieve group goals. Nature's design would be incomplete without another reward system to encourage successful and repeated deployment of the skills we already possess.[1]

I don't want to belabor this point because it is self-evident that skill deployment (achievement) is rewarded with positive feelings. The rewards are regulated by the neurotransmitter dopamine and dopamine 1 and 2 receptors in the basal striatum. Dopamine's reward is intense, but short lived. When we win a race, or get an "attaboy" or "attagirl" from the boss, we are rewarded with a brief dopamine-induced euphoria that fades over a period of minutes to hours. When the euphoria drops back to the baseline, nature's message is, "Okay, now do it again—deploy another skill." If we ignore this message we get punished with boredom, a gnawing and persistent form of discomfort. Mice that have had the gene for dopamine deleted from their genome are lethargic, lose interest in food and sex, and quickly starve to death.[2] Dopamine, it seems, is a *very* important neurotransmitter.

People with Parkinson's disease have abnormally low levels of dopamine, which can make them unable to experience positive rewards, including rewards associated with achievement. Rewarding a Parkinson's patient with an "attaboy" or "attagirl," money, or some other reward will not make them feel good and will not influence their future behavior because they don't experience the reward. Parkinson's patients can also lose their ability to learn from their successes because their successes are not felt as pleasurable.[3] When Parkinson's patients are treated with dopamine-enhancing drugs, they often develop the opposite problem. Winning becomes overly pleasurable, and they often develop problems like gambling addictions.

This skill-deployment pleasure has many names, such as joy, elation, euphoria, ecstasy, exhilaration, and the pleasure of achievement. This important pleasure motivates a huge swath of productive human behavior. The main goal of this chapter is to figure out how to structure the work environment so the skill-deployment appetite gets fed and employees feel rewarded on a daily basis. In other words, we are going to design a dopamine-rich work environment that boosts the emotional paycheck and helps give the workplace a positive emotional return on investment.

I assume that your employees have already bonded together into a superorganism as described in Chapter 4 and that they are already getting their daily dose of oxytocin and vasopressin (that warm family feel) in the workplace. I also assume that their competency appetites are being fed. In other words, I assume your employees are highly skilled, respected as experts, and experience feelings of high self-esteem in the workplace. If we tested their blood for the neurotransmitter serotonin, we would presumably find high levels.

The next step is to create a dopamine-rich work environment. This step requires some artful design work. We approach the design task the same way Jack Nicklaus, Tom Fazio, and Pete Dye approach a golf course design project. We are going to design a championship course that is challenging, but fair, and where a solid effort results in a win. We want to create a work environment full of hoots, hollers, and high-fives because these are the sounds of good shots being struck!

Type A high achievers live for the euphoria of the win. To some extent, we all do. Human beings participate in sports, play Monopoly, solve math problems, and pull the one-armed bandit at the casino for one reason—we love dopamine. Men produce three times more dopamine than women in response to drugs like methamphetamine.[4] Men also rate the methamphetamine-induced high as more pleasurable than women do. This explains why men are more likely to become meth addicts than women. It may also explain why men are so darned competitive: they have a hyperactive dopamine-reward system.

Creating a dopamine-rich work environment takes two simple steps: make sure employees value the game, and then design the game so a strong effort results in a win.

STEP 1: VALUE THE GAME

Step 1 is simple. We must teach employees to value the work-game or they will not feel rewarded for playing it. A game that employees don't value is a chore. We already know from the Gallup Organization's employee engagement surveys that 69 percent of employees do not value the game they are playing. These employees are the corporate world's version of high school underachievers.

We should not be surprised that 69 percent of employees don't value the game. The modern work world is frighteningly complex, and finding one's place in it is a daunting task. For every employee who discovers his or her passion, makes an enlightened career decision, and finds a supportive tribe, I suspect that five others drift into unsatisfying jobs due to random circumstances. After employees enter the workforce, other factors come into play that can cause them to mentally check out of the corporate game, even if they had a lot of enthusiasm coming in. Demanding bosses, for example, who never have a kind or supportive word to say, can easily turn committed employees into disengaged underachievers.

Another cause of disengagement is the hyperrational, bureaucratic business model that Western companies are based on. This model devalues human beings and treats them as replaceable components in a machine. The default message to employees is, "You're a replaceable cog with little inherent value to the organization." This is hardly a formula for encouraging employees to value the game! The question in my mind is not why 69 percent of employees are disengaged, but how 31 percent somehow find meaning and intrinsic reward inside the impersonal corporate machine. Perhaps individual managers create pockets of sanity within an otherwise dysfunctional system.

Our Ice Age ancestors had it easy. They automatically valued the game. Nobody had to explain to them why hunting, gathering, weapon-making skills, fighting skills, shelter-making skills, and food-preparation skills were important to the tribe. In other words, the tribe's survival priorities were straightforward and obvious. The target was clear. The straightforward survival dynamic of our ancestors can be re-created inside superorganisms today, as long as employees are bonded to one another and the company as a whole. If employees care about their tribe, then they will automatically value the corporate game and want to contribute to its success.

Let's Play Golf

Golf is a game that many businesspeople value and enjoy playing so I will use it to explore game playing in general. I think corporate America can learn important design lessons by examining the games people naturally enjoy playing—like golf.

People who don't play golf often shake their heads in amazement. They wonder why sane adults would spend large chunks of their disposable incomes and free time hitting white, dimpled balls around a parklike course. If human beings can find motivation and reward in the game of golf, then they can probably find similar rewards in *any game of skill*, including the corporate game.

The golfer's motivation can be explained in terms of the skill-deployment appetite that is the focus of this chapter. Golfers belong to a golfer tribe. This tribe considers golf as an important skill and values the challenge of mastering it. Some businesspeople even look at the game of golf as a microcosm of life. If you can't control your frustrations on the golf course, they reason, then you probably can't control yourself in the workplace either. If you cheat at golf, then you are likely to cheat in the business world, too. Golfers also understand something that the uninitiated do not—it feels really good to hit a well-crafted shot, thanks to dopamine.

From an engineering standpoint, the golfer must control an incredible number of variables to produce a good golf shot. Each ball-and-socket joint in the human body, like the shoulder and hip joints, can take on many configurations. Golf stretches the information-processing ability of the human brain. All of the muscles and joints must be precisely choreographed to make the clubface square up at impact and thereby produce a reliably straight shot. If anything is out of alignment, the clubhead will impart a spin to the ball that will cause it to curve right or left of the target. From the player's perspective, golf is the ultimate sports challenge and a Herculean test of mental and physical self-control. There is no such thing as a perfect golfer because the game is so infuriatingly difficult. Even Tiger Woods has his share of duffed golf shots. Golfers value the game precisely because of its daunting complexity and challenge.

Golfers, if they are good, experience lots of dopamine-induced highs. Whenever they hit a good shot, their brains instantly and automatically compare the intended outcome with the actual outcome. If the two match, dopamine is released and the golfer experiences pleasure. If golfers didn't value the game, they would not experience the dopamine reward, and would quickly stop playing.

Converting a Chore into Rewarding Work by Understanding the Big Picture

Most managers, I propose, simply assume that their employees value the corporate game as much as they do. This, I believe, is a *grave* mistake. As I mentioned above, there are many reasons in our complex society why employees might not value their role in the corporate game the same way we do. How might a manager rehabilitate someone who views their work as a distasteful chore instead of rewarding work?

I dealt with a situation like this in 1985 when I tested some of the ideas in this book on a group of high school underachievers. These were hard-core underachievers whose parents had already tried a number of conventional solutions, like sending their students to tutors or to school psychologists. Underachievers, by the way, are smart kids who view school as a thankless chore—effort expended without emotional compensation.

The dilemma I faced with these underachievers is identical to the dilemma faced by managers with disengaged employees: how to convert a hated chore into an intrinsically rewarding game that employees will enjoy playing. I first devised a simple exercise to show the students how to find pleasure in a seemingly thankless chore. I asked the students to pick one thing they hated the most. The consensus of the class was doing the dishes. I then asked them to imagine what would happen if nobody in the family ever did the dishes. Here are some of the consequences the students came up with:

- The house would stink.

- My friends wouldn't come over anymore because of the mess and the smell.

- We'd get sick.

The students then determined that maybe they did have some responsibility for taking care of the family, and perhaps doing the dishes could be part of their contribution. After establishing that doing the dishes was *not* worthless or stupid, I then asked the underachievers to go home and do the very best job they could on the dish-washing task. I predicted that they would feel good about completing an important survival task for their tribe.

I asked the students the following week if they had gotten any pleasure from doing the dishes. The response was unanimous and enthusiastic. One boy commented, "My parents thought I was nuts. They freaked out. They couldn't believe it when I cleared the table and did the dishes without them asking." Everyone had a similar story. Remarkably, they had all enjoyed doing the dishes.

The next step, I told them, was to do the same thing with the school chore. We had to convert it from something stupid and hated into something valuable and rewarding. I started the chore-conversion process by giving students a big-picture perspective so they could understand how the educational system worked and why they were justified in having negative feelings about it. Modern education, I told them, is a good-faith effort to make the best of a very difficult and unnatural situation. Education, at its essence, boils down to mastering the survival skills of one's tribe—skills that have been painstakingly acquired over thousands of years of exploration and trial-and-error experimentation. The sheer volume of survival skills we have compiled since the invention of writing makes it hard to figure out what to teach our children and how to teach it without overwhelming them. Do you teach a lot, with little depth, or a little, in rich detail?

I next explained that modern education is profoundly unnatural compared to the way children are designed to learn. The natural mode of learning for human beings, I explained, is for children to observe adults performing routine survival skills and then mimic the adult behaviors during play. Play is therefore the primary vehicle for learning in natural human societies.

The modern educational system couldn't be more unnatural. First of all, it separates children from adults so the children can't see the adults in action and teaches the tribe's survival skills out of context in a classroom. Play in the modern context is viewed as a counterproductive distraction, rather than as a vital vehicle for learning. In modern society, I explained, we cannot allow children into the workplace to observe adults in action because this would be highly disruptive. The modern educational system, I suggested, was an honest attempt to deal with a profoundly unnatural situation. I suggested that the students stop resisting this unfortunate reality and try to make the best of a difficult situation. The students were grateful for the big-picture overview and commented, "Nobody bothered to explain the game to us before." Once the students understood the inherent complexity of the situation, they stopped blaming their teachers and their resistance to learning melted away.

I proceeded to teach the students how to experience the five productive pleasures that are the subject of *Primal Management*. I figured that once they had tasted the pleasures that nature incorporated into the system to encourage learning, the process would become self-sustaining. I believe I was correct in my calculation. The students' attitudes and grades improved and they were still enjoying the learning game a year later when we had a reunion.

Managers, I suggest, should never assume that employees view their jobs as inherently valuable. Employees, just like my students, need to understand the big picture and how they fit into it. Don't automatically assume that your employees value the game. It is far better to assume the opposite and explain to each and every employee how to identify value and purpose within their workplace role.

STEP 2: DESIGN A FAIR GAME IN WHICH A GOOD EFFORT RESULTS IN A WIN

I believe that all companies should structure the workplace as an intricate game of skill, like golf. Just like a golf course, the corporate game has the equivalent of sand traps, trees, long grass, water hazards, dog legs, and out-of-bounds areas. The course should be laid out so it is challenging but fair and where a solid effort results in a win. If the game is too easy or too hard, employees will lose interest in it.

The players, your employees, should celebrate artfully placed shots (good decisions made, problems solved, and goals reached). If your company is not filled with whoops, hollers, high-fives, attagirls, and attaboys, then it should be. Hoopla in the workplace is a sure sign that employees value the game and are hitting good shots.[5] It is a sign that employees are getting their skill-deployment rewards, their dopamine. If employees don't get the requisite dose of dopamine, they probably feel and act like losers instead of winners.

The corporate game should not be too difficult. Human beings become frustrated if the ratio of good shots to bad shots falls below a certain critical number. I played golf as a child and adolescent but got progressively frustrated and eventually quit playing. The warning signs were the clubs I chucked into the air or slammed into the ground. For me, the critical ratio of good shots to mediocre or bad shots was around one to one. I got upset and frustrated when the ratio fell below this critical number because the emotional return on investment shifted to the negative column (painful instead of pleasurable).

John Gottman, in his research on divorce, came up with a similar ratio for spousal interactions. He found that stable and healthy marriages exhibited five positive interactions for every negative interaction (five to one ratio). When this critical ratio reached one to one, Gottman discovered that divorce was likely.[6] A healthy work environment, just like a healthy marriage, should be dominated by positive interactions. If the emotional return on investment turns negative, the predicted outcome is obvious: Your employees are going to either quit the game or disengage from it.

Part of the art of management is designing a course that is tough but fair. If an employee seems ready to "chuck it," then set up some lessons with the "club pro" or sit down and discuss why your game is the best and most rewarding one available. If the employee still doesn't value the game, then suggest that she or he find a different, more compatible game to play.

I became disengaged from the game of golf because I started having a negative emotional return on investment (negative EROI). I invested effort but didn't receive enough emotional compensation to make it worth the trouble. I later returned to the game when I rediscovered it in an entirely new format that included drinking beer, betting, telling jokes, smoking cigars, and grappling with my hypercompetitive friends. This new format added emotional incentives to the mix and changed golf's EROI from negative to positive. I significantly improved my skills under the new, more rewarding, format. You can make your corporate game memorable by celebrating, recognizing well-placed shots, and generally having fun.

PERSONAL IMPLEMENTATION

By now you should know the implementation drill. Step 1 on the road to creating a rewarding, dopamine-rich workplace is to check the Tune-Up Metric. If your employees value the game and are experiencing energizing wins during the course of their workday, then their score for the skill-deployment appetite should be positive (pleasurable).

If the score is strongly positive (plus 4 to 8), then you have already designed a game that your employees enjoy playing and you are doing a fabulous job recognizing your employees' contributions and boosting their emotional paycheck—bravo! If the skill-deployment score is strongly negative, then employees are starving and managers need to take a long hard look at their personal standards and attitudes. Are they me-based managers seeking to dominate their employees and push them to the bottom of the hierarchy? Do they feel somehow threatened by them? Do they feel they are better than their employees? Are they expecting black-belt performance from the martial artists under their care when they are actually only green belts? If managers answer "yes" to any of these questions, then they need to return to Chapter 4, the one dealing with interpersonal bonding.

Implementing the suggestions in this chapter is not rocket science. It starts with a deep examination of one's own motivation and assumptions. If we change our fundamental assumptions and realize that achievement is just as important as eating or drinking for human beings, then we will begin acting accordingly. Once managers have their heads in the right place, here are some specific suggestions for designing a workplace game that employees will instinctively enjoy playing.

Design Suggestion 1: Feed the Skill-Deployment Appetite with Plenty of "Attaboys" or "Attagirls"

My golf anecdotes were humorous, but the message was serious. If you want employees to stick with the corporate game, then the benefits (pleasure) must exceed the costs (pain) and the course should be challenging but fair. At least one out of every two shots should be a winner.

Tom Rath, a global practice leader for the Gallup Organization, has uncovered some disturbing statistics regarding positive versus negative feedback in the workplace. For example, he found that 65 percent of employees got no "attaboys" or "attagirls" in the past year.[7] What's going on here? Didn't these employees hit any good shots? Part of the problem is that our society is competitive and hyperrational and giving support is often seen as a sign of weakness. Domineering, me-based managers wouldn't even consider giving support because it would feel like helping a competitor.

I encountered a nightmare, me-based manager early in my career who nearly drained the life out of me. His overall attitude was condescending—I am better than you because I'm an engineer who graduated from a prestigious university and you are just a lowly geologist. It didn't seem to matter to him that I was also an engineer and had an MBA from one of the world's top business schools.

Working for this guy was hell. I got zero attaboys and every report I wrote for him came back bathed in red ink. The nicest thing he ever said to me was, "The client liked your report but I didn't." I was ready to quit when my nightmare manager's niece, who was working for us for the summer, bounced into my office with some interesting intelligence. She said coyly, "Guess what we talked about at dinner last night?" "I haven't got a clue," I responded. "Well, my aunt told my uncle that she would have preferred marrying you, rather than him, if you had only showed up a little sooner."

At that point it was pretty clear why I hadn't gotten any attaboys from my nightmare boss. He probably felt threatened by me and/or saw me as a competitor. I was rescued from this predicament when I began doing projects for my boss's boss. Whereas I could do nothing right for my nightmare manager, I could do nothing wrong for my new one. He respected me, and mentored me, and we are still great friends to this day.

This is hardly a unique situation in a competition-based hierarchical ecosystem. For managers interested in creating a superorganism, however, there is no excuse for being stingy with praise. Well-deserved praise is the cheapest and easier way to improve employee motivation and performance. Praise releases dopamine and contributes mightily to the emotional paycheck. Employees need praise as much as they need food and they are not going to hang around long if they are starving to death! I nearly starved to death, so I know precisely what I'm talking about.

Focusing on just negative feedback is a ruinous proposition. How many friends do you think we'd have if we pointed out only their bad golf shots? "Wow, Bob, that was a real stinker. I think you dented the car across the street!" Your friends would soon "divorce" you. If you do this sort of thing at work, your employees are going to emotionally check out as well. As I mentioned in Chapter 5, nature doesn't allow us to self-administer emotional rewards by giving ourselves undeserved attaboys or attagirls, because, if it did, we would self-administer them *all the time*. Since we can't effectively praise ourselves to get our dopamine rush, managerial praise becomes all the more salient.

Recent brain imaging research has demonstrated that receiving a monetary reward and receiving praise activate the same emotional reward circuits in the brain. Paying our employees with money, or paying them with praise, in other words, are the same thing as far as the brain is concerned.[8]

Design Suggestion 2: Establish Clearly Defined Performance Standards

In some situations employees don't need praise because there are objective performance standards. In other words, the finish line is clearly marked. In these instances, employees automatically know if they've won or lost. For example, we don't need praise if we win a race. The objective outcome is praise enough. We either won or we lost. If we won, dopamine is automatically released.

Clear performance standards are obviously *a good thing*, at least within the context of a bonded peer group where everybody cares about the corporate survival game. Performance metrics help players delineate good shots from bad shots—just like the out-of-bounds stakes, fairways, and greens on a golf course. If corporate goals are valued and achievable with a reasonable expenditure of effort, they will trigger dopamine and be a source of hoopla and celebration. If the performance goals are unreasonable, or are used to punish rather than encourage, they can backfire and cause frustration, resentment, and "divorce."

Design Suggestion 3: Tailor Performance Standards to the Individual

When companies set performance standards, one size does *not* fit all. Some managers praise only achievements that meet their own exceptionally high standards. Everything else is simply expected. Some organizations set zero-sum goals where only the top 2 or 5 percent of producers are recognized and rewarded. Such win-lose reward systems are guaranteed to demotivate the bulk of the workforce. It is far more sensible to set challenging win-win goals, and then recognize *everybody* who reaches them—even if you end up recognizing everybody.

How many students do you think our karate studio would have if our world-class instructors praised students only for world-class performances? Simple—they would have "zero" students. The studio is wildly successful because it rewards incremental improvement from whatever baseline skills the student began with. White belts are not held to the same high performance standards as brown or black belts, but they are expected to improve their skills over time. This dopamine-rich environment results in the steady, incremental improvement of the entire group, not just the super-skilled. Most of the students in my studio look forward to karate class, progress steadily, and end up earning their black belts within three to five years. Few people drop out of the karate game, because it has a superb motivational design.

In terms of the golf analogy, the corporate game should be based on a handicap system. Beginners should not be held to the same standards as experts. This approach will motivate the beginners to become experts, one jolt of dopamine at a time.

Design Suggestion 4: Remember That Praise Is Particularly Important When Objective Performance Standards Are Lacking

Few outcomes in the workplace are as obvious and unambiguous as a well-placed golf shot or a properly executed karate move. If we write a report for our boss, for example, we might be left wondering if it was a good shot or a bad shot. Maybe the ball just disappeared into the fog and we are left wondering where it landed.

If employees get criticized and punished for their bad shots but never praised for their good ones, then work will have a highly negative EROI, effort expended without compensating reward. The logical thing to do is to quit the game and find a more emotionally satisfying pastime. The U.S. Department of Labor reports that the top reason employees quit their jobs is because they do not feel appreciated. In other words, they are not getting their "attaboys" or "attagirls."

There is an art to praise and recognition. Most important, it should be appropriate. There is nothing more irritating than receiving praise for an errant shot. We should all get in the habit of scanning the workplace for praiseworthy accomplishments and good-looking shots.

Design Suggestion 5: Schedule an Intramural Game

Some excellent companies use internal competition as a motivational tool. Human beings naturally tend to compare themselves to one another. In the case of golf, buddies compare who hit the longest drive (drive for show, pitch and putt for dough). The same thing happens in the animal kingdom in the form of good-natured sparring and play fighting. This is how animals naturally size each other up and determine their rank in the dominance hierarchy.

Companies like Procter & Gamble do something similar. They pit brand managers against one another in the same product category, such as laundry detergent (Tide, Cheer, Era, and Gain are all P&G brands). This may seem inefficient, but it's not. A good-natured sporting match gets the competitive juices flowing and provides sustained focus and motivation to achieve difficult goals. The extra cost to the organization for duplicating brand-development efforts is compensated by the benefit of improved productivity.[9] Such competition is fine as long as it stays good-natured. If the competition turns cutthroat and creates enemies, then it will cause more harm than good. Competition that is mean-spirited creates interpersonal warfare that ruins the feelings of solidarity and cooperation that characterize a superorganism.

ORGANIZATIONAL IMPLEMENTATION

The CEO of an organization obviously plays an important role in designing a corporate game that employees will enjoy playing. In fact, he or she should be the chief architect. The three mavericks—Iverson, Quadracci, and Semler—saw game design as their chief responsibility. They dedicated themselves to designing exciting workplace games that fostered good decisions (good shot making) and kept everybody's head in the game. An important fringe benefit of a well-designed corporate game is that it is self-managing, self-organizing, and self-motivated—which means that it will operate fine on its own, even if the CEO takes a few weeks off to hike through the mountains, lounge by the seashore, or take a golf vacation.

Design Principles of the Maverick CEOs

The corporate survival game is every bit as difficult as the game of golf or any other game of skill I can think of. It's a game that pushes the limits of human creativity, intuition, and logic. There is certainly no lack of challenge to playing this daunting game.

The three mavericks described in the Introduction were expert game designers, and their employees were highly committed, highly innovative, and highly productive on account of it. Employees of Nucor, Semco, and

Quad/Graphics were skilled participants in the corporate survival game and they greatly enjoyed the challenge of playing it. Whatever the mavericks were doing, it seemed to mesh harmoniously with human nature, so let's take a look at some of their key design principles.

Make Sure Everyone Gets to Play

Traditional bureaucratic, hierarchical companies, I argue, create a corporate game that very few human beings enjoy playing. Employees inhabiting the lower tiers of the hierarchy are more like disinterested spectators or caddies than active participants because the main shots (decisions) are taken by a small group of specialists at the top.

According to the traditional view, only specially trained experts can be trusted to make good shots and employees are more likely to be seen as unthinking pawns on the chessboard than as full-fledged players. CEOs and executives typically make all the key decisions, solve the most pressing and interesting problems, and enjoy the most dopamine. Here is how Ricardo Semler, the Brazilian maverick, described how the corporate game is generally stacked against employees:

> The heart of the problem is the pyramid, the basic organizing principle of the modern corporation. It gets narrower as it rises, rewarding the few who keep climbing but demoralizing a far greater number who reach a plateau or fall by the wayside. What can be expected of employees at the lower levels, whose opinions are never sought and to whom explanations are rarely given? They know that the decisions that matter, the decisions that will affect them, are made on high.[10]

All three mavericks encouraged everyone—right down to the janitor—to have their heads in the game. After all, the corporate game is enormously difficult and warrants *all* the brainpower a company can muster. According to the mavericks, important ideas can sprout from unexpected sources—like from a crane operator at Nucor or a machine-tool operator at Semco.

All the mavericks treated their employees as competent adults who were fully capable of playing the corporate game and of making their own intelligent moves (making their own decisions and solving their own problems). Ken Iverson, the architect of Nucor Steel, created a highly decentralized structure that pushed the power to set strategy, spend money, make decisions, and create policies to the folks closest to the action—employees and supervisors on the front lines.[11] These maverick leaders seldom took shots themselves, but contented themselves with laying out the course.

According to Semler, it takes a special humility, or ego restraint, for a CEO to resist taking all the key shots. Leaders will not hand the clubs over to their subordinates until they first admit to themselves that maybe, just maybe, they aren't the smartest person in the building and that the collective wisdom of the tribe is smarter than any individual executive. CEOs who don't reach this key realization, Semler argues, are naturally going to hog all the shots and turn everybody else into caddies and spectators.[12]

It should hardly be surprising that employees at Quad/Graphics, Nucor Steel, and Semco SA enjoy playing their corporate games. What would you rather be, a player or a pawn? Inside a *self-managing* superorganism, everyone is a player as well as a manager (at least of oneself).

Design the Corporate Game Around Your Employees' Passions

Ricardo Semler's most important principle was to design Semco around the passions and interests of his employees. This, he figured, would ensure maximum engagement and maximum productivity. Semler designed his corporate game to help his employees "feel alive with a purpose" and to make their life journeys worthwhile. He accomplished this by allowing his employees to customize the corporate game to their own unique specifications.

Semler's approach, the most extreme among the three mavericks, has resulted in a rather disorderly looking company that has its fingers in a bewildering array of products and services ranging from controlling inventories inside Wal-Mart stores to building turnkey biscuit factories for making Ritz crackers and Oreo cookies, to managing environmental investigations at polluted industrial sites. The unifying principle underlying this chaos is encouraging employees to follow their passions and keep a sharp eye out for emerging opportunities. Semler claims he has no idea what Semco SA will look like in the future because his company is an organic, evolving organism based upon authentic delegation of shot making. He therefore cannot anticipate what niches his fired-up, alert employees will feel their way into.

As a side note, Semco SA has one rigid requirement that must be satisfied before it enters a new niche—the niche must be sufficiently complex that standard companies, populated with standard employees with traditional motivation, would have a hard time competing in it.

The mavericks' approach is brilliant because involving employees in decision making and problem solving invites them to freely invest in the company, and, as we already know, consensual investment results in psychic bonding via the mysterious process of cathexis.

Allow Employees to Swap Roles in the Corporate Game

Any game, even one that employees had a role in designing, can get boring after awhile. The mavericks were therefore flexible regarding work roles. Financial executives at Semco, for example, are encouraged to do a stint running the marketing department and welders are encouraged to run forklifts, operate lathes, or take finance or engineering courses at the local university. The primary reason for all this flexibility is to keep the corporate game from becoming stale and boring—you master one skill and then move on to the next. A secondary reason has to do with flexibility and adaptability—not only is a multitalented workforce more motivated, confident, and skillful, but one individual can also fill in if another unexpectedly becomes ill or leaves the company. Managers who rotate through various business functions develop a more accurate metal map of the organization and therefore make better overall decisions.

In summary, all three mavericks got kudos from the business press for being brilliant strategists and innovators. In actuality, however, Iverson and Semler claim that they made few decisions themselves. Rather, they created conditions where good decisions (good shots) could be made throughout their organizations. If we want our organization to become a superorganism, I recommend that we emulate the three mavericks by elevating our employees from caddies to full-fledged players. This is how we can design a corporate game that our employees will intrinsically enjoy playing. If you'd like to learn more design tips from the three mavericks, read the following books:

- *Plain Talk: Lessons from a Business Maverick* (1998) by Ken Iverson

- *Maverick: The Success Story Behind the World's Most Unusual Workplace* (1993) by Ricardo Semler

- *The Seven-Day Weekend: A Better Way to Work in the 21st Century* (2003) by Ricardo Semler

- *Ready, Fire, Aim* (2006) a book about Harry Quadracci by John Fennel (this book is not widely available but can sometimes be found on Amazon.com)

SUMMARY

This chapter was short and sweet because the message is simple: Nature wants human beings to win (achieve) and rewards us with powerful pleasures when we do so. Companies that strive to build high-performance cultures that excel in the marketplace must tap into nature's powerful skill-deployment appetite: Appetite #3 in the motivational mechanism. We will know when the skill-deployment appetite is fed because our workplace will be filled with whoops, hollers, and high-fives. Social Appetite #3 will misfire if our employees don't truly value their employer and their role within the company. In this case, our employees are probably disengaged and trapped in jobs that are perceived as unrewarding chores.

CHAPTER 7

SOCIAL APPETITE #4: THE INNOVATION APPETITE

How to Foster Innovation by Encouraging Employees to Explore the Edge of the Known World

INTRODUCTION TO THE INNOVATION APPETITE

In the animal world, human beings are slow, weak, and poorly armed. If we did not compensate for these physical and physiological shortcomings, we would certainly be extinct. Our primary equalizer is technology: the tools and skills we invent to extend our capabilities and make ourselves more formidable than our physical attributes would suggest. We are, above all, the technological primate—the toolmaker.

The bottom line is that human beings need to innovate—to put resources together in novel ways in order to survive. Logically, therefore, there should be incentives for innovation. I call this system of incentives the innovation appetite. The innovation appetite is Social Appetite #4 in the motivational mechanism. Like the other social appetites, innovation is not an option but an absolute necessity for our species, so nature rewards us when we innovate.

Nature's innovation appetite is designed to solve problems and cope with complex and changing environments. The innovation appetite is what makes human beings the most adaptable and successful mammal on the planet. Human beings thrive in every ecosystem because of our technological genius and our ability to innovate and adapt. In the corporate world, change is ubiquitous and accelerating, so understanding the innovation appetite should be a top priority! Most managers are ill-equipped to manage innovation. Managers are trained to oversee, control, and administer. Managers are taught how to make employees diligent and obedient but not creative and committed.

We now pop the hood on nature's innovation appetite and describe the essential experience of innovation. In other words, how does it feel to innovate and how can companies encourage these natural feelings in the workplace?

Incremental Versus Disruptive Innovation

According to University of Chicago professor Harry Davis, innovations can be either:

- *Incremental.* Step-wise improvements on existing inventions (left-brain innovation)

- *Disruptive.* Radically new ideas that cause entire industries to reorganize themselves (right-brain intuitive leaps)[1]

I think this is an excellent distinction so I will use it to start our discussion of the innovation process.

Incremental Innovations (Left Brain)

According to Dr. Davis, the bulk of practical innovation occurring inside companies is incremental in nature—lots of small improvements to existing products and services. Davis argues that many small, incremental changes add up to substantial aggregate change over time.

Incremental innovations, according to Dr. Davis, can be tackled from a rational, engineering approach, which has traditionally been considered a left-brain talent. The left hemisphere of the brain, as you probably know, is specialized for language, problem solving, analysis, and planning. In other words, it's cool, practical, efficient, and tradition minded.

The left hemisphere is "you," the marble, the conscious mind we discussed in Chapter 3, and the right hemisphere is its multitalented and emotional helper. When cognitive scientists describe the human brain as computerlike, they are talking about the left hemisphere, not the right. Above all, the left brain is practical. Its fundamental purpose is to create order by parsing reality into categories, causal relationships, and patterns that aid survival.

In a sense, the left brain is like a hunter. It captures raw experiences and butchers them into their essential parts. It remembers what might prove useful in the future and leaves the rest. It then arranges the useful parts into categories and builds knowledge structures out of them. In this sense, the left brain is a builder as well as a hunter.

The left brain is also linear. It puts thoughts and actions together in strings, like a computer program, step by step, because this is how life events unfold. When the left brain innovates, it adds another step to the sequence or another branch to the structure, but *it does not invent another structure from scratch.*

Disruptive Innovations (Right Brain)

If incremental innovation is done logically and step-wise, disruptive innovations occur in intuitive leaps. Intuition is a mysterious, nonverbal, right-brain, holistic process. Because it is more mysterious and difficult to understand, I focus on it in this chapter. Besides intuition, the right brain excels at manipulating mental imagery, drawing, facial recognition, coordinated movement, navigating through three-dimensional space, and music. The right brain can understand language, but, in most cases, it cannot speak. Both hemispheres of the brain are vital for survival, and damage to either hemisphere causes profound malfunctions that put survival at risk.

The Innovation Barrier

Logically, human beings should innovate sparingly because the creative act focuses attention on the internal world of thoughts and images and distracts us from the external reality where danger and opportunities lurk. If human beings had behaved like distracted "absent-minded professors" during the last Ice Age, for example, survival would have been imperiled.

Innovation is also disruptive to culture—the database of hard-won survival wisdom acquired by our ancestors. If we had been overly encouraged to innovate, it would have spawned chaos instead of survival. Standardization and cooperation would have been impossible because everyone would have invented his or her own, idiosyncratic, ways of doing things. Unbridled innovation would have destroyed culture instead of serving it.

Both innovation and standardization have crucial survival benefits: Standardization is useful during stable times, and innovation is useful during times of rapid environmental change. Our minds need to be rigid and tradition minded on one hand and flexible and innovative on the other. Managers face a difficult challenge in finding the right balance point between practical tradition and disruptive, but essential, innovation. I believe that there is an activation barrier built into the innovation mechanism to inhibit its unnecessary and frivolous use. Writers call this barrier "writer's block," but its real name should be "idea block." If we did not have this barrier, peak experiences wouldn't be "peak" anymore, but the norm.

The innovation appetite, like the others, is designed to serve the tribe. Innovation will occur most readily within the context of a bonded tribe composed of experts. If employees don't deeply care about the corporate tribe, then they are unlikely to have the motivational momentum to scale the energy barrier that guards the entrance to innovation. They are also unlikely to have the determination to develop a spark of an idea into a finished product.

STEPS IN THE INNOVATION PROCESS

In this chapter I break the innovation process into four crucial steps:

1. *Information-Gathering Phase.* This phase is driven primarily by curiosity—the pleasure of novelty.

2. *Ideation Phase.* The ideation phase involves the mysterious process by which human beings get ideas. This process is motivated by two pleasures. The first pleasure doesn't even have a name. It is the brief burst of pleasure that announces the arrival of an idea. As I mentioned in the Introduction and Chapter 1, I call this pleasure that accompanies the moment of ideation the eureka pleasure. Researchers at the University of Southern California recently implicated endomorphins and mu-opioid receptors in the ventral visual pathway as regulators of the eureka experience.[2]

    There is a second type of ideation pleasure that sometimes occurs after we struggle with important problems over extended periods of time. This pleasurable state is sometimes described as a peak experience: the effortless and exhilarating flow of ideas. Peak experiences are most common at 2 o'clock in the morning before an important term paper or project is due. Psychologist Mihaly Csikszentmihalyi calls this peak-experience phenomenon "flow."[3]

3. *Reality-Testing Phase.* Getting an idea is generally the easy part. It is followed by the difficult part—demonstrating that the idea is practical and serves the interests of the tribe. Reality testing is the "99 percent perspiration" in Thomas Edison's famous proclamation, "Invention is 1 percent inspiration and 99 percent perspiration." In

order for an idea to qualify as a true innovation, it must prove itself on the real-world test track. It has to work.

4. *Jury-Trial Phase.* The final step of the innovation process is convincing one's peers that the innovation has merit—survival benefits that outweigh its costs. If the tribe agrees that the innovation has benefits, the group will applaud it. Applause, as we discussed in Chapter 5, imbues the innovation with value and desirability and causes it to spread through the tribe.

This chapter explores each of these four steps and discusses ways of incorporating them into your innovation plan.

Step 1: Information Gathering and the Pleasure of Exploration

The first step of the innovation process is information gathering. Innovation will not occur unless human beings are first motivated to explore their environment and create an internal cache of mental images that will serve as the raw material for innovation later on.

Curiosity is the pleasure that encourages exploration. In the modern world, curiosity motivates us to watch nature and science shows on TV, visit zoos, and go on exotic vacations. Curiosity is also the force that motivates scientists to journey to the ends of the known world, peer into the abyss, and confront the unknown.

My first research experience occurred in 1978 in the wilderness of the Central Alaska Range, not far from Mt. McKinley, the tallest mountain in North America. My thesis adviser, Dr. Campbell Craddock, had recommended the Central Alaska Range as a fascinating and scenic place to study. My thesis work in Alaska combined the physical adventure of spending two months in the uncharted wilderness with the intellectual adventure of being the first person, ever, to study the geology of a fascinating piece of real estate located along the Denali Fault: Alaska's version of the San Andreas Fault. The physical adventure and the intellectual adventure felt the same—exhilarating. I found myself on the edge of the civilized world and had the experience of a lifetime.

It's exciting to be on the intellectual edge, and research scientists have more fun there than their carefully worded papers suggest. If you've ever done research, you know what I am talking about. The thrill of research is a closely guarded secret. When I wrote my thesis, for example, I did not gush about my physical and intellectual adventure. I stripped out all the emotional juice, just like any cautious scientist should.

Fortunately, the adventurous part of the experience was documented in my assistant's field journal, which he titled *Alaska Diary*. He wrote about the wildlife, grizzly bear encounters, storms, near-fatal climbing accidents, and other misadventures during our summer of fieldwork. The seldom-revealed truth about innovation is that it contains a strong emotional component. It is emotionally rewarding because nature wants us to explore the edge.

A recent study published in the journal *Science* reported a strong correlation between hands-on research experiences for undergraduates and subsequent improvements in their attitudes regarding careers in science, technology, engineering, and mathematics. The effect of the undergraduate research experience was not subtle. Sixty-eight percent of the 15,000 students in the study who participated in hands-on research reported increased interest in science after experiencing the rewards of being on the edge. The researchers concluded "the earlier the better" regarding the impact of research exposure.[4] The researchers recommended exposing students to research as soon as elementary and high school.

Managers can encourage employees to explore the edge in the business world by allowing experimentation and research. Superorganisms encourage employees to innovate by encouraging lots of rapid and inexpensive tries (experiments). They realize that research and development is an inherently risky business, like drilling wildcat oil wells, and that nine out of ten attempts will come up dry. Tom Peters recommends encouraging inexpensive experiments in every department from accounting to IT and from engineering to sales. Constant experiments will keep your superorganism moving forward rather than backward. It is also energizing and adds substantially to the emotional paycheck.

The best way to stamp out curiosity in the workplace and chase away your most creative employees is to create rigid rules and bureaucracy that prohibit experimentation and research. Keep them away from the edge by telling them that the world is flat and that you have already figured out the best way to do everything. Tell them that innovation is disruptive, unpredictable, and messy and you just don't want it.

On my first day of work for an environmental consulting company, my boss, an engineer, told me *not* to make my assignments into research projects. This was equivalent, in my mind, to him saying, "Don't do good science, don't learn from other people's mistakes by reading the literature, and by all means, stay away from the edge." The between-the-lines message was, "Get it done quickly and inexpensively because quality doesn't really count." For a curious and creative person, working for this kind of engineer was tantamount to torture. This sort of conflict is not rare. Geologists and engineers have different personality profiles and emotional needs.

Geologists are curiosity driven and thrive on complexity and the unknown. Geologists seldom reach a simple, definitive solution because the natural world is exceedingly complex and does not fit easily into equations. Geologists are most likely to conclude, "It could be this or it could be that, and we need more data to decide." Engineers don't want to hear this kind of talk. Engineers are more left brained. They thrive on getting the right answer in a world of numbers, formulas, and rules. To engineers like my first boss, the complexities of the real world were a constant source of annoyance, expense, anxiety, and delay instead of a source of curiosity and wonder.

I later worked for Don, a senior engineer at the same company. Don had a more enlightened attitude toward geologists and had been taught by his professors that engineers must respect and listen to geologists or they will eventually get burned. Engineers, he was taught, have an instinctive tendency to simplify problems to fit their equations and thereby make their solutions mathematically workable. This simplification tendency can cause important facts to be ignored, and eventually result in failed dams, subsiding buildings, and ineffective environmental cleanups.

Don and I respected each other's strengths and formed a synergistic, whole-brained team. We completed our projects with engineering precision and a geologist's knack of considering all the angles. None of the projects we completed over a fifteen-year period collapsed, subsided, or otherwise failed—although we were often called in to investigate engineering projects that had.

Whatever field you are in, it probably has the equivalent of engineers and geologists. Finance executives are likely your "engineers" and your marketing department is probably filled with "geologists." The moral of this story is that both groups have their strengths and weaknesses. Engineers are efficient, precise, and tradition minded, while geologists like to explore, discover, and innovate.

Since we all possess both right and left hemispheres in our brains, we must also possess both sets of attributes. In other words, we can wear our engineer's hat in some situations and our geologist's hat in others. This flexibility of thought is precisely what is needed for practical innovation: the innovator should wear a geologist's hat in order to get an idea and an engineer's hat to prove that it works. This suggestion is consistent with the advice of Roger Sperry, the scientist who won the 1981 Nobel Prize in medicine for his work on split-brain patients. Sperry recommended that all scientists should be ambicerebral—able to draw on the strengths of both the right and left hemispheres.[5]

Exploration, Curiosity, and Dopamine

Curiosity is regulated by the neurotransmitter dopamine. Dopamine, as you may recall, is the same neurotransmitter involved in rewarding skill deployment (controlled by dopamine-1 and -2 receptors). The pleasure of novelty is controlled by a specific type of receptor, however—the dopamine-4 receptor.[6]

Studies of novelty seeking in children indicate 30 to 35 percent of children are born curious and exhibit a predisposition to approach that which is novel or unfamiliar. In other words, 30 to 35 percent of us are born with exploratory leanings. Around 15 to 20 percent of children are born with the opposite disposition. They actively avoid novel situations.[7] Children with the first type of predisposition might logically gravitate to fields like geology, while children with the second predisposition may be attracted to more predictable and orderly fields like engineering.

Science has advanced to the point where indications of one's novelty-seeking temperament can be determined with a genetic test. Human beings born with a certain version of the dopamine-4 receptor gene (DRD4) are prone to exploratory excitability[8]—like me. Mice that have had their DRD4 gene removed altogether are unusually fearful. They hide even when nothing is threatening them.[9] This research may help managers understand why some employees hunger for innovation more than others. If you want your organization to be innovative and cutting edge, then you should design it to support, encourage, and channel the exploratory instinct—especially for employees with a strong predisposition to explore.

Exploring the Edge in the Modern World

Our hunter-gatherer ancestors were surrounded by the unknown. The edge lay just outside their door. Each day must have felt exciting, like my research expedition to Alaska, because there was plenty of novel territory to explore.

The modern world is faced with something of a curiosity crisis. The modern educational experience, for example, does not stimulate the same sense of curiosity and wonder that I experienced in Alaska. For those of us born with the excitable version of the DRD4 gene, the modern educational system is stifling. In the early years of education, in my case a Catholic grade school staffed by nuns, the focus is on rote memorization of the "three R's": reading, writing, and arithmetic. Once those skills are mastered, we are expected to learn ideas out of context in unnatural school settings (think back to the discussion I had with the high school underachievers in Chapter 6). Knowledge is presented as fact—as truth— and the exciting edge is nowhere to be seen.

I enjoyed my educational experience the closer I got to the edge. I liked high school more than grade school, and I enjoyed college more than high school because it became increasingly clear that humanity still had lots of unsolved mysteries to grapple with—I could finally see the edge! Graduate school at the University of Wisconsin, Madison and my research experience in Alaska were best of all. I finally had a chance to peer over the edge myself and confront the unknown up close. I also got to work with fired-up professors who loved their work. It's too bad that it took seventeen years of education to discover the edge!

In 1984 I traveled around the country visiting major universities. I was investigating the academic community's current understanding of emotions. I interviewed prominent research scientists along the way regarding their educational experiences, including physics Nobel Prize–winner Emilio Segrè. To my surprise, almost every professor I interviewed had a similar story. They generally disliked their primary and secondary school experiences for the same reason I did: It was stifling and kept them away from the edge.

Managers can create passion in the workplace by encouraging employees with the exploratory excitability gene to explore the edges of the business or technological universe. Managers can encourage employees to explore the edge by allowing them to attend seminars where cutting-edge ideas are discussed or by bringing in speakers from academia and elsewhere who make their living on the edge. Best of all, managers should encourage invention and experimentation. In the long run, this will keep your superorganism moving forward rather than backward as it feels its way into the future.

Ricardo Semler, the Brazilian maverick, encourages his superorganism to feel its way forward with a policy called "rambling into the future." Rambling into the future means that employees are expected to follow their gut intuitions in whatever directions they lead. Monthly go/no-go meetings are held to allow the Semco tribe to give embryonic ideas the thumbs-up or thumbs-down.[10] Sadly, Semler's rambling concept would qualify as heresy inside most traditional companies, even though it aligns magnificently with the exploratory nature of human beings. Companies that want to avoid corporate extinction in an unpredictable and rapidly changing world, I suggest, should emulate Semler's example and encourage their employees to ramble into the future too.

Step 2: Ideation and the "Eureka" Pleasure

Curiosity, as we just discussed, motivates human beings to explore and gather raw information. The next step in the innovation process is to mine the storehouse of collected data for useful ideas that solve thorny survival problems.

Most animals don't innovate. They are instinctive, and their behaviors are largely automatic. They don't need to think ahead because they are preprogrammed to react in certain ways to life's challenges. When I greet my beagle, Lucy, in the morning, she instinctively licks her lips. I'm the alpha male in her mind, and she is programmed to lick the muzzle of the alpha male when she greets him. She doesn't actually lick my face, but her tongue starts going anyway. If I give Lucy a bone, she instinctively runs outside and buries it. When she goes to bed, she instinctively scratches at her bedding to remove sticks and debris, even though there are no sticks and debris. Lucy's actions are predictable and stereotyped. She learns from experience, but she doesn't think ahead. She lives in the moment and is stirred to action only by food, intruders, and her daily walk. The rest of the time she sleeps.

Human beings are different. We can plan ahead and anticipate. We can run through alternate scenarios of the future by manipulating mental imagery. We can simulate the future before it arrives and select the option with the greatest rewards and chance of success. This is a marvelous ability that makes us special and different. This is our genius! Here is how renowned neurobiologist Antonio Damasio makes this point:

> [W]e can, more or less deliberately, more or less automatically, review mentally the images which represent different options of action, different scenarios, different outcomes of action. We can pick and choose the most appropriate and reject the bad ones. Images also allow us to invent new actions to be applied to novel situations and to construct plans for future actions—the ability to transform and combine images of actions and scenarios is the wellspring of creativity.[11]

In case you doubt the importance of mental imagery in the innovation process, Roger Shepard, a famed Stanford University psychologist, reviewed the writings of famous scientists from the past several hundred years to determine what sort of thought processes they used to make their greatest discoveries. Many of the scientists reported using nonverbal mental imagery as their main idea-generating tool. The list of imagery-manipulating scientists includes some of the all-time greats: Albert Einstein, James Maxwell, Michael Faraday, Hermann von Helmholtz, Sir Francis Galton, James Watson, Francis Crick, and others.[12] We shouldn't be surprised that mental imagery is the key to innovation. Our brains are bathed in images arriving through our senses of touch, hearing, vision, and smell. These images are processed in the sensory cortices. We often take these splendid, multisensory images for granted.

Human beings evolved the miraculous ability to multitask the image-making machinery to not only sense what is actually there, but to antici-pate a virtual future.[13] We can hold an image in the mind, turn it around, bring in other images from memory, and organize them into new images or rationally slice and dice them into their constituent components. In the process of all this image manipulation, we just might get an idea!

Antonio Damasio asserts that all thoughts are images and that images are the fundamental substance of human thought. The evidence he cites to support his claim comes from neurobiology and advanced brain-scanning techniques like functional MRI and PET scans. If one thinks about a dog, for example, the early visual cortices of the brain will light up on a PET scan in the same way they would while observing a real dog. If you think about the smell of coffee brewing in the morning, then the olfactory cortices will light up, just as they would if you smelled real coffee brewing. As you read the words on this page, your auditory and motor (movement) cortices light up just as though you were reading and listening to the words aloud. If we placed sensitive electrodes around your mouth, they would pick up patterns of muscle activation identical to actually speaking the words.[14]

Thinking about an act or performing the act use precisely the same image-making mechanism—the early sensory and association cortices. The only real difference between the images you see and the ones you imagine is that the internal images are much, much fainter and less de-tailed than the sensory ones coming in from outside. If the opposite were true, thoughts would imperil survival by interfering with sensory vigi-lance. If your early visual cortices were somehow destroyed, you would be blind in both the real world and in your virtual world of dreams and thoughts.[15] You would still be able to imagine the texture, odor, and sound of an object, but not its visual image!

Some highly left-brain individuals deny the very existence of mental images, except, perhaps, when they dream. What is going on here? The answer, I believe, is twofold: (1) mental images are inherently subtle phenomena and (2) the left brain processes mental images quickly and over-prints them with verbal descriptions and interpretations. If this labeling and interpreting happens too quickly, some individuals could be unaware of the underlying images that triggered the verbal-labeling process in the first place. Nonetheless, it is the images flickering behind the words that give them meaning, substance, and context. Without images, words would be unintelligible sounds with no meaning whatsoever.[16]

My eleven-year-old daughter complained recently that her history class was boring. I explained to her that she could make learning as interesting as she wants by creatively imagining the topic of the day. The quality of her learning, I told her, was directly related to the quality, accuracy, and interest value of the internal mental images she creates. I told her that it's not always the teacher's responsibility to make learning fun and that she could add some emotional "juice" herself through mental imagery. If she were learning about the Revolutionary War, for example, then she could imagine what it would have been like for a young girl living in those difficult times. She understood the point and is now adding emotional juice to her reading assignments and class discussions.

Failure to find school interesting is a failure of imagination more than anything else. I taught this same lesson to the high school underachievers I mentioned earlier. Mental images are vital in the workplace as well, because innovation will not occur unless your employees can clearly picture the problems they are trying to solve. The clearer and more detailed these pictures, the more likely it will be for solutions to present themselves.

Idea Generation and Resonance

We have thus far determined that innovation involves the manipulation of mental images. We can even go a step further and investigate what happens at the miraculous moment when an idea pops into existence. Roger Shepard, one of the first scientists to rigorously study mental imagery, gave me an article titled "Ecological Constraints on Internal Representation: Resonant Kinematics of Perceiving, Imagining, Thinking, and Dreaming" when I visited his office at Stanford University in 1984. This article, which I dug out of my basement recently, suggests that ideas occur through the phenomenon of resonance.

Resonance is a term used in physics to explain how objects vibrate. Every physical object has a natural resonance frequency. In other words, if you tap an object, it gives off a specific sound: its resonance frequency. If you have a roomful of objects lined up on shelves, and the objects have various natural resonance frequencies, then what would happen if someone struck a large tuning fork in the room? The objects that have the same resonance frequency as the tuning fork would begin to rattle on the shelves because they are stimulated to vibrate in unison with a tuning fork vibrating at their special frequency. Objects with other natural resonance frequencies would not rattle because the tuning fork frequency does not stimulate their natural resonance frequency.

Shepard proposed that ideas occur in much the same way. The objects on the shelves, in Shepard's view, are analogous to the mental images stored in long-term memory. When we hold a specific mental image in working memory, it acts like the tuning fork. It gives off waves of specific frequencies that radiate through the brain and cause memories of the same, or similar, frequency to resonate in unison. The activated images collide with the tuning fork image held in working memory to generate an idea and the eureka pleasure.

Shepard's concept of resonance is alive and well in the scientific community. It's now called adaptive resonance theory.[17] Scientists researching artificial intelligence have developed resonance-based computer models that attempt to mimic the neural networks of the human brain. These resonance-based models can vastly outperform standard computer programs in complex tasks like facial recognition; the control of mobile robots; remote sensing; target recognition; medical diagnosis; electrocardiogram analysis; signature verification; tool-failure monitoring; chemical analysis; circuit design; protein/DNA analysis; 3-D visual object recognition; musical analysis; and seismic, sonar, and radar recognition.

I'm a big believer in the mental-imagery approach to innovation because it is precisely how I wrote this book. Every morning I go for a one-hour walk with my beagle, Lucy. I stop at a coffee shop along the way for a large latté. As I walk my standard route, I ponder the topic of the day. This pondering process is dominated by images: images of past experiences, images of things I've read about, and "what-if?" simulations. This flow of images invariably coalesces into one or more ideas. The ideas appear suddenly, as if from nowhere. I'm in charge of manipulating images during my walk, but the ideas seem to pop in on their own. Resonance is the best explanation I have come across to explain this miraculous process.

As you probably know, it feels good when the lightbulb finally turns on. This pleasure doesn't even have a name, so I refer to it simply as the "eureka pleasure." If my experience is typical, innovative companies should design themselves around the brain's peculiar ideation process. I am only half kidding when I suggest that companies should provide beagles, free lattés, walking paths, and woodlands around their corporate campuses.

Thinking Inside the Box

The logical, verbal, left side of the brain is you: the conscious mind. The conscious executive has two habits that limit creative, outside-the-box thinking. First of all, the left-brain executive automatically interprets reality.[18] It instinctively and immediately classifies experiences, assigns meaning, and slaps verbal labels onto everything. If the left brain is presented with disconnected, random facts, for example, it will immediately knit them into a plausible theory—like the conspiracy theories that inevitably arise whenever there is a traumatic public event like 9/11 or the John F. Kennedy assassination.

The left brain builds knowledge structures based on its preexisting interpretation of the world at large. It is therefore tied to this preexisting knowledge tree ("the box"). Left-brain ideas represent incremental innovations, new branches to the existing tree, or rearrangements of branches rather than something altogether new. In this sense, the left brain is tradition bound. It cannot think outside the box because *it is the box.*

Left-brain thinking is ideal for situations that conform reasonably well to past experiences. In these situations it can reach a workable solution quickly and efficiently because prepackaged response rules are already prepared. Adding a new feature to an existing product is a good example of incremental innovation in the business world.

Thinking Outside the Box

The right side of the brain experiences reality in its full, multisensory glory but does not interpret or put verbal labels on it. The right brain lives in the sensory present and does not plan or anticipate. Right-brain mental imagery is therefore the key to developing truly novel solutions to difficult problems. If the left brain dissects mental images into their component parts, the right brain puts them back together again into coherent wholes. It deals with complex reality, not the left brain's simplified interpretations of reality. The term commonly used for this holistic, or Gestalt, thought process is *intuition*.

In order to think outside the box, the logical left brain needs to let go and keep quiet. It needs to sit back and watch the show. The left brain cannot, on its own, produce the raw, integrated mental images that result in intuitive leaps. Rather, it needs to politely request these images from its nonverbal partner. The right brain can respond to these left-brain verbal requests because it possesses a large vocabulary and considerable grammatical knowledge.[19] The essential creative experience is therefore one of watching and requesting rather than creating and controlling mental imagery.

A number of respected scientists, inventors, and mathematicians have reported making important discoveries either during dreams, or immediately upon waking (Helmholtz, Hadamard, Watt, Kekulé, and Hilprecht).[20] Perhaps this is because the conscious mind is in a passive, observing mode during sleep and is therefore less likely to interfere with the right-brain's holistic, pictorial, intuitive process that results in great leaps of insight and radically new ideas.

Professional artists report that they need to turn off the left-brain interpreter in order to draw. A popular book titled *Drawing on the Right Side of the Brain* describes numerous exercises for achieving this.[21] As long as the left brain is involved in the drawing process, the artist's pictures will be simple, stylized, and childlike because the left brain perceives the essential features of objects rather than the details of the objects themselves. In a sense, the left brain thinks in simplified, cognitive shorthand. Perhaps it is no coincidence that Leonardo da Vinci, an artist, was one of the greatest inventors of all time. Perhaps his artistic talent for quieting his analytical left brain provided a conduit for truly original thought.

Perhaps managers in charge of new product development should emulate the artist's method. If you want a truly revolutionary idea, don't overanalyze or overcontrol your creative staff because these left-brain analytical processes will cause the intuitive side to clam up and shut down.

Take Care of Your Champions

As I described above, when I get ideas during walks with my dog, they announce themselves with bursts of pleasure. The message of this pleasure is "Congratulations, you have just made a correlation between the image you were manipulating in working memory and images stored in long-term memory." When I get a really good idea, perhaps created by the collision of many separate images resonating at once, the ideation pleasure can be quite intense. Without this pleasure, I wouldn't even know that I had had an idea. The ideation pleasure imbues the idea with a sense of value—like discovering a gemstone on the beach. It motivates me, the discoverer, to share the idea with others.

The simplest way to get your employees to innovate is to tell them it's okay to do so. Innovation is a natural process that nature wants us to engage in. If your employees truly care about the company and its success and you give them freedom to experiment and explore, then innovations will literally come knocking. Employees will barge into your office full of enthusiasm to share their latest finds. Few of the ideas will be major innovations that will make you rich, because such innovations are exceptionally rare.[22] Nonetheless, try to resist the natural analytical temptation to shoot the ideas out of the sky like so many clay pigeons.

The man or woman walking through your door is a potential champion, someone who believes in an idea and has the guts and gumption to push it through to reality. Only a champion with a vision will be resolute enough to stumble, dust him- or herself off, and keep on going. Thomas Edison captured the indomitable spirit of the champion when he stated, "I failed my way to success." Rather than blast your champions, you might want to lock them up in a garage, give them a pittance of resources and an unreasonable deadline to come up with something practical, and hail them as heroes when they succeed.

Another Ideation Pleasure Called Flow

There is another pleasure associated with ideas called *flow* or *peak experience*. *Flow* is the term Mihaly Csikszentmihalyi coined for the effortless and exhilarating flow of ideas that sometimes occurs when human beings immerse themselves in a problem that is challenging but not overwhelming. Csikszentmihalyi does not confine the term *flow* to the intellectual realm. In his formulation, expert musicians and expert athletes experience flow during their best performances when they are "in the zone" and the mind is functioning at its best.[23]

The term *peak experience* describes a related concept. It was coined by Abraham Maslow to refer to the experience that occurs when the thought process jumps to a higher plane of functioning with an extrapersonal perspective. Maslow used the term *extrapersonal* to refer to a sense of being outside of the standard routine of everyday life where you see things in a different light. According to Maslow, a peak experience can be a life-altering event that changes one's perspective, permanently. It is also a nonverbal experience that human beings have difficulty putting into words.[24] Regardless of whether we call this experience flow or peak experience, it is intensely pleasurable and generally corresponds to exceptional performances. If human beings had the choice, they would probably choose to be in this exhilarating state most of the time.

My first recognizable peak experience occurred while trying to write a term paper for an English literature class in college. I had to write a paper on Thomas Hardy's book *Tess of the d'Urbervilles*. The night before the paper was due I still had nothing, just a sheet of white paper staring back at me. About 2 A.M., after struggling for hours, I had a breakthrough. I wrote the entire paper in about twenty minutes, all in one shot. The ideas flowed effortlessly, but I didn't feel as though they were my ideas. My role was simply to write them down. Wherever the ideas came from, they earned me an A for the paper.

This experience suggests that much of the ideation process takes place in the background, outside of conscious awareness. Background processing makes sense because it relieves the conscious mind of distractions and allows external vigilance to be maintained. This subconscious mechanism is balky, however, like an old lawnmower that is difficult to start. If we keep at it, however, the subconscious mind eventually kicks in. When the subconscious solution is finished, it is fed into consciousness fully formed. All we have to do is write it down.

The same thing happened during my thesis work in Alaska. My thesis adviser, Dr. Campbell Craddock, accompanied me to Alaska. He ran out of time as we were hiking into my study area. He said he had to catch a flight to Svalbard, an island in the Arctic Ocean, and had to leave. He pointed toward a mist-shrouded valley in the distance and said, "There are some geologic puzzles in that valley and others nearby. Good luck." With that brief introduction to my thesis area, he left.

I was mortified. My assistant and I were on our own without even a radio to communicate with the outside world. Three weeks passed and I still had no idea how to solve the geologic puzzles of my study area. The rocks were jet black and covered with black lichens. I couldn't even locate a bedding plane with any confidence, which is not good when you're doing a structural geology thesis. I started to panic. Would this be the end of my graduate-school career?

I eventually found a valley where a retreating glacier had scraped all of the bothersome lichens from the rocks so I could finally see some details. A few days later a storm blew in, and I had to spend the day huddled inside the tent. During that day in the wind-whipped tent, I developed the main ideas for my thesis. The ideas came quickly and effortlessly, just like during my term paper–writing experience.

We might call the period of struggle preceding ideation, *incubation*. As far as I can tell, a peak experience requires a period of struggle to activate the subconscious mechanism that ultimately does most of the work. The struggle component is related to the innovation barrier that I discussed at the start of this chapter. This phenomenon of sudden illumination following a period of struggle has been described by many of the most creative thinkers.[25]

Recent experiments by Ap Dijksterhuis and Loran F. Nordgren at the University of Amsterdam support the idea of subconscious incubation. Their research indicates that unconscious thought is superior to conscious thought when solving complex problems with many variables. Rational thought, as one might guess, was superior for solving simple problems.[26]

It makes perfect survival sense for us to manufacture ideas in the subconscious, the basement. The hunter-gatherer lifestyle was hazardous, much more hazardous than modern humans can imagine. I have probably come closer to the hunter-gatherer lifestyle during my fieldwork in Alaska than most. I had two encounters with grizzly bears and numerous opportunities to get killed or injured. I have personal respect for the vigilance required to survive in the uncharted wilderness with formidable predators wandering around. It would have been hazardous for me to take my eye off the ball under these circumstances. It therefore makes sense, from a design perspective, for nature to bury as much of the innovation process in the subconscious as possible. The primary duty of the conscious mind is to scan the external world, recognize problems, collect data, and wait for the subconscious mechanism to kick in and spit out a solution.

Regardless of the reasons, we have an innovation mechanism that is quirky and difficult to operate. The steps to operate the mechanism are:

- Care deeply about your group, its survival, and its problems.

- When you confront a problem, tackle it with determination and persistence because the innovation mechanism somehow senses the seriousness of the problem at hand and may refuse to engage without a good reason to do so. In other words, immerse yourself in the problem.

- Read, research, ponder, and explore in order to feed in as much raw data as possible. The final innovation will be a creative recombination of these inputs.

- Have some sort of deadline to provide motivational momentum to scale the innovation barrier. This has been an essential feature of my peak experiences.

If all of these pieces come together, human beings can make startlingly original connections that would not occur during the routine of a typical day. These experiences are rare, but exhilarating. They create a sense of awe at the hidden processing potential of the human mind.

Step 3: Reality-Testing Phase

Ideation is the fun part of the innovation process because it involves the playful and exhilarating manipulation of mental images intermixed with dopamine. Now it's time to get serious and sift the wheat from the chaff.

It's time to put on our engineer's hat and prepare for the "perspiration" part of the innovation process. It's time to prove that our idea is better than the incumbent idea, using data, cool analysis, equations, and evidence; it's time to get rational. If your innovation is a product, it's time to make and test a prototype and conduct focus groups.

Many people get ideas, but ideas are cheap. Most of them are impractical or have already been thought of. If you want to call yourself an inventor, you'd better have the stamina and drive to turn your raw idea into a practical reality that benefits the tribe. This is where champions come in. Champions have a near-fanatical belief in the value of their ideas, just like I have a near-fanatical belief that emotions have been maligned and underappreciated as the drivers of business success. Every neuron in my brain is convinced of this and the idea will not leave me alone. This idea has sat by my side for thirty years, prodding me to take action. I suspect this is true of many champions—they are pestered into taking action by their own creations.

Step 4: The Applause or Jury-Trial Phase

The "applause phase" of the innovation process might also be called the jury-trial phase. The applause phase is the endgame in the innovation process in which the inventor trots out his or her innovation before the tribe and demonstrates its benefits. The tribe is the judge, jury, and executioner. If the jury applauds the innovation it immediately and magically becomes valuable and spreads, viruslike, through the tribe.

The corporate tribe *always* resists disruptive innovations because they are inherently threatening to prior investments in the status quo. Disruptive innovations also imply a mandatory expenditure of effort to learn, master, or manufacture the innovation. The tribe will automatically reject all innovations unless they provide compensating emotional benefits to counteract these inherent emotional and monetary costs. The tribal jury will instinctively run an emotional cost-benefit analysis to decide the fate of the innovation. If this analysis results in an overall positive EROI, the innovation will be accepted and applauded.

In the corporate context, the innovator (champion) takes on the role of defense attorney during this judging process. The champion needs to demonstrate to the skeptical jury how the innovation serves the tribe. It's easy to demonstrate the survival value of incremental innovations because they represent straightforward, predictable extensions of existing ideas and knowledge. They do not require relearning and they do not really threaten prior investments. The hard innovations to sell to the jury are the intuitive, disruptive types because they will not make initial sense to the tribe. The members of the tribal jury will evaluate the innovation by trying to connect it to what they already know. If the tribe cannot detect a logical connection between the known and the unknown, the innovation will be dead on arrival. It will seem strange, threatening, and unfathomable.

The first step for the disruptive innovator is therefore to create a logical, step-by-step bridge from the known to the unknown. This is the hard part that many innovators dread.[27] Disruptive ideas arrive in an intuitive flash. To craft them into practical innovations, however, they must be logically connected to the known world with words and analysis. It takes a skilled "defense attorney" to make a convincing case.

I've been a "defense attorney" throughout this book. My client, human emotion, had been accused of irrational and harmful acts in the workplace. I hope I've proved, beyond a reasonable doubt, that my client has a positive and productive side that outweighs its negatives.

PERSONAL IMPLEMENTATION

Is your organization innovative? If you are not sure, just check your Tune-Up Metric, because innovation, just like the rest of human behavior, is driven by emotions. If you provide your employees with the freedom to explore and experiment, then they will experience two innovation-related pleasures on a regular basis: curiosity, the pleasure of being on the edge, and the eureka moment experienced when ideas pop into existence. These pleasurable feelings contribute to the emotional paycheck and show up on the Tune-Up Metric as a positive (pleasurable) score for Social Appetite #4, the innovation appetite.

If your score for the innovation appetite is positive, it means that you allow your employees, especially those with the novelty-seeking version of the DRD4 gene, the freedom to explore, experiment, and solve problems. When they barge into your office full of enthusiasm, you listen intently, provide a modicum of resources to flesh out the idea, and encourage them to become new product/service champions. More often than not, the ideas will prove impractical or uneconomical, or will already have been thought of and patented. Managers who score high for Social Appetite #4 on the Tune-Up Metric are not fazed by these inevitable setbacks because they come with the territory of cutting-edge innovation. Instead, they dust off the champion, thank him or her for the idea, and encourage him or her to try again. Eventually, if you stick with it, you will bring in a gusher—an innovation so remarkable that it sets you well ahead of the competition and secures your organization's future, at least for the time being.

The manager or leader of a superorganism has a distinct advantage on the innovation front because he or she already has a tightly bonded team composed of confident experts. If a challenge arises for your organization, all you need to do to solve it is to unleash your superorganism and watch the solution arise organically and naturally because your organization already aligns with human nature and the built-in hunger to innovate.

If your organization is a cool and dispassionate bureaucracy, on the other hand, where efficiency, rules, systems, punctuality, and making money are more important than people, and where employees are unbonded and don't really care about their employer, then it is highly unlikely that your employees will have the motivational momentum to scale the energy barrier that guards the gates to innovation. Employees in such organizations will feel stifled instead of free to explore and innovate, so their scores for the innovation appetite will be in the negative (painful) range. Dispassionate organizations fall flat in regard to innovation, which is why they need to be restructured sooner, rather than later!

Role-Based Approach to Innovation

There are numerous consulting firms that specialize in helping companies innovate. Many facilitate brainstorming sessions. The success of these services is mixed. If they are executed skillfully, they can improve the quantity of ideas generated during a group session, and if they are executed poorly they can be counterproductive and cause employees to disengage.[28]

Dr. Harry Davis, the University of Chicago professor I mentioned at the start of this chapter, is skeptical about group brainstorming sessions. He proposes a different solution whereby employees are taught to unleash their creative sides by changing the personas they wear into work in the morning. Most of us have been taught to come to work in business clothes and assume a cool, dispassionate persona—a hyperrational role. This role, unfortunately, is ill suited to the messy and emotional process of innovation.

Davis points out that human beings have multidimensional personalities. He calls these dimensions "roles" or "characters," like the roles and characters in a play. Even the most hard-core CEO, he argues, relaxes and assumes a different role within the context of close friends and family. This CEO has a work character and a home character. Davis proposes that managers often take on the role of skeptic and judge in the workplace. Employees often see their roles as rational and efficient worker bees. These self-imposed roles stifle innovation, according to Davis. To encourage innovation, Davis recommends that employees and managers allow themselves to take on varied roles in the workplace, like the adventurous explorer, mad scientist, and perceptive artist—in other words, to draw on elements of their personalities that are normally checked at the door. The more of ourselves we bring to the workplace, he argues, the more skills, knowledge, and creative juices we have to work with.[29]

I agree with Dr. Davis. The innovation process requires more than one character. Personally, I like to alternate between the roles of passionate explorer, intuitive dreamer, and analytical perfectionist.

Got an Emergency? Try the Skunk Works® Approach

If you have an urgent problem in need of an immediate solution, you might want to try the Skunk Works approach to innovation. It involves sequestering a bonded team of experts (a superorganism, in other words) at a spartan location, and then tasking them with a compelling but difficult problem with an impossible deadline. The manager also hints that the team will be hailed as heroes if they pull it off. I like this approach because it provides the motivational momentum needed to scale the innovation barrier and thereby come up with a creative solution quickly.

The term *Skunk Works* was coined by Lockheed Martin to describe its Advanced Development Projects Unit, the research arm of the company that has been responsible for a number of famous aircraft designs such as the U-2, SR-71 Blackbird, and its latest innovation, the Joint Strike Fighter. The Lockheed Martin Skunk Works was initially housed in a tent! The name refers to an advanced or secret project group working within an organization with a high degree of autonomy and unhampered by bureaucracy. Another way to describe it is, "Lock five guys in a garage and let them go crazy on a difficult problem."

Kelly Johnson, the leader of the Lockheed Martin Skunk Works, insisted that his engineers get dirty on the shop floor, like guys building hot rods in their garages. Kelly's informal, nonbureaucratic process produced the most important planes of the twentieth century.[30]

This is also how Steve Jobs and Steve Wozniak created the first Apple computer—futzing around in a garage. I recently visited an advertising school here in Madison, Wisconsin, called Extra Bold Portfolio School. I got a kick out of the student lounge. It was decorated to look like a garage, because this is where many of the best ideas come from. Maybe all innovative companies should have garagelike spaces designed into their facilities: a place where employees can playfully tinker with new ideas with their buddies.

The Skunk Works remote location helps create a tribal identity out of an assembly of separate individuals. The remote location should have a mystique that will be the grist for folk stories for years to come. Let your Skunk Works participants know that they will be celebrated as heroes if they succeed. In other words, add a self-esteem bonus to the process.

There is nothing traditional about the Skunk Works process, but it makes sense in relation to nature's motivational mechanism. If your goal is to develop motivational momentum to scale the innovation barrier, Skunk Works are probably the way to go. Such small, passionate bands routinely out-innovate much larger and better-funded mainstream labs working inside plush quarters. If human beings were hyperrational computer-like creatures, the labs would out-innovate the Skunk Works. Curiously, this is not the case.

ORGANIZATIONAL IMPLEMENTATION

As the CEO or owner of a company, it is perfectly understandable if you are a bit bewildered by the innovation process. The psychological phenomenon of resonance, which underlies innovation, is not linear and steplike but subconscious, intuitive, and hidden. In addition, there's that pesky energy barrier that naturally inhibits innovation. Here are some approaches to innovation that work harmoniously with nature's balky mechanism that corporate leaders can implement to make innovation more-or-less predictable.

Implementation Step 1: Encourage Exploration and Experimentation

Innovation is not conceptually difficult, because human beings are already prewired to do it. In essence, all managers need to do is give employees the okay to explore and experiment and then develop systems to support and reward the process. Tell them it is okay to innovate and back up your words with actions.

Entrepreneurial companies, like 3M, have developed more formal processes to encourage, evaluate, sort, and implement ideas. To start with, 3M allocates 15 percent of each researcher's time to pursuing and developing their hunches. Google, Genentech, and W. L. Gore use this approach in their R&D departments too. The 3M process encourages internal entrepreneurs and champions to run with their pet ideas. In other words, 3M throws lots of mud at the wall. The mud that sticks gets additional resources and is developed further. If an idea turns out to be a dud, then the innovator is encouraged to quickly abandon it and start again.

The 3M research process is motivationally efficient because it harnesses the innovator's natural energy and enthusiasm for his or her discovery and uses this motivational energy to propel the innovator through the difficult "perspiration" part of the innovation process—the reality-testing phase.

At Ore-Ida, the failures are actually celebrated and awards are given out for the perfect failure.[31] The message to the inventor is an uplifting one: Get back in the saddle and try again! Bill Smithburg, the former CEO of Quaker Oats, used a skiing analogy to make the same point: "It's just like learning to ski. If you're not falling down, you're not learning."

"Lots of inexpensive failures" is precisely how nature designs sophisticated organisms such as ourselves. The "tries" are random mutations—experiments with no intelligent thought behind them whatsoever. Despite the randomness of nature's design process, many, many trials along with many, many failures eventually lead to nature's spectacular innovations.

Nucor Steel doesn't even have a research and development department, yet it has successfully out-innovated larger rivals that do. Nucor has achieved this miracle by encouraging everyone from crane operators to college interns to constantly search for cost-saving ideas and by rewarding them when they discover something useful. In other words, Nucor gives the entire organization permission to innovate and takes employee suggestions seriously. This serious approach to innovation encourages serious thinking in return.

Ricardo Semler fosters innovation by encouraging his employees to question absolutely everything. If you don't continually question the status quo, Semler argues, you will be unable to identify when a system or rule or procedure has become an artifact that no longer serves a useful function. Allowing employees to question and probe is one way companies can keep themselves and their employees on the cutting edge of change.[32]

Implementation Step 2: Create a Marketplace for Ideas

Gary Hamel, in his book *The Future of Management*, describes an exciting approach to innovation that aligns nicely with the ideas in *Primal Management*. Hamel calls this approach a *marketplace for ideas*. This approach, according to Hamel, is gaining in popularity and has been tested successfully by a number of innovative organizations like W. L. Gore, the maker of Gore-Tex fabric, and Rite-Solutions.

An *open marketplace of ideas* is exactly what the name implies—a forum, or bazaar, where employees can showcase their ideas and seek volunteers to help turn them into practical innovations. Companies using this approach provide discretionary time, what Gore calls *dabble time*, to either come up with innovative ideas or to invest in developing other people's ideas. As Hamel describes, employees at Gore receive a half day of dabble time each week.[33] Employees can accumulate their dabble time and use it in blocks—like an entire day spent at a library or research institution, or tinkering in their garage. Employees without their own pet project are encouraged to volunteer their dabble time to help advance other promising ideas.

Gore's use of dabble time might seem like a waste of time. Then again, this is a company with $2.1 billion in sales, 8,000 employees, and over 1,000 products. I think Gore's approach aligns perfectly with the innovation appetite because employees are allowed to explore the edge and work on projects that intrinsically interest them.

There is nothing soft about Gore's approach because it contains a rigorous jury-trial phase. In order to get past the dabble stage of development and receive serious funding, ideas must survive a cross-functional peer-review process called "Real, Win, Worth" to make sure the opportunity is *real* and not some kind of flaky idea, one where Gore can *win* in the marketplace by becoming a market leader in the product category, and that it is *worth* the time and effort in terms of profit potential.[34]

According to Hamel, Rite-Solutions took the dabble time concept to an entirely new level by building an internal stock market around it. Ideas that bubble to the surface at Rite-Solutions, a software company, are given their own Web page on the company's intranet. Rite-Solutions calls these posted ideas on the intranet *initial public offerings* (IPOs).[35] The internal entrepreneur who posts the IPO also describes its potential benefits and lists the initial steps needed to test or develop the idea.[36] Management does not need to approve an IPO under the Rite-Solutions stock market format, so it is truly a grassroots, or bottom-up, approach to innovation that taps the creativity of everyone in the organization.

Employees who would rather develop the ideas of others than come up with their own ideas can invest their discretionary time in promising IPOs. Each listed IPO includes a threaded public discussion group, similar to an Internet news group, where potential investors can discuss the merits and drawbacks of each IPO (creating "buzz on the street").

Employees are allotted $10,000 in fantasy money to purchase stock in the various IPOs. These stocks can then be traded in the company's internal "stock market." The IPOs' fantasy values are adjusted periodically by experts in the company based upon how they are progressing and how much discretionary time has been invested in them by colleagues. Ideas that don't attract followers (employees willing to volunteer their discretionary time) die a natural death and are delisted from the internal stock market.

The top-rated IPOs at Rite-Solutions, based upon the number of volunteer hours invested, the buzz on the street (discussion group postings), and amount of fantasy money invested, are given a pot of real money to invest in serious development. Employees who invested their discretionary time in these IPOs receive cash bonuses or stock options (this time with real money) if the IPO turns into a successful product launch. In its first year of operation, Rite-Solution's IPO stock market accounted for 50 percent of the company's new business growth.

Rite-Solutions' marketplace for ideas aligns with human nature because it provides freedom to explore and it uses the consensus opinion of the tribe (Web page hits, blog comments, and fiddle-time investments) to organically determine which ideas are valuable (serve the survival of the tribe) and which aren't. It also draws upon the wisdom of the crowd to select the most promising ideas. This approach to innovation is brilliant because it turns the work of innovation into an organic, human-friendly game that employees instinctively enjoy playing.

Implementation Step 3: Create an Innovation "Battle Plan" for a World Characterized by Rapid Change

What's in store for your company in the years ahead? The Internet, I propose, is causing an innovation explosion because it effectively makes every society on earth our neighbor and greatly speeds the flow of ideas and information by reducing transaction costs. If companies want to thrive in this dynamic, interconnected world then they had better be prepared for a bumpy and turbulent ride. The company you manage today will probably be quite different from the one you manage five years from now.

One of the most turbulent business environments on the planet today is China. Western companies have lost hundreds of billions of dollars in its shifting political, regulatory, and cultural sands. The business environment in China is buffeted by many unpredictable forces, including:

- Hypercapitalism, where a good idea is immediately copied by a hundred imitators

- Tenuous rule of law, where whom you know is often more important than what the rules are

- Uncertain property rights

- Corruption

- An opaque Communist government that has little love of Western societies or their corporations

- Tacit governmental support for intellectual property transfers—both legal and illegal

- A huge population with many mouths to feed

- Tensions between the mainland and Taiwan that could explode into violence at any time

- A regulatory landscape that is constantly changing as China races to catch up to international standards

Professor Donald Sull, of the Harvard Business School, provides guidance for operating businesses in such turbulent environments in his 2005 book, *Made in China*. Sull suggests that businesses operating in turbulent environments should adopt a Marine Corps model characterized by decentralized planning and real-time decision making. In a battle, Sull argues, military planners operate in a chaotic fog of war.

The U.S. Marines, to give a concrete example, are often thrust into rapidly changing and unfamiliar situations replete with unexpected threats and opportunities. Marines spend much of their time conducting reconnaissance by groping their way through unfamiliar terrain and assessing circumstances that shift constantly with changes in weather, enemy movements, and the deployment of their own forces. Facing these conditions, Marines follow a simple rule that can be summed up as "recon pull versus headquarters push," which encourages Marines to rely on their understanding of the emerging situation based on local knowledge in real time rather than to blindly execute a preconceived plan from headquarters. This rule allows Marines to capitalize on their local knowledge to spot opportunities and threats quickly and grants them the autonomy to improvise a response to the facts on the ground.[37]

I propose that companies should adopt a similar "recon pull" approach to innovation. Advance planning, such as three- or five-year plans, is largely irrelevant in turbulent environments because the plan is likely to be overtaken by events and made obsolete. Perhaps this is why Harry Quadracci's rule was "no planning allowed." He believed that if you start planning, "you blind yourself to opportunity."[38] Harry modified his battle plan on the fly as the business environment morphed around him. Harry constantly updated his mental map of the "battlefield" and searched for emerging opportunities and developing threats rather than wasting a lot of time with long-range planning and budgeting. Harry told me in 1986 that he didn't need to worry about the future if he had his finger on the pulse of his organization and the marketplace today. Harry concentrated on current opportunities and threats rather than spending time trying to predict a complex future that may or may not have materialized.

Sull's recon pull approach delegates much of the decision making to the frontline troops who have the best view of the emerging situation on the ground. Companies that want to innovate should do something similar—perhaps by implementing Hamel's marketplace of ideas approach. They should empower their employees to probe the marketplace with lots of innovative initiatives. This will require a participatory style of management that empowers employees to explore, experiment, and innovate. In other words, let your corporate superorganism feel its way into the future by delegating decision making and creativity to the folks closest to the action. Your troops will be more than happy to oblige, because innovating on the edge is something many human beings like to do. You, the leader, will allocate resources to those probing actions that identify weaknesses in the enemy's lines.

This is precisely what Ken Iverson did at Nucor Steel. Iverson realized that he could not possibly map out a future for Nucor's twenty-one diverse divisions. Nobody could. Instead, he empowered his general managers to make their own decisions. They, in turn, empowered supervisors and hourly employees to make major decisions and take responsibility for the consequences of those decisions. Iverson claimed that his role was not to make decisions but to create an environment where good decisions and ideas would emerge at all levels of the organization. The business press hailed Iverson as a brilliant innovator. He felt sheepish about all this adulation because he actually didn't come up with any of Nucor's major innovations himself! Here is how Iverson expressed the importance of getting everyone's head in the game:

The great and terrible irony of modern business is that so many managers feel overburdened with responsibility, while so many employees feel unchallenged and unfulfilled in their jobs.

The way to a happier and more prosperous state is clear: Concede once and for all that employees, not managers, are the true engines of progress, and dedicate your management career to creating an environment in which employees can stretch for higher and higher levels of performance.

Shaping the work environment has always been an acknowledged part of the manager's responsibility. But to my way of thinking, it's the manager's primary job. Instead of telling people what to do and then hounding them to do it, our managers focus on shaping an environment that frees employees to benefit themselves and the business. We've found that their answers drive the progress of our business faster than our own.

Is there a better way for managers to invest their time and energy? I doubt it. The manager who devotes him- or herself to this endeavor is on the side of the angles. Employees will sincerely appreciate your efforts to help them explore and develop their capabilities. Customers and investors will appreciate the superior performance of your employees, and as a direct

*result, of your business. Last, but not least, you and your fellow managers
will appreciate all the fine things people will say and write about you. True,
it'll be more than you deserve. But is that your fault?*[39]

I suggest that managers heed Iverson's suggestions because both he
and Nucor triumphed in the face of intense international competition in
the steel industry while many of the conventional competitors floun-
dered. He achieved this in a modern high-tech steel industry without a
research and development department! Unleashing the creative, decision-
making abilities of your employees creates a world where everybody wins.
Win-win!

SUMMARY

The good news in this chapter is that human beings are wired to innovate
and help their tribes solve difficult survival problems. This process will
occur naturally and organically inside a superorganism where employees
truly care about their managers, their coworkers, and the organization as
a whole.

The bad news is that many traditional, bureaucratic, hierarchical organizations are ill equipped to adapt to the accelerating pace of change
created by global competition and the Internet. Innovation, I suggest, is
the Achilles heel of traditional management because innovation cannot
be scheduled and systematized using hyperrational, impersonal business
practices. Innovation requires a radically different, employee-centric approach, because only organizations firing on all cylinders will have the
motivational energy to scale the innovation barrier on a regular basis.

I hope the suggestions presented in this chapter will help you unleash
the creative potential of your employees. If you need additional guidance,
you might try emulating the three mavericks—all of whom worked harmoniously with human nature to create highly adaptive and innovative
organizations.

CHAPTER 8

SOCIAL APPETITE #5: THE SELF-PROTECTION APPETITE

How to Avoid Triggering Defensive Behaviors in the Workplace

The self-protection appetite is the fifth and final social appetite in the motivational mechanism. This regulatory system does what its name implies: It *protects* human beings from physical and psychological harm. We are all familiar with this social appetite because it's the source of ballistic emotions like fear, jealousy, anger, and rage. The self-protection appetite also has a subtle side that exists below the waterline, such as the barely perceptible anxiety that coaxes us out of bed in the morning or motivates us to do the many routine chores that we would otherwise avoid.

I propose in this chapter that there are only three types of management: fear-based management, pleasure-based management, or a mixture of the two. I argue that pleasure-based management, utilizing the five productive pleasures described in *Primal Management*, is generally the way to go because it creates more winners than losers and maximizes gain for the overall business ecosystem.

THE "SELF" IN SELF-PROTECTION

I now pop the hood of the self-protection appetite and explore its main component, sense of self, or self-worth. We start here because it's impossible to understand the *self*-protection appetite without first having a clear and concise definition of *self*.

What do you understand the word *self* to mean? I described self earlier as the very core of the motivational mechanism. Before proceeding, however, I will describe self in a bit more detail because it is a vital concept for understanding the self-protection appetite. Every interaction in the workplace can be viewed as an economic transaction that adds value to or subtracts or transfers value from the self-worth of the participants.

Body Assets

Part of self is simple—our physical bodies. Our bodies represent our starting allotment of assets—the ones we were born with. Our bodies obviously belong to us, and self-protective feelings are instantly and automatically triggered whenever we are threatened with bodily harm by a criminal, wild animal, or accident. The fear reaction is triggered by the amygdala and a score of affiliated brain areas, hormones, and neurotransmitters. The amygdala is the vital nerve center of our crash-avoidance system.

The amygdala scans the torrent of sensory information flooding in from our senses for any signs of danger. Whenever we feel anxious, angry, or threatened, the amygdala is at work. Much of the bad rap associated with the word *emotion* stems from the extreme emotions that result when the amygdala is triggered. Much of this chapter is dedicated to learning how *not* to trigger the amygdala and its extreme and harmful emotions in the workplace.

In many ways, the amygdala is designed like a hair trigger to respond rapidly to dangerous situations. It receives two types of signals: (1) a torrent of preprocessed sensory information originating in the cerebral cortex and (2) a trickle of unprocessed sensory information that reaches the amygdala directly, tens of milliseconds ahead of the processed signal. Tens of milliseconds might not seem like much, but it's enough time to dodge a striking snake or to duck a rock thrown at your face. These sorts of ancient threats are preprogrammed into the amygdala and thereby allow us to instantly react to certain threats before our conscious minds even know what's happening.[1]

Social Assets

I have already described how the things into which we freely invest effort become merged with our sense of self, our personal identity, our vault. The things we invest in are automatically brought inside through the process of cathexis and thereby become owned assets in our frontal lobe vault. I will refer to these acquired assets as *social assets*. Not surprisingly, the amygdala watches over these social assets with the same vigilance with which it protects our physical bodies. As you may recall from Chapter 4, my vault contains my kids, my wife, friends and family members, my karate and golf skills, Houston, my theory of social emotions, and many other assets.

Social assets are acquired, one by one, from a lifetime of investment. The overall portfolio of social assets includes both hard assets, like money or property, and soft assets consisting of the skills, relationships, and knowledge we acquire during our lifetimes. Our social assets constitute a vast and diverse collection of people, places, and things that are important to us. We fret over and tend these investments like a gardener obsesses over his or her roses. Our lives and actions revolve around our social assets like the earth revolves around the sun.

The frontal lobe vault is the brain's version of a bank account or safety deposit box. Life successes are recorded as deposits to this account and life failures are recorded as withdrawals. The overall balance in our account determines our sense of self-worth—whether we feel good or bad about ourselves. Managers who help us succeed and achieve in life contribute to this bank account. Managers who criticize us and make us feel like failures withdraw assets from the account.

This bank account is not just theoretical, it is real. It resides in the ventro-medial prefrontal lobes. People with damage to this vital brain area behave strangely with regard to assets and money. They have a distorted sense of value, tend to squander both their monetary and social assets, and, as we learned in Chapter 4, do not react angrily when their assets are threatened.

The amygdala, which watches over our bank accounts, triggers a cascade of biochemical events the moment a body asset or social asset is threatened. A threat to a major social asset, like one's career, will spark just as vigorous a protective response as a threat to the body proper because the amygdala *does not make a distinction* between the bodily assets we are born with and the social assets we acquire through investment and achievement. Both body and social assets belong equally to *self* and damage to either type of asset triggers the same pain-sensing areas in the brain, the anterior cingulate cortex and anterior insular cortex.[2]

Managers, especially respected managers, intuitively understand nature's accounting system and strive to make deposits instead of withdrawals. A compliment from a respected leader, for example, is a deposit to the social-asset vault that boosts self-esteem and self-confidence and contributes powerfully to the emotional paycheck. It creates *real*, but hidden, value. Abusive, or overly critical, managers who motivate with fear destroy value and lower self-esteem. This is the essential dynamic we will explore in this chapter—value creation versus value destruction.

DESTRUCTIVE, FEAR-BASED MANAGEMENT

In the previous chapters I mainly described the social appetites that power superorganisms—passionate companies where employees think and act as one. In this section I turn my attention to the average, hierarchical, bureaucratic company—the nonsuperorganism that runs on just a few social appetites.

The self-protection appetite is the social appetite that dispassionate hierarchical companies rely on most. This social appetite is powered by a spectrum of feelings ranging from anxiety, anger, and fear on one side, to feelings of safety and security on the other.

Superorganisms strive to keep their employees on the safe and secure side of the pain-pleasure spectrum by not threatening their core investments. Hyperrational hierarchies, on the other hand, are much more likely to rely on the fear of being fired as their primary motivational tool. It is the "stick" in their simplistic carrot (money) and stick (fear) approach to management.

The stick is easy to use. Even novices with little understanding of human nature can get people moving by threatening them with the stick. Overuse of the stick, however, triggers the brain's defensive systems via the amygdala and spawns a workforce composed of angry enemies who work against a company's interests rather than for it—hardly a prescription for improved productivity.

"Chainsaw" Al Dunlap, the corporate downsizing guru and Wall Street darling of the 1980s, serves as a striking example of stick-based management. Dunlap relied almost exclusively on the stick to run companies like Scott Paper and Sunbeam. Dunlap lived up to his reputation as a corporate demolition expert—a Rambo in pinstripes. He announced the shutdown or sale of two-thirds of Sunbeam's eighteen plants and the elimination of half its 12,000 employees.[3] Here is how John Byrne described Dunlap in his book *Chainsaw*:

> *Chainsaw Al was a creation of the Street and its ceaseless lust for profit at any cost. He came of age when the market routinely rewarded layoffs with lofty stock prices. The more people he tossed out in the street, the higher stock values went.*[4]

Dunlap was eventually fired from Sunbeam, settled a class-action shareholder lawsuit for $15 million, and was banned by the SEC from ever serving as an officer or director of a public company.[5] His management-through-intimidation style resulted in $4.4 billion in shareholder losses and led Sunbeam into bankruptcy.[6]

Relying on the stick to motivate employees will breed enemies in the workplace. Al Dunlap's employees—and even his own family members—were happy to see him fall. This may be an extreme example, but there are still plenty of me-based managers like Dunlap out there and the system cranks out more of them every day.

In this chapter I prove that fear-based management ignores hidden costs to society and does not maximize the financial wealth or well-being of investors, employees, customers, or society at large. Fear-based management is also incompatible with building a superorganism.

Oil Company Case Study—Personal Example of a Value-Destroying Manager

The following case study examines a personal run-in I had with a destructive, fear-based manager whom I will call Ron. There are, unfortunately, lots of Rons running around in the corporate world, so we need to understand what makes them tick and learn how to recognize them and ban them from positions of power and authority inside our organizations.

I began my career in the oil business in Houston, Texas, in 1980. I was hired during an oil boom caused by the Iranian revolution. Every company I interviewed with offered me a job. Then a bidding war broke out. Company A asked me if I liked to ski and then offered to station me in Denver. Company B offered me more money and promised to put me in Dallas instead of steamy Houston. I ultimately took a position with Company C in Houston.

The recruiter for Company C told me that it was planning to move the exploration staff from Houston to the West Coast—partly to be closer to the region where we explored for oil, but mainly to make the geologists and geophysicists happy. Before I even arrived in Houston I had received several salary increases. I almost had to pinch myself!

My first manager at Company C was gracious and welcoming. He reminded me of a genteel Southern gentleman. The first assignment he gave me went well. When the project was complete, he called me into his office and told me I had done a great job and that everyone was impressed. He made me feel good about myself. He gave me a self-esteem bonus. My manager was we-based rather than me-based. He created a bonded work group and fed our social appetites. One way he promoted bonding was to encourage young geologists to conduct fieldwork together during the summer months.

During my second year at Company C, my manager sent me to Alaska with a small team of geologists in preparation for a major government lease sale. We were stationed in Nome, Alaska, and got to fly around in a helicopter collecting rock samples. My manager admitted to me that the fieldwork was probably not absolutely necessary, but that it built esprit de corps among the staff. In other words, sharing an exciting adventure in Alaska built lasting relationships and enhanced employee morale and cooperation. Using the tribal analogy, sharing an adventure in the wilderness molded separate individuals into a connected group.[7]

This manager retired from Company C in 1983, at the same time that oil prices fell and Houston went bust. If he was the enlightened egalitarian manager, his replacement, Ron, was quite the opposite.

Ron became livid when he saw young geologists hired at salaries it had taken him years to attain. He viewed us as pampered and spoiled. Ron also disliked the retiring manager and anyone associated with him— like me. When Ron took over the position, he immediately called the staff into the conference room. He got right down to business. "Regarding the move to the West Coast," Ron said, "forget it! Regarding future raises, forget them, too." He went on to explain how spoiled and pampered we were and that layoffs were just around the corner. He also canceled all fieldwork, effective immediately.

In the following weeks a predictable ritual played itself out. Ron would enter the office of a young geologist and close the door. Several minutes later Ron would emerge and the geologist would either be stunned or crying. By the time Ron got around to me, I was ready for him. I wasn't worried, because I had already decided to leave Company C to start a business in my hometown of Milwaukee. Within a few weeks Ron entered my office, closed the door, and got right to the point. "Herr, you think you're a hot shot—but not to me." I cut him off. I said, "Ron, if you have nothing constructive to say, then get the hell out of my office!" He was stunned and speechless. After several seconds of awkward silence, he spun around and left my office. I figured I had just committed career suicide, but it didn't matter. I was leaving anyway.

A couple of weeks passed and I still had my job. Ron continued his destructive march around the office and began firing my colleagues. When he finally summoned me to his office, he greeted me with a friendly tone. He said, "Herr, I like your attitude—I like aggressive guys like you." By standing up to his bullying tactics, I had paradoxically earned his respect. As I stood there dumbfounded, Ron invited me to his son's football game, which I politely declined. I had no intention of socializing with this guy.

I share this example because Ron is a classic example of a me-based manager who lacks empathy and controls through fear and intimidation. He sowed destruction and pain, but the young geologists in his cage had nowhere to go. The oil industry was in the tank and there were no jobs available. People hunkered down and cowered at the feet of the alpha male. Fear-based hierarchies function best in this sort of powerless environment.

This manager destroyed employee morale, engagement, commitment, and discretionary effort. He withdrew assets from the vaults of his employees by the sackful. He did not build relationships between employees and did not create an interpersonal network that allowed knowledge and skills to flow to where they were best needed. I also suspect that Ron's bullying took a terrible toll on the physical health, mental health, and family lives of his employees. Working for Ron was an all-around losing proposition that yielded a highly negative emotional paycheck by starving the social appetites.

POISONOUS LEADERS

Daniel Goleman describes three destructive personality types, what he calls the *dark triad*, in his book *Social Intelligence*. The dark triad consists of narcissists, Machiavellians, and psychopaths. Here is Goleman's unflattering description of the dark triad:

> *All three types share to varying degrees an unappealing, though sometimes well-concealed, core: social malevolence and duplicity, self-centeredness and aggression and emotional coldness.*
>
> *We would do well to familiarize ourselves with the hallmarks of this threesome, if only to better recognize them.*[8]

All three members of the triad treat other human beings as objects rather than people. They either lack empathy completely, or have the ability to selectively turn it off.[9] All three of these personality types would be highly poisonous to a developing superorganism, because they are either unable or unwilling to bond and form meaningful relationships with fellow human beings. They are also value destroyers instead of value creators.

I focus my attention on the wiliest member of the bunch, the narcissist. Narcissists are socially skilled, ruthless, and highly ambitious, and they often claw their way to the top levels of corporate hierarchies. Goleman, Boyatzis, and McKee cite Al Dunlap as an example of a narcissistic leader in their book *Primal Leadership*.[10]

Freud coined the term *narcissist*. It was one of his three primary personality types. Extreme narcissism, however, is defined as a personality disorder, a type of mental illness. Here are the nine diagnostic criteria for recognizing a hard-core narcissist.

1. Has a grandiose sense of self-importance

2. Is preoccupied with fantasies of unlimited success, power, brilliance, beauty, or ideal love

3. Believes that he or she is "special" and unique and can be understood only by other "special" people

4. Requires excessive admiration

5. Has a strong sense of entitlement

6. Takes advantage of others to achieve his or her own ends

7. Lacks empathy

8. Is often envious or believes others are envious of him or her

9. Shows arrogant, haughty behaviors or attitudes[11]

Hard-core narcissists are not bound by societal norms or moral codes, and they do not experience guilt or shame for their crimes or empathy for their victims. Extreme narcissists can end up in prison or deftly climb to the highest levels in industry and government.

All human beings are somewhat narcissistic because we want to be seen by our tribe as capable, competent, and respected. We all tend to accept praise and deflect criticism. Extreme narcissists, however, do this to an unhealthy extreme. This is why extreme narcissism is defined as a mental illness called narcissistic personality disorder (NPD). This disorder affects approximately 1 percent of the U.S. population.[12]

NPD is thought to be caused by abuse or trauma during childhood, especially abuse by the primary caregiver.[13] Most children are supported by their parents, and each small success is celebrated and thereby converted into a social asset that goes into the "vault" and boosts the child's self-esteem. Well-adjusted children enter adulthood with a substantial portfolio of social assets in their vaults—life successes that boost their feelings of self-worth. They have an emotional war chest to help them weather the many challenges of adulthood.

Most parents use their influence to build their child's self-worth and add assets to their vaults. Some parents, unfortunately, do precisely the opposite. They turn on their children and destroy their child's fledgling sense of self. Narcissists experience rejection as children and enter adulthood "penniless" (without social assets). Narcissists, at a subliminal level, feel fundamentally flawed and incompetent because their competency appetites are in a state of extreme starvation.

In order to ward off further feelings of rejection and low self-esteem, narcissists attempt to control how others view them. In other words, they compensate for their shattered sense of self by projecting a false image of invincibility and perfection to the outside world.[14] Creating this false front is an all-consuming preoccupation for the narcissist. Preoccupation with appearances distracts narcissists from paying attention to the reality of their situation or to the feelings and boundaries of others.

I have had intimate contact with a number of hard-core narcissists during my life. Their most disturbing and baffling characteristic, in my view, is how they twist and warp reality by selectively ignoring their mistakes and weaknesses and by grabbing undeserved glory for themselves. They are charismatic and attract supplicants and followers with their grandiose plans and larger-than-life personalities.

Narcissists, because their competency appetites were starved in childhood, crave respect and admiration, and they are willing to lie, cheat, or steal to get it. They crave all forms of social assets: money, fame, property, and respect. They lack a moral sense, so they are motivated to acquire social assets by legitimate or illegitimate means. Their appetites for success, acclaim, and power are insatiable. If these appetites are not fed, or if their false front of invincibility is punctured by cold, hard facts, narcissists can experience psychological meltdown (depression, delusions, psychotic behavior, and suicide).

Narcissists are like the wizard in the *Wizard of Oz*. They project a fiery alter ego to their audience, but when you pull back the curtain, there is a timid and shattered person cowering at the controls. They are quick to anger and quick to assign blame because their social-asset vaults are, in reality, empty. This makes them feel fundamentally incompetent and vulnerable and sets their amygdalas on high alert. They see enemies around every corner and are exceptionally thin skinned regarding criticism. Narcissists are quick to blame others for their own mistakes because they can't endure further deductions from their social vaults.

The High-Functioning Narcissist

Narcissists are skilled in the social arts because they are hypervigilant in the social world from childhood onward. They are therefore skilled observers of human behavior and can detect an opportunity or threat from a long way off. They are also clever manipulators and undetectable liars. They seem confident and bigger than life from the outside, even as they suffer from painful feelings of inadequacy on the inside.

Psychiatrist and anthropologist Michael Maccoby argues in the *Har-*

vard Business Review that a healthy dose of narcissism is a desirable trait in corporate leaders and that many high-profile CEOs are, in fact, clinical narcissists. Maccoby bases his insights on twenty-five years as an adviser and psychoanalyst to top corporate leaders. Narcissists, he argues, possess the courage, vision, and drive to take corporations in new directions. "Throughout history," he claims, "narcissists have always emerged to inspire people and to shape the future."[15]

Maccoby suggests that narcissistic leaders need to surround themselves with down-to-earth sidekicks who keep the leader's grandiose visions rooted in reality. He also recommends psychotherapy to address the narcissistic leader's underlying feelings of social inadequacy. Maccoby claims that leaders such as Jack Welch and George Soros are examples of productive narcissists.

The Argument Against Narcissistic Leadership

Maccoby's conclusions about the benefits of narcissistic leadership are directly opposed to Jim Collins's great-company research. Collins found that the leaders of great companies, what he calls Level-5 leaders, are unassuming, selfless individuals who put the welfare of the group ahead of personal glory.[16] Boards of directors, according to Collins, are seduced and hoodwinked by larger-than-life, charismatic leaders. This, he argues, is why there are so few Level-5 leaders and why few corporations sustain greatness over the long haul. Collins discovered charismatic leadership at two-thirds of the not-so-great companies he studied.[17]

Who's right here? Are narcissistic leaders the heroes of modern corporate America, as Maccoby claims, or are they unrealistic, self-absorbed egotists who fail to sustain corporate profits over the long run, and who often engage in criminal activities?

Perhaps we should look to history for the tiebreaker on this issue. The ancient Chinese philosopher Lao Tzu described the best leaders as follows:

> *As for the best leaders, the people do not notice their existence. The next best the people honor and praise. The next, the people fear, and the next*

*the people hate. When the best leader's work is done, the people say, "We
did it ourselves."*[18]

Lao Tzu was an ancient Chinese philosopher and contemporary of Confucius. Confucius met Lao Tzu at the imperial library near modern Luoy-
ang in the fourth century B.C. and was greatly influenced by their
discussions there. It is said that Confucius learned more from his talks
with Lao Tzu than from all the scrolls in the library.

Lao Tzu's description of the best leaders makes sense from an
emotional-paycheck viewpoint. Leaders who allow the troops to take
credit for the organization's successes deposit self-esteem-building social
assets into employees' vaults. These benefits represent real income from
the brain's perspective. Sharing credit is therefore a value-building transaction that improves the emotional paycheck and promotes discretionary
effort and productivity in the workplace.

Self-absorbed narcissists cannot nurture a superorganism or run a
company that feeds the social appetites. Superorganisms are built by
leaders who value others, commit to others, and invest in others. Superorganisms are "we-based," not "me-based." Words like *commitment,
mentoring,* and *investment in others* are simply not part of the narcissist's
vocabulary. Narcissists care only about themselves and their own success
and glory. They cannot create a superorganism, because bonding requires
respecting and investing in the people around you.

It is understandable why boards select narcissists as leaders. The
boards are pressured by Wall Street or investors for dramatic, short-term
results. Selection of new leadership often occurs within the context of
chaos and crisis where the narcissist's outgoing personality, self-promotion,
and aura of invincibility feel reassuring. When boards feel themselves
under siege they turn to strong, bigger-than-life leaders to make tough
decisions and save the day. Narcissists are more than happy to make hard
decisions, like laying off half the workforce, because they fundamentally
lack empathy. They don't agonize or lose sleep over things like layoffs.
They don't even blink. They are equally likely, however, to ignore rules,
regulations, laws, and boundaries of all sorts in order to protect their
false front—their projected Superman image. Finally, narcissists are often

shattered and timid individuals on the verge of psychic meltdown—hardly the person you would want at the helm of a major corporation.

Jim Collins concluded from his great-company research that great leaders have the guts to confront the brutal facts of reality.[19] Narcissistic leaders could not be further from the mark on this vital point. Narcissists hold reality in contempt—they warp and distort it. If they cannot find glory in reality, they sometimes make a clean break from reality altogether and become delusional. Their entire beings are directed at creating a sham of reality in order to protect their damaged egos.

I think the evidence is clear. Corporate America needs more Harry Quadraccis (Quad/Graphics), Ricardo Semlers (Semco SA), and Ken Iversons (Nucor), not more narcissists like Al (Chainsaw) Dunlap. Something is wrong when the economic system allows narcissistic leaders to rise to the top and take charge of large organizations. Perhaps a better understanding of human nature, the motivational mechanism, and the value-building transactions of great leaders will help decision makers avoid the mistakes of the past and resist the quick-fix allure of the narcissistic leader.

PERSONAL IMPLEMENTATION

It's time to check the Tune-Up Metric to determine whether or not your employees feel safe and secure in the workplace, or attacked and threatened. If employees feel threatened or attacked in the workplace, then the score for the self-protection appetite will be strongly negative (painful) and your workplace will be characterized by fear, anxiety, anger, and defensiveness. You can probably determine your score for this social appetite without even checking the metric because the self-protection appetite is the most visible of the five social appetites on account of the ballistic emotions it controls. A negative score will be readily apparent in the form of angry, anxious, and fearful expressions on the faces of your employees and in workplace behaviors that are more focused on defending turf than getting the job done in a collaborative and efficient fashion.

If you followed the bonding recommendations in Chapter 4 by valuing your employees and then investing in the relationships for four months, then I already know your score for the self-protection appetite. It is strongly positive and your employees feel safe and secure because you watch over them and protect them like any consensus leader would.

The investments you made in your employees by mentoring them quite literally made them part of you. You would not harm or threaten your employees' interests because it would feel like you are hurting yourself. A bonded consensus manager would no sooner harm an employee than throw a treasured possession out the window. We-based managers automatically treat employees with respect and add to their social-asset vaults rather than destroying assets—and this results in a positive score on the Tune-Up Metric.

Are We Going Soft?

Perhaps it's time to do another *hardness check* because I promised you a hard solution to employee motivation. I can imagine a number of objections from traditional managers to the pleasure-based management approach I am proposing. Let's examine these issues logically according to the theory.

Let's start with the assumption that the workplace we are dealing with is typical for the United States and consists of 31 percent engaged employees, 52 percent disengaged employees, and 17 percent actively disengaged employees. The expedient and hard solution would be to identify the 69 percent of employees (disengaged plus actively disengaged) whose heads are not in the game and fire them. They should be easy to identify by their underachievement and negative attitudes.

This is precisely the solution recommended by Jim Collins in *Good to Great*. Collins observed that great companies get the wrong people off the bus as soon as they realize they are wrong. Dedicated employees, Collins warns, will exit the bus at the next stop if companies let the wrong people hang around. If the Gallup employee-engagement research is accurate, however, companies would need to jettison 69 percent of their employees, on average, in order to retain only their engaged employees.

Tossing more than half the workforce off the bus will not solve anything, I suggest, so long as we are dealing with a traditional, bureaucratic hierarchy populated with self-interested, me-based managers. Such organizations deny the very existence of the motivational mechanism and therefore starve the five social appetites. In other words, they don't deserve engaged employees. The enthusiastic new recruits who walk through the door will look just as gaunt and undernourished as the old ones after being exposed to the impersonal conditions that reign inside many companies. They will go unmentored, uninspired, unrecognized, and unprotected. They will wither on the vine and hence become disengaged, just like the first batch we threw off the bus. This hard approach to hiring and firing doesn't look so rational after you factor in the motivational aspect. It looks more like a dog fruitlessly chasing its tail.

A Better Solution to the Disengagement Dilemma

Let's start the scenario over again, but this time assuming we are dealing with a superorganism run by a consensus leader. Let's assume that the superorganism has just acquired a traditional bureaucratic hierarchy with the same breakdown of engaged, disengaged, and actively disengaged employees we started with in the previous scenario. Let's see how a superorganism handles the influx of disengaged employees.

Bob Carpenter dealt with large numbers of disengaged employees in the companies he took control of, so we will use him as our model. Bob Carpenter, the corporate turnaround artist mentioned in Chapter 2, inherited entire busloads of enemies and mercenaries in the Third World countries he operated in and turned them into buses full of warriors. When he started a turnaround project, essentially 100 percent of the employees hated him. Carpenter sympathized with his employees. They had been abused and disrespected by management and treated like slaves, so their extreme negativity was justified.

Carpenter invested four months, on average, to rehabilitate his disengaged employees and convince them he wasn't just another gringo trying to manipulate them. He eventually reached a tipping point when his employees finally "got it," accepted him as their leader, and started investing in return. Carpenter repeated this impressive feat thirteen times in Third World countries around the world, and productivity typically doubled as a result.[20]

This is a cautionary tale. Before you chuck 69 percent of your employees off the bus, you should first demonstrate to them that you are a different kind of leader: a consensus leader who respects employees and is committed to their development and success. Your employees deserve a second chance because they, just like you and me, have been exposed to an abusive, hyperrational business culture that earns a failing grade for employee motivation. By giving both employees and yourself a second chance, you will not only convert many of your mercenaries and enemies into warriors, but you will also ensure that your existing warriors remain warriors.

Harry Quadracci checked out employees carefully and personally before letting them on the bus, but he had a very hard time tossing loyal employees off once they were on board—even if their performance flagged because of age or other factors. Quadracci bonded with his employees. They were part of him, just as his own hands were part of him. He could no sooner fire a loyal warrior than lop off one of his hands.

Quadracci had another reason to be generous—the tremendous investment he had made building a trust-based superorganism. He couldn't fire a loyal partner without causing his trust network to disappear in a puff of smoke. The seemingly rational decision to fire an underperforming employee could have catastrophic implications in the intrinsic economy. It would be a value-destroying proposition that would severely impact the bottom line. Quadracci must have intuitively realized that it would be "penny wise but pound foolish" to toss warriors off the bus the minute their performance lagged. This sort of treatment would have invalidated Quadracci's implicit social contract of mutual commitment and mutual investment.

Okay. Let's assume that you accept the second scenario—that it's better to rehabilitate disengaged employees than it is to toss them off the bus. There is still one thorny issue to deal with. What do we do with employees who don't respond to the we-based approach? What if we invest in employees, carefully mentor them, create a workplace game that is challenging but fair, inspire them to find their passion, give them a sense of purpose, help them become respected experts, recognize their contributions, and protect them from harm—and they are still disengaged?

The answer, based upon my study of the three mavericks and the superorganisms they created, is that you don't need to do anything. Superorganisms are intense and energetic places to work and disengaged employees will stick out like a sore thumb. There is nowhere for disengaged employees to hide inside a superorganism because they lack the strength of numbers to create a credible counterculture of their own. Their peers are going to detect their lack of commitment and effort and take it personally. You therefore don't need to toss these folks off the bus because they will either leap from it willingly or the other passengers will show them the door. This is precisely what happened at Nucor, Quad/ Graphics, and Semco SA if somebody didn't buy into their intense trust-based cultures.

ORGANIZATIONAL IMPLEMENTATION

Let's shift our discussion from a focus on managers within an organization to the CEO or owner of the organization. What can be done at the senior executive level to add value and avoid triggering the self-protection appetite and the destructive emotions it controls? My best suggestion is to treat every interpersonal interaction and every decision as an opportunity to create value in the minds of your employees.

Here are some of the value-enhancing practices used by (1) the three mavericks (Quadracci, Iverson, and Semler), (2) the great companies researched by Jim Collins, and (3) the excellent companies reviewed by Peters and Waterman. We will discover that the seemingly wasteful and ludicrous policies of these companies were actually highly rational, value-building transactions when viewed from a social appetite (intrinsic reward) perspective.

Management by Walking Around

Peters and Waterman coined the phrase, "management by walking around," in their classic 1982 book, *In Search of Excellence.*[21] It sounds, at first glance, like a silly prescription for competent corporate governance. I'm sure that many managers and CEOs rolled their eyes in 1982 and said things like, "Do they want me to waste half my valuable time wandering aimlessly around the workplace instead of spending that time productively by analyzing the competition or developing a smart strategic plan?" Tom Peters argues that there is nothing more important than wandering around, and I wholeheartedly agree. There is one caveat, however. Management by walking around will work only if you are the respected, consensus leader of your tribe.

A consensus leader is someone who is applauded and respected by his or her tribe. This applause magically gives the leader the ability to create value. The leader becomes a competent authority with the ability to create social wealth out of nothing by complimenting the performances of others.

Management by walking around makes perfect sense from this perspective. The leader, by devoting attention to various employees in various work roles, enriches his or her workforce. When the CEO visits a factory's "lowly" maintenance staff, for example, it sends the message that maintenance is a valuable function that is worthy of the leader's time and attention. This simple act alone can convert a hated chore into rewarding work.

Is management by walking around a silly concept that should be ridiculed by hyperrational managers? I think not. Rather, it is a brilliant and insightful idea that all managers and corporate leaders should practice! This practice alone will feed two of the social appetites: the competency appetite and the skill-deployment appetite.

Management by Walking Away

If you think "management by walking around" is a silly idea, get a load of this. Harry Quadracci took Peters's and Waterman's suggestion one step further. Harry not only practiced "management by walking around," but "management by walking away"—a yearly ritual called Spring Fling, during which he and his managers would leave the hourly workers running the entire show.[22]

What kind of madness is this? What sort of sane manager would leave inexperienced hourly employees in charge of factories full of multimillion-dollar printing presses where even a tiny mistake can quickly add up to thousands of dollars in scrapped printing jobs?[23] Isn't this lunacy?

Quadracci's lunacy was, in reality, a brilliant value-enhancing transaction. It sent the message, "You are competent and perfectly capable of running the show by yourself. In other words, I trust that you will perform with distinction—even without anyone watching you or telling you what to do. You are an adult and a decision maker—a partner who can be trusted with the keys to the factory." Once Harry created this self-esteem enhancing challenge at Quad/Graphics, his employees never let him down. No Quad manager has ever been called back from the Spring Fling to deal with an emergency.

The first time Harry engaged in this unusual form of management hooky, it was by accident. Harry had planned to close the plant for the day so he and his management team could have a day free for planning and socializing. A last-minute rush order made closing the plant impossible, so Harry decided to leave anyway and trust the employees to get the job done.[24]

If employees are truly connected with their employer, as many were at Quad/Graphics, they would rather shoot themselves in the foot than take advantage of the Spring Fling situation. In bonded companies there is no clear boundary where the employee ends and the employer begins. The two entities have been merged into a greater whole—a superorganism. If you cannot leave your troops in charge for the day, then you probably don't qualify as a superorganism.

Treat Everyone as Equals

Here is another bit of management heresy that smacks of communism—"treat everyone as equals." Hyperrational managers working inside bureaucratic hierarchies would have a hard time uttering this phrase. A hyperrational manager might feel, "I have worked my entire life to climb up the corporate hierarchy and achieve status and monetary reward inside the organization. How can you say that I am equal to someone without even a high school diploma working in the mailroom? I'm a winner and those guys are losers. If I treat everyone as equals, then I am giving up the very thing I worked so diligently to achieve—status and respect!"

The hyperrational manager would be right. He played the hierarchy game with skill and industry and therefore deserves to rake in the chips. From an ecosystem standpoint, however, the hierarchy game produces many more losers than winners, so it is ultimately dysfunctional. It leaves the bulk of the workforce powerless and demoralized. In addition, the leaders in a hierarchy are usually not consensus leaders, so they do not have the ability to create value or to grab the organization's emotional rudder. They therefore default to the only other alternative available, money and *fear*. A corporate world populated with fear-based hierarchies *cannot* feed all five social appetites. This is why Gallup found that only 31 percent of employees are engaged in the corporate mission. The simple fact is that bureaucratic hierarchies are not excellent or great. They do not deliver sustained performance, so they should be remodeled and flattened. Better yet, they should be flipped upside down.

Excellent companies, according to Tom Peters, do not have lavish corporate headquarters, private executive bathrooms, private executive dining rooms, lavish corporate jets, private parking spaces for executives, or any other trappings of superiority.[25] These policies send a strong message to the rest of the company: "Ha, ha, you guys are the lowest, least-skilled, worthless monkeys in the dominance hierarchy."

Some leaders, like Liz Claiborne's CEO William McComb, not only treat employees as equals, they also serve them. Bill McComb commented at a recent conference, "I expect managers to check their egos at the door and practice servant leadership. They should have no qualms about delivering coffee to employees six layers below them in the hierarchy."[26]

McComb has just begun to deconstruct the hierarchy at Liz Claiborne. He is committed to reengineering the culture because he spent his formative years at Johnson & Johnson, an employee-centric superorganism and one of the United States' most respected companies.[27] McComb knows from experience that "culture leads performance," so reengineering the hierarchy will be one of his top priorities at Liz Claiborne.

Harry Quadracci, as we already know, believed in equality and service. He referred to his employees as partners and treated each and every one of them as crucial to the organization. One of his favorite sayings was, "we all put our pants on the same way, one leg at a time." Ken

Iverson, the down-to-earth social architect of Nucor Steel, summed up the essence of servant leadership in his book *Plain Talk* as follows:

> *Well, it's pretty hard to treat someone fairly when you view him or her as inherently unequal. Across corporate America, managers look down on the people they manage and distance themselves from employees with layer after layer of hierarchy and management privileges.*
>
> *Managers are supposed to do what's best for the business. And what's best is to remember we're all just people. Managers don't need or deserve special treatment. We're not more important than other employees. And we aren't better than anyone else. We just have a different job to do.*
>
> *Mainly, that job is to help the people you manage to accomplish extraordinary things. That begins with remembering who does the real work of the business (something managers, with their outsized egos, often forget). It means relying on employees to make important decisions and take significant risks. And it means shaping a work environment that stimulates people to explore their own potential.*[28]

Servant leadership is an excellent concept because it essentially turns the standard hierarchy idea upside down and balances the pyramid on its point. It takes the people at the bottom of the hierarchy who feel inferior, shamed, humiliated, insignificant, worthless, and disrespected and boosts their dignity and self-respect. An upside-down pyramid has many confident winners on top and a few humble, but well-compensated executives at the bottom. If emotional rewards and monetary rewards are essentially made of the same stuff (feelings) then this sort of upside-down arrangement leaves everyone feeling rewarded in one way or another. It is therefore brilliant from an economic-transaction point of view.

Nucor Steel, Quad/Graphics, and Semco SA are the purest examples of egalitarian superorganisms I have identified to date. They developed independently of one another in different industries (steel making, printing, and manufacturing, respectively), but their policies and attitudes toward employees are remarkably similar. All three companies did away with time cards and job descriptions; delegated much of the day-to-day decision making to frontline employees; and founded a workplace based on mutual trust and mutual respect. All three believe in long-term job security and complete transparency regarding financial and operational decisions.

Most important, all three superorganisms have been structurally flat and fervently antihierarchy. In 1998, Ken Iverson managed Nucor Steel, an organization with $3.6 billion in revenue, with only four levels of hierarchy. Semco is even flatter, with only three levels. The typical Fortune 500 corporation has eight to twelve layers of management.[29] Harry Quadracci was said to "lob hand grenades" whenever he spotted even a hint of hierarchy or empire building.

Ken Iverson dedicated an entire chapter in his 1998 book, *Plain Talk*, to the evils of hierarchy.[30] Here are two excerpts:

> *Inequality still runs rampant in most business corporations. I'm referring now to the hierarchical inequality which legitimizes and institutionalizes the principle of "We" vs. "They." . . . The people at the top of the corporate hierarchy grant themselves privilege after privilege, flaunt those privileges before the men and women who do the real work, then wonder why employees are unmoved by management's invocations to cut costs and boost profitability.*[31]

> *Our executives wouldn't have it any other way. They see our egalitarian culture serving their interests as much as the interests of our employees. For one thing, our managers don't have to waste time fretting over their chances to get the fancy corner office or arguing over who gets to use the company plane. We don't have those perks, and we imagine they would cause more stress than fulfillment. What a bunch of nonsense! Chasing meaningless status symbols and tokens of power. When you look back on your career, will those things seem important?*[32]

Harry Quadracci reinforced his egalitarian philosophy with a dress policy that required everyone (management, sales, and office staff) to wear the same blue uniforms as the hourly workers. Iverson did the same thing at Nucor with hard hats. He made executives, managers, and supervisors wear the same green hard hats as hourly employees. Prior to Iverson's arrival, managers and supervisors wore distinctively colored hard hats as a badge of honor and status. The supervisors complained bitterly when the same-color policy was adopted but came to accept it after a few months of complaining.

Harry Quadracci, Ken Iverson, and Ricardo Semler were practical, nuts-and-bolts businessmen. They did not decide to build egalitarian organizations just for philosophical or moral reasons. As Iverson put it:

> *The best case for promoting equality rests on practical considerations like productivity, efficiency, profitability and growth. A business needs motivated employees to compete over the long term, and an egalitarian business culture is an extraordinarily practical way to sustain employee motivation.*[33]

Nucor has grown into a $14 billion dynamo in the steel industry based on Iverson's simple idea, "aligning worker interests with management and shareholder interests through an egalitarian meritocracy largely devoid of class distinctions."[34] In other words, Nucor's path to dominance in the steel industry was to become a very large tribe—a superorganism just like Quad/Graphics and Semco SA.

Nucor, in 1998, ran a $3.5 billion corporation from a corporate headquarters with only twenty-five employees. Nucor's headquarters was the size of a small dental practice and cheap veneer furniture decorated the lobby. The corporate staff at Nucor's main domestic rival, Bethlehem Steel, was housed in a twenty-one-story tower with all the trimmings. When Nucor's revenue finally topped Bethlehem's in 1999, Nucor's profit per employee was *200 times* that of Bethlehem's.[35] When Nucor hit hard times during the 1982 recession, workers took a 25 percent pay cut, officers' pay went down 60 percent, and the CEO's pay went down 75 percent.[36] Iverson called this policy "pain sharing," as opposed to "profit sharing." This is the sort of "crazy" corporate governance that builds a workforce composed of engaged employees. Nucor is now a $14 billion corporation with a "whopping" corporate staff of sixty-two! It still has only four layers of management and has thrived in a challenging industry without layoffs for thirty years.[37]

Egalitarian policies make sense from an economic-transaction standpoint. Companies that elevate executives above other employees simultaneously devalue other workers and make them feel inferior, incompetent, and impotent. In other words, hierarchical behavior subtracts assets from the vaults of the most vulnerable, numerous, and least-paid employees, thereby adding insult to injury. Hierarchical behavior threatens the workforce's social assets and sets the stage for an amygdala meltdown and crippling class warfare. It's hard to pay attention to the corporate mission and customers when management and labor are at each other's throats.

Quadracci, Iverson, and Semler eliminated class warfare by making sure they had only one class of employee. Their policies blurred the distinction between management and labor and created confident employees who walked tall and inspired fear in the hearts of their competitors. The mavericks elevated the self-worth of their employees and were repaid with skill, efficiency, innovation, and a workforce that could basically manage itself!

If you are interested in deconstructing your fear-based hierarchy and turning it into a superorganism, here are some reengineering tips from Ricardo Semler. Semler turned a bloated, fear-based hierarchy into a dynamic and successful superorganism by flipping the hierarchy upside down. If you want to follow in Semler's footsteps, and nurture a superorganism, try implementing some of these unconventional ideas:

- Remove time clocks because they imply that management doesn't trust employees to do the right thing.

- Practice job rotation so employees don't get bored.

- Let employees be self-managed and self-governing, which includes choosing their own leaders and hiring their own managers.

- Treat employees as responsible adults and then trust them to do the right thing.

- Get rid of norms, manuals, rules, and regulations and let employees regulate themselves by taking personal responsibility for their actions.

- Remove car-parking privileges, executive dining rooms, and other symbols of superior management status.

- Transfer operational decisions and target setting from managers to workers.

- Let the staff collectively determine their own salaries and bonuses.

- Promote complete, unwavering transparency by allowing complete access to company books.

- Promote informality in communications, dress, and decision making.

- Provide job security for those over fifty.

- Break up large units into smaller ones consisting of 150, or fewer, individuals to promote stronger interpersonal bonds.

- Align your company's goals around things that really matter to employees and the greater community.

- Create an environment where employees are recognized and valued.

- Encourage managers and employees to wholeheartedly immerse themselves in the group and its mission and thereby lose their egos in the group. Semler called this "ego leveling."[38]

Between 1980, when Semler took over the family's traditional, bureaucratic hierarchy and 1993, when he wrote *Maverick*, Semco had grown sixfold, productivity improved sevenfold, profits rose fivefold, and the company went as much as fourteen months without losing a single employee. Not a bad result for a guy with "crazy" egalitarian ideas.[39]

Hire Your Friends and Relatives

One of the ten commandments of hyperrational management is to never, ever, hire your friends or relatives because you might need to ax them at some point or they might seek favoritism and preferential treatment.

Harry Quadracci did precisely the opposite. He hired every friend and family member he could get his hands on. He trusted his employees to recommend only their hard-working relations. By 1996, fully 58 percent of employees had familial relations at Quad/Graphics.[40] Harry recognized family connections as a source of power. After all, who wants to screw up in front of their personal tribes—their peers and family members? Who wants to damage precious relationship assets that have taken a lifetime of investment to create? Harry also recognized that a strong work ethic tended to run in families. A hard-working employee, more often than not, came from a "hive" of hard workers.

Superorganisms are built from bonded relationships, so relationships with friends and family members plug right in to the existing trust network. Relationships are the muscle and sinew of a superorganism. Relationships also provide the conduits for the right skills and knowledge to flow to where they are most urgently needed. Most companies probably should not hire friends and family members, but if you're a superorganism built on trust, it's a value-enhancing proposition that greatly improves efficiency and productivity.

Economies of Scale Don't Work

Tom Peters attacked the holy grail of management wisdom in *A Passion for Excellence*. He claimed that the theoretical efficiencies of large, centralized organizations are seldom realized because large, hierarchical organizations inherently cause the motivational engine to stall. Whatever economic gains and synergies are realized from centralization and economies of scale are counteracted by reduced quality, productivity, and innovation. Peters argued that small groups of 50 to 300 people are optimal, even if each group has its own, duplicative accounting and control systems.[41]

Peters's suggested group size comes intriguingly close to the estimated size of hunter-gatherer groups. Human work groups should not go above this size because our minds and emotions just can't deal with the complexity of large groups. This is a very rational reason for keeping things small.

It's Not About Money

Wall Street analysts will scream "heresy" and "blasphemy" regarding the next excellent company policy: It's *not* about the money. It's hard to believe, but Jim Collins concluded in *Good to Great* after 15,000 hours of researching great companies and six years of academic research at Stanford University before that, that the best of the best sustain excellence over the long haul by *not* focusing on making money. Money, for the truly great, is a fringe benefit of having a companywide focus on a greater moral purpose—an energizing set of core values that transcends money and keeps everyone moving in the same direction with focus and fervor.[42] Collins cited companies like Hewlett-Packard and Merck as great companies that were motivated by high ideals and a greater purpose.

What Collins is claiming is that human beings value, above all, a desire to make a lasting contribution to society and to thereby achieve a sort of immortality. Having an overarching moral purpose makes everyone feel that their work is valuable, and hence motivating. Having an overarching purpose is therefore a value-enhancing proposition. It is like an incoming tide that raises all the ships in the harbor!

A purpose, or moral imperative, must be authentic to be effective. According to Gary Hamel: "A moral imperative can't be manufactured by speech writers or ginned up by consultants. . . . [It] must grow out of some genuine sense of mission, possibility, or outrage. . . . To be regarded as authentic, it must be an end, not a means."[43]

Hamel believes that many large corporations are morally bankrupt, which is why only 31 percent of employees are engaged in the corporate mission. As he put it in *The Future of Management*:

Think about the management processes in your company. How much time and priority do these rituals give to conversations around purpose or destiny? Not much, I warrant. Sit in on a typical management meeting—to discuss strategy, budgets, employees, or anything else—and not only will you observe a distinct lack of right-brain thinking, you'll also hear virtually nothing that suggests the participants have hearts. Beauty. Truth. Love. Service. Wisdom. Justice. Freedom. Compassion. These are the moral imperatives that have aroused human beings to extraordinary accomplishments down through the ages. It is sad, then, that the vernacular of management has so little room for these virtues. Put simply, you are unlikely to get bighearted contributions from your employees unless they feel they are working toward some goal that encompasses bighearted ideals.[44]

We have just reviewed some peculiar policies that make no sense from the traditional hyperrational viewpoint. They seem irrational, but, when you take the hidden emotional cash flows into account, they are revealed as brilliant value-enhancing transactions that mesh with nature's motivational mechanism. These are precisely the policies required to convert the enemies and mercenaries inside your company into dedicated warriors.

How do you want to run your company? The choices are clear. You can motivate through fear and intimidation like "Chainsaw" Al Dunlap or you can deploy nature's carrot—the pleasures associated with the social appetites—like Quadracci, Iverson, and Semler. If we view positive feelings as the ultimate currency of the human mind, the carrot approach clearly provides greater incentives and hence motivates better long-term performance.

SUMMARY

The self-protection appetite is, perhaps, the easiest to understand because we can see its handiwork everyday in the form of extreme emotions. Consensus leaders seldom trigger the self-protection appetite because they emotionally bond to their employees and bring them inside. The focus of a consensus leader is to build employees up, rather than tear them down, so there is little chance to run afoul of this defensive appetite.

In *A Passion for Excellence*, Tom Peters described how managers at excellent companies get the small stuff, the daily interactions with employees, right. They treat every employee interaction as an opportunity to boost employee confidence and self-esteem and thereby add value to the feeling-based economy.

Artful managers handle these day-to-day exchanges deftly so they contribute to the vault instead of stealing from it. This behavior amounts to a hidden bonus system that can increase the size of their employees' asset base and bump up their emotional take-home pay.

By contributing social assets instead of destroying them, skilled CEOs avoid triggering the amygdala. Careless managers unwittingly or callously threaten assets and thus create enemies and disengaged employees instead of allies. The intrinsic cash flows in these day-to-day feeling-based transactions have a lot to do with differentiating great companies from average ones. I hope this chapter has convinced you that, in the long run, it makes sense to manage with the carrot rather than the stick.

CHAPTER 9

IS IT TIME TO FLIP THE HIERARCHY UPSIDE DOWN?

HIERARCHY VERSUS SUPERORGANISM

There are millions of ways to rationally structure an organization, but only a few of the many options engage one or more social appetites of the motivational mechanism and result in a viable, functional company. The dominant form of corporate organization in the world today is the bureaucratic hierarchy. A bureaucratic hierarchy is a serviceable organizational structure that feeds some, but not all, of the social appetites.

I propose, in this chapter, and as I have been throughout *Primal Management*, that the traditional hierarchy underperforms the market because it generates emotional friction (interpersonal conflict), creates more losers than winners, and does not optimally engage the cooperation, competency, or innovation appetites of employees. Hierarchies, I argue, do not efficiently harvest the potential energy that is inherent within human nature—which is why only 31 percent of employees are engaged in their work.

The most productive organizational structure, I argue, is the flat, trust-based superorganism that has been the focus of this book. Superorganisms are held together from the inside by invested relationships and trust networks. Invested relationships provide the emotional glue, or connective tissue, that bonds separate human beings into a coordinated unit—a group of human beings who think and act as one.

Hierarchies, because they focus on individual performance and aggressive competition between employees for positions of power, perquisite, and prestige, are inherently unbonded. They do not encourage the mutual mentoring and investment required for authentic relationships—despite corporate propaganda about mission, culture, and teamwork. Managers who occupy the same tier in the hierarchy are unlikely to fully cooperate with one another because they are competing for the next rung on the corporate ladder. Helping a peer would be as unthinkable as helping the opposing team during a football game.

Since the individual employees in a hierarchy are generally unbonded, hierarchies, by default, require rules, regulations, sanctions, and coercive use of power to provide a structural backbone. In other words, hierarchies are primarily held together by the fear of being demoted and by the anticipation of advancing to the next level of power and prestige. Motivation in a hierarchy is primarily extrinsic in the form of money and perks. Motivation within a superorganism is primarily intrinsic in the form of the five productive pleasures that energize tightly bonded groups. I believe that the future belongs to the superorganism—the most fearsome creature in the corporate ecosystem.

Benefits of Bureaucratic Hierarchy

I do not mean to imply that hierarchies are without important benefits. The primary benefit of hierarchical, top-down, command-and-control management is the instant, unquestioning obedience it fosters. This is why militaries are commonly organized hierarchically. If the general says "attack," for example, a lengthy set of discussions or negotiations is not required. Failure to obey is met with immediate and serious sanctions. The same sort of reasoning probably explains why hierarchies predominate in the primate world, where sudden crises, like attacks from predators, are commonplace.

Human hierarchies are typically rule based, so they offer the added benefit of consistent quality according to strict standards. Hierarchical organizations thus tend to predominate in industries where standardization of products or services is crucial for business success.[1] Hierarchies require thick policy manuals and small armies of supervisors because employees are basically not trusted to think independently or do the right thing. The Herculean task of running a large organization is broken into manageable bits and the duties of each bit are carefully defined with detailed job descriptions. Each bit can be learned relatively easily, which eliminates the need for highly skilled employees. In this highly structured environment, human beings degenerate into inexpensive, unskilled, replaceable cogs.[2]

The downside to hierarchical organizations is their behavioral rigidity, centralized decision making, and employees' inability to think independently when the leader is not available. I encountered this sort of thought paralysis one day at a fast-food chain in Milwaukee, Wisconsin. I ordered a salad, which was promptly and courteously delivered, but without a fork. When I asked for a fork, the store manager walked over and said in an apologetic tone, "I'm sorry, but we ran out of forks." I pointed to the grocery store across the street and responded, "Why don't you send someone over there to get some forks?" The manager replied, "I'm sorry, but we are not allowed to buy from outside vendors." This simple transaction epitomized both the benefits and costs of hierarchical, rule-based organizations—they are efficient and standardized, but inflexible and myopic. Employees are trained to focus strictly on the task at hand with little understanding of the overall enterprise or why their task is important. The human experience inside hierarchical organizations can be dehumanizing and alienating because it "runs against the grain of human nature."[3]

Bureaucratic hierarchies are the antithesis of superorganisms. They are motivationally undernourished because they don't feed the social appetites that drive human achievement. For example, hierarchical organizations do not promote relationships (Social Appetite #1), innovation (Social Appetite #4), or self-protection (Social Appetite #5), and employees live in constant fear of attack from above and below as they compete for rungs on the corporate ladder. Most of the employee's attention in a hierarchy is therefore distracted from the marketplace and the customer and devoted, instead, to self-defense and political maneuvering. Hierarchical organizations are therefore primarily anxiety driven (pain driven). It is unrealistic to expect employees to be emotionally engaged within such a mechanistic and anxiety-ridden environment.

The human experience aside, which type of organization is more fit for survival in today's economic jungle? The fitness analysis boils down to the trade-offs between efficiency, adaptability, and motivation. The hierarchical organization might have the efficiency edge in a stable ecosystem where there is little need for nimbleness and adaptability and when there are plenty of hungry job applicants in the labor pool (a captive group of job seekers that can be manipulated with fear). In this situation, the rational efficiencies of an orderly hierarchy with direct lines of communication and clearly defined roles, responsibilities, and rules might outweigh the hierarchy's disadvantages—rigidity, inertia, and decreased productivity caused by a misfiring motivational engine. Hierarchical management is also simple—all you really need is a big stick, lots of supervisors, a thick policy manual, and some cash.

Leadership theorist and Harvard Business School professor Joseph S. Nye, Jr., would agree with my contention that hierarchical management is past its prime. Nye writes that organizations are becoming flatter and more cooperative, participatory, and integrative.[4] The chief executive of IBM echoes Nye's sentiments when he says, "Hierarchical, command-and-control approaches simply do not work anymore. They impede information flows inside companies, hampering the fluid and collaborative nature of work today."[5] Iverson and the other mavericks, it seems, were way ahead of their time. Egalitarian superorganisms, I predict, will eventually become the norm in the twenty-first-century corporate ecosystem.

Benefits of a Trust-Based Superorganism

This entire book has focused on the motivational advantages of a trust-based superorganism. A superorganism is flat, decentralized (with decision making widely dispersed across the organization), self-managing (which reduces oversight costs and paperwork/reporting costs), and innovative (because employees truly care about their workplace and are given the freedom to explore and experiment). In other words, it feeds all five social appetites. Resources within a superorganism are distributed equitably between members, just as our Ice Age ancestors presumably divvied up a wooly mammoth kill, but with the choice cuts going to the hunter who inflicted the fatal wound.[6]

Employee turnover and absenteeism within a superorganism are low because employees experience the workplace as intrinsically pleasurable and rewarding. Employees are loyal because of the authentic relationships they've developed with their employer and workmates. Health-care costs are low because the work environment is less stressful than in a hierarchy where there is lots of interpersonal warfare and wasted energy. The reduced stress inside superorganisms results in fewer sick days. Indeed, it has been proven that stress has a negative effect on employee health.[7]

Most important, a superorganism is like a human Internet. The network of invested relationships allows skills and knowledge to flow to where they are most needed. This does not happen in a hierarchy, because hierarchies are not relationship based. There are few interconnections between employees in a hierarchy. A manager in a hierarchy would not volunteer to help a peer because the peer is a competitor. The manager would prefer to see his peer crash and burn and get demoted. Cooperation is therefore rare within a tooth-and-claw, competition-based hierarchical system. Knowledge is hoarded for the same reason—knowledge is power, so why share it with your competitors?

We-based superorganisms, I would argue, are also more disciplined and attentive to the marketplace because employees truly care about their workmates and the survival of the enterprise. In me-based hierarchies, employees primarily care about their paycheck and muscling their way to the top. If a better job comes along—they are gone.

Superorganisms are not devoid of hierarchy, because human beings instinctively rank themselves within any group. The hierarchy within a superorganism is organic and consensual versus artificial and imposed. The individuals who are most skilled and competent are respected and relied upon by the group. These individuals become consensus leaders who naturally attract followers. Their opinions carry more intrinsic value because they were blessed by the consensus. Leaders don't need to fight their way into positions of authority because the group installs them there based upon competency, merit, and commitment to the group.

It is difficult for Western cultures to spawn superorganisms. We are taught, from an early age, to compete aggressively with one another. We put a genteel guise on this competition by calling for "good sportsmanship" and "fair play," but deep down many of us (particularly men) subscribe to Vince Lombardi's motto: "Winning isn't everything, it's the only thing." It is extremely difficult for Western countries to create cooperative superorganisms, because head-to-head competition is in our blood.

NATURAL SOCIETIES: THE FIRST SUPERORGANISMS

The challenge corporations face in making the transition from conventional hierarchy to trust-based superorganism can be glimpsed by studying the few egalitarian hunter-gatherer societies that have survived into modern times. The San of the Kalahari are one such group.

The San, until recently, were among the most untouched societies on earth in terms of both their genetics and culture. They were protected from genetic and cultural dilution by their remote and inhospitable desert home. They failed to make the shift from hunter-gatherer to agrarian lifestyle because the Kalahari has no permanent standing water and cannot support agriculture. The San provide a rare and precious glimpse of the long-lost lifestyle of our Ice Age ancestors. They represent how human beings behave in their natural setting—outside the sterile cages of modern society.

Japanese anthropologist Jiro Tanaka spent nearly three years during the late 1960s and early 1970s living with the San in the Republic of Botswana. Here is his description of their remarkable, egalitarian lifestyle. His account underscores the profound cultural changes that Western companies would need to make to transform themselves into truly egalitarian superorganisms.

> There are almost no signs of competitive behavior among the San: competition is fundamentally at odds with the egalitarianism that underlies their society. Rather than trying to outdo one another, they strive to live in harmony and on the same level with others. The person who stands out becomes a target of envy and jealousy, of almost unbearable hostility; therefore, possessions are given away (and) people help each other out. Even among children's games, there are no wrestling matches, foot races, or other competitive games with "winners" and "losers." Aggression finds its outlet in the hunt, where it is directed at the prey; children similarly displace aggressive feelings onto the lizards, rats, and so forth, which they pursue in their hunting game. The San avoid at all costs aggressive behavior toward their human colleagues.[8]

The San compete indirectly with one another for the respect of the tribe and to be treated as leaders within their specific areas of expertise. Here is how Tanaka describes the organic competition among the San:

> A great bowman who is young and sturdy may become respected as a famous hunter, and his opinion in hunting matters will carry much weight.

There are also people skilled at incantations to cure illnesses, or at making tools, or at storytelling, and while they do not become specialists, they do take a leading position in activities in their sphere of ability and receive prestige.[9]

It is important to note that corporate superorganisms like Quad/ Graphics and Nucor Steel display the same system of dispersed responsibility and decision making as the San. Individuals and small groups are trusted to do the right thing without someone watching over them. In other words, both the San and a corporate superorganism are self-managing and leaders are selected by the group consensus.

Western societies have strayed far from the egalitarian lifestyle of the San and we are paying a high price for it in terms of stress and mental illness. There is no way to reclaim our hunter-gatherer heritage, but we can add a touch of egalitarianism to the mix to make our lives more rewarding and productive.

The medical community recently waded into the egalitarian superorganism versus hierarchy debate. Medical and health researchers have known for many years that low income correlates with poor health and high mortality rates. Researchers failed, however, in their many attempts to discern exactly how low income impacts health. They looked at variables like lower nutrition, decreased access to health care, higher smoking rates, higher rates of drug and alcohol abuse, and excessive exposure to air pollution. Their studies indicated that material factors, like access to health care, were *not* responsible for the bulk of the health problems of the poor. The researchers finally determined that perceived status, seeing oneself on the bottom of the pecking order, was the primary culprit.[10]

Life at the bottom of a hierarchy *hurts* because it triggers painful low self-esteem and chronic anxiety. Being low in the hierarchy, any hierarchy, triggers the amygdala and results in chronically high levels of stress hormones. Low social status in humans and in animals is now associated with worse HDL:LDL ratios, obesity, glucose intolerance, increased atherosclerosis, raised basal cortisol levels, and attenuated cortisol responses to stress.[11]

The bottom-line message from the medical community is that egalitarian, socially cohesive societies are healthier than hierarchically structured ones.[12] Homicides and violent crime are substantially higher in the less-egalitarian countries.[13] In other words, hierarchies are not only less productive than superorganisms, they are also less healthy!

Recent brain-imaging studies have confirmed that the human brain is exquisitely sensitive to unequal rewards like reserved parking spaces for executives. Unequal rewards are perceived as unfair and activate brain areas involved in malevolent, angry decisions.[14] If you want a workplace full of engaged employees, the rational thing to do is to limit perquisites like corner offices and reserved parking spaces.

At some point investors are going to realize the advantages and sustained financial results produced by trust-based superorganisms. The hunt will then be on to identify gifted leaders, like Ken Iverson of Nucor Steel, who can grow structurally flat, relationship-based organizations. Building a superorganism is a complex process that takes time to implement. It simply will not work until investors overcome their short-term mind-sets and allow superorganisms to germinate and grow.

THE EMERGING FIELD OF NEUROECONOMICS

In Chapter 8 I discussed how the social assets in individuals' "vaults" are the true assets in human transactions. These assets are acquired through investment and are rigorously tracked by a sophisticated emotional mechanism located in our ventromedial prefrontal lobes. When this asset-tracking mechanism is damaged by injury and disease, even money loses its value for the affected party. In other words, both emotions and the value placed on money are generated by precisely the same stuff—feelings of pleasure and pain.

This may seem like a radical proclamation, but economists are slowly coming to the same realization. The field of neuroeconomics, for example, acknowledges that emotions and feelings are deeply involved in the concept of economic *utility* and in economic decision making.[15] The latest neuroeconomic thinking postulates that the mesolimbic dopamine-reward system creates a common reward metric for perceiving value in economic decision making. Brain activity in this area reliably correlates with magnitude of monetary reward or punishment.[16]

A recent review article in the respected journal *Science* concluded:

> *In addition to the rewarding or punishing effects of social interactions,*
> *these scenarios also illustrated the prominent role emotions play in social*
> *decision-making. Classical models of decision-making have largely ignored*
> *the influence of emotion on how decisions are made, but recent research*
> *has begun to demonstrate the powerful effect these factors play.*[17]

Articles dealing with neuroeconomics are emerging with increasing regularity in the nation's top science journals and business magazines like the *Economist*. Andrew Lo, the director of MIT's Laboratory for Financial Engineering, predicts that, "Within five years, neuroeconomics will become mainstream . . . in fifteen to twenty years, it will be fully accepted."[18]

The concept of *utility* is defined in economics as a measure of the relative happiness or *satisfaction* (gratification) gained by consuming different bundles of goods and services. According to this definition, the social and biological appetites described in this book are economic concepts because they determine whether we feel satisfied (satiated) or dissatisfied (starved).

It seems, in other words, that we have been discussing the internal workings of economic utility all along. *Primal Management* is therefore a neuroeconomic textbook that maps out economic transactions at a very fundamental and detailed level. The concept of utility can be exploded into its ten component parts that correspond to the biologic and social appetites that regulate human survival and thereby allow us to feel satisfied. In other words, the ten biologic and social appetites depicted in Figure 1-1 in Chapter 1 produce ten types of feeling that are the underlying currency of the human mind and the underlying phenomenon behind economic utility.

Let's take this thought a step further. If economics is about utility, and utility is about feelings, then money is just a stand-in for feelings-based transactions. The true currency of all economic transactions is therefore *feelings*.

Who would have thought that a discussion of emotions would eventually lead us to the very heart of modern economic theory? Feelings, it seems, are not irrelevant to business at all: rather, they are its lifeblood. If we could turn off regulatory feelings, all economic activity would come to a screeching halt.

I am certain that emotions will continue to creep into discussions of economics because this is where the logic of survival leads. The ultimate value is *survival* value, and this is what emotions and feelings are all about.

The Neuroeconomic Superiority of Corporate Superorganisms

As discussed in Chapter 8, every interaction between human beings can be viewed as either a value-producing event that adds social assets to the vaults of the participants or a value-destroying event that withdraws assets. Excellent companies, as I said before, intuitively understand these hidden "monetary" transactions and skillfully manage them. Fear-based companies do the opposite—they destroy social assets at every turn, degrade the corporate ecosystem, starve the social appetites, and foster a workplace populated with underperforming and disengaged employees.

The implications of a subterranean feelings-based economy are immense. If economists measure only, say, the visible one-fourth of all economic transactions, then what are the ramifications in terms of poor economic decisions such as mergers and acquisitions that fail to live up to their advance billing because they have a negative feelings–based ROI? Rational analysis that ignores key variables or is conducted with incomplete data is likely to be flawed, no matter how brilliant the analyst.

Errors happen every day in the world of finance, as the dismal success rate of mergers and acquisitions will attest.[19] Here are some historic facts regarding merger and acquisition failure rates:

- A 1998 *Barron's* article entitled "Merger Mayhem" indicated that between 60 percent and 80 percent of mergers (and acquisitions) are financial failures.[20]

- In a 2001 study of 118 mergers and acquisitions, KPMG found that 70 percent of them did not create shareholder value for the combined companies.[21]

- A McKinsey & Co. study of 160 acquisitions by 157 public companies across eleven industry sectors found that only 12 percent of acquirers managed to accelerate growth, while 42 percent of acquirers had lower growth rates than their industry peers after the acquisition.[22]

- A *Business Week* analysis of 302 major mergers and acquisitions revealed that 61 percent of the merged companies destroyed shareholder wealth.[23]

What is going on here? Are investors and analysts irrational, or are they missing something fundamental? I think they are missing something fundamental—they fail to account for the emotional transactions that power the companies they are analyzing. They also fail to tally the social transaction costs that occur when hyperrational decisions are made. Finally, they fail to account for the emotional paycheck, the one that really counts for human beings.

The hyperrational analyst in charge of such a failed merger ought to hang his head and say, "I'm so sorry, but I'm not a psychologist, anthropologist, sociologist, or neuroeconomist, so how could I have known that the productivity of the merged companies would plummet and that innovation would cease? How could I have anticipated the merger would starve the social appetites and result in a motivational meltdown? If I had known that this transaction would destroy the acquired superorganism, I never would have proposed it."

I hope such excuses will be less acceptable in the future. The hidden "cash" flows in the subterranean economy are not really all that difficult to understand. Nature's system of emotional regulation is simple, elegant, and eminently logical. All analysts really need to do is stop ignoring one of the most vital factors in sustained success—the regulatory feelings that drive the show!

Here are some simple dos and don'ts for analysts who evaluate mergers and acquisitions:

- *Do not* let a hyperrational hierarchical company acquire a superorganism. This acquisition will quickly self-destruct because the acquiring company has no skill in running a finely tuned superorganism.

The standard operating procedure following an acquisition is to pick management's brains for a year or so and then axe them. This sort of corporate decapitation is sure to destroy a superorganism because the leader of a superorganism is a hub in the interpersonal network that holds the superorganism together. If you decide to go ahead and acquire the superorganism anyway, be sure to make a major downward adjustment to its projected productivity and innovativeness—probably by 50 percent, or more.

• *Do* let one superorganism swallow another superorganism. This will produce an acceptable outcome consistent with analyst forecasts because both organizations are "we-based" and know how to feed the social appetites that motivate high performance. The merged entities should perform similarly to their premerger levels.

• *Do* let one hyperrational hierarchy swallow another hyperrational hierarchy, but don't expect much in the way of productivity improvement or improved innovativeness. The merged entities in this instance will likely perform the same as they did before the merger. In other words, the merged entities will continue to sputter along as they did before the acquisition.

• *Do* let a superorganism acquire a hyperrational hierarchy because the superorganism will, after a period of adjustment and organizational flattening, create a human-friendly ecosystem that feeds the social appetites. This is a value-added transaction that will yield major returns.

THE PATH FORWARD

Hyperrational management and conventional hierarchies are inherently flawed because they do not acknowledge the elegant, feelings-based economy that underlies business success. Hyperrational management, because it is blind to the feelings-based cash flows of the subterranean economy, cannot possibly maximize utility in economic transactions or create great companies. This is why seemingly rational policies so often go disastrously wrong and why mergers and acquisitions fail more often than they succeed.

Hyperrational management is aggressive, me-based, and blind to emotions, and it treats people as objects. It promotes cold-blooded, self-serving managers and cold-blooded, hierarchical organizations ruled by money, bare-knuckled competition, and fear. It produces a win-lose scenario instead of a win-win scenario.

Life inside a hyperrational company is impoverished and leads to high rates of stress, illness, and premature death.[24] Hyperrationalism promotes self-serving managers like Al Dunlap instead of brilliant consensus leaders like Harry Quadracci, Ken Iverson, and Ricardo Semler. Someday hierarchical, hyperrational management will be viewed as archaic, inefficient, and primitive. Hyperrational management is not truly rational at all because it denies human history, human biology, human behavior, and the fact that excellent and great companies are balanced, not hyperrational.

I suggest that corporate America make a drastic, 180-degree course correction. Hierarchical, bureaucratic management is deeply flawed. It creates a dysfunctional, disengaged world with many losers and only a few spectacular winners. It is my fervent hope that Wall Street will make the correction I recommend by recognizing the many advantages of superorganisms and the many disadvantages of centralized, hierarchical organizations run by egotistical, narcissistic leaders who promise the world but deliver little in the way of tangible, sustained results. My suggestion is for Wall Street to demand superorganisms because they provide more value to all parties over the long run because they work with human nature rather than against it. Superorganisms feed all five social appetites and therefore create the sustained motivational horsepower required for long-term financial success.

Great leadership and great management is an art. Unfortunately, this art is not taught in business schools, and most Wall Street analysts have not been trained in this sort of art appreciation. I hope this book helps to nudge leadership from an art to a more easily taught and understood hard science.

Put Up or Shut Up

I am willing to put up or shut up regarding the five social appetites that motivate high performance. Chapter 2 introduced an emotional health survey to assess whether employees are being motivationally fed or starved and two metrics to visualize the results. The emotional health survey is feelings based because human beings and economic utility are feelings based. Life, in general, is feelings based.

Wall Street now has a tool, "magic glasses" if you will, to look inside companies and determine if they are superorganisms or not. The Horsepower Metric allows analysts to correlate motivational horsepower with hard financial results. If I'm right, this correlation will be robust and will prove once and for all that traditional bureaucratic hierarchies are unbalanced and ignore the motivational engine that propels corporations to greatness.

The Horsepower Metric can detect whether a company's motivational engine is tuned or sputtering. This metric can also detect great leadership because it takes great leadership to create a well-fed superorganism operating on all five social appetites. There is no parameter that is more relevant if you want to make money over the long haul with your investments!

Hyperrational managers may object to the survey and metrics by saying, "Why on earth should I care how employees feel? They get paid so they should do their work regardless of how they feel." Such managers are hyper-left-brained, so they don't understand other people's feelings and are only vaguely aware of their own. I hope my hard analysis of emotions will help convince even hyperrational managers to accept the central role of emotions in business, even if they can't quite see it themselves. I have taken a hard, engineering approach to emotions and feelings based on the latest scientific breakthroughs in neurobiology, deductive logic, empirical data from great companies, and statistics, with the hope of getting my message through to the hyperrational world. The hard path that I followed for the past thirty years leads to an incontrovertible conclusion—feelings drive performance and are, therefore, central to organizational excellence. This conclusion is as hard as the laws of physics because it was derived in a similarly rigorous way.

Becoming a superorganism is not a strategy or tactic. Rather, it's a life change, like being "born again." To truly make the transition from bureaucratic hierarchy to superorganism, we will need to hit the cultural "eject" button and reject our hyperrational, hypercompetitive upbringing. As I said in the Introduction, there's only one way to pull off the transition to superorganism: Value employees, commit to employees, invest in employees, and go to bat for employees. We've got to jump in! Our employees, after a period of four months or so, will detect our commitment and investment and begin to invest in return. We will also need to learn to share decision making, status, and rewards, and to treat our employees more like competent and capable peers rather than as supplicants. If we follow this prescription, our corporate tribe just might help us bring down a wooly mammoth or two!

HIERARCHY-FLIPPING SUGGESTIONS

Dismantling the bureaucracy and hierarchy inside our companies is not going to be easy. Harry Quadracci built his flat, egalitarian superorganism from scratch, so he didn't need to deconstruct a preexisting hierarchy—he merely had to keep one from sprouting up.

Ken Iverson started purging Nucor of hierarchical thinking way back in 1962 by knocking down the walls separating white-only and black-only dressing rooms in Nucor's South Carolina Vulcraft division. Iverson continued to knock down figurative walls of hierarchy and prejudice throughout his illustrious career at Nucor.

Ricardo Semler took over his family's struggling manufacturing business at the tender age of 20 and immediately began molding himself into the prototypical tough businessman. He soon concluded that his company's problems were caused by a lack of discipline, organization, accountability, and internal controls. Accordingly, Semler started a law-and-order campaign by hiring tough, autocratic, hard-driving, aggressive managers. Semler and his hired guns issued policies, rules, and procedures with abandon. They went on a bureaucracy-building spree.

Semler's organizing binge made the company look efficient, but it also created a listless malaise that showed up in missed shipping deadlines, quality problems, and stalled innovation. Semler eventually came to the realization that his bureaucracy binge had caused his employees to stop thinking and stop caring and had smothered their initiative.

Semler decided that his bureaucracy initiative was a giant mistake and set out to undo it. Semler's new approach was to treat employees as responsible, intelligent adults who could be trusted to make decisions and do the right thing, without an oppressive bureaucracy and external controls. He had no grand plan, just a desire to try a more natural approach to management where employees could participate and find genuine pleasure in their work.

Semler started by getting rid of the most obvious symbols of disrespect, like executive parking places and the policy of frisking employees as they left work. In the headquarters building he removed all the walls and created one large space with work areas separated by rows of plants and flowers. The dress code he had installed was uninstalled.

His next big move was to open up a dialogue with his alienated employees by forming factory committees. This step started out awkwardly because his employees were initially suspicious and expected some kind of gimmick. Once they figured out that the committees were legit, a long list of grievances was aired. Wages and job security were immediate concerns, and the committees commissioned a study to assess whether Semco lagged behind industry average wages. Once the backlog of grievances had been dealt with, the tone of the committees changed from adversarial to collaborative and the committees began to participate in problem solving and decision making.

This collaborative process accelerated and the factory committees soon formed subcommittees to run the plant cafeterias, remodel locker rooms, set production goals, suggest changes to products, and even to decide who should go when layoffs were required. The factory committees became the primary vehicle for getting everybody's head in the game. The committees, Semler notes, went beyond just asking employees for their opinion. Rather, they involved authentic delegation of decision making—the employees now ran their own shop.

Following the hierarchy-and-bureaucracy-busting initiative, the orderly arrangement of equipment inside Semler's factories disappeared. Instead of linearly arranged machines spaced at regular intervals, the machines migrated into disorderly looking clumps called *cells*. Those disorderly clumps, however, served the human beings actually doing the work. Machines and equipment that belonged together migrated into functional groupings that made life easier for employees and improved efficiency and increased motivation.

Semler warns that flipping the hierarchy upside down is not for the weak of heart. In 1993, after years of hierarchy dismantling, Semler wrote:

> *We have been ripping apart Semco and putting it back together again for a dozen years, and we're just 30 percent finished. Still, the rewards have already been substantial. We've taken a company that was moribund and made it thrive, chiefly by refusing to squander our greatest resource, our people.*[25]

Semler didn't have a blueprint to guide his hierarchy-and-bureaucracy-busting efforts. He knew that he wanted to align Semco with human nature, but he didn't have a clear picture of what, exactly, human nature looked like. He started with a vague notion of creating a natural tribal workplace, using a process he termed *natural management*.

The social appetite concept in *Primal Management*, I suggest, is the missing blueprint that would have greatly accelerated Semler's efforts to flip the hierarchy and align his company with human nature. The five social appetites constitute the core of human nature, so companies that feed these appetites will automatically align themselves with nature's motivational mechanism.

Removing the bureaucratic shell from an organization, with all its attendant rules, regulations, control systems, and organization charts, will unleash the energy of the humans inside. Once the shell is gone, employees will naturally and organically configure themselves into a superorganism. The superorganism, just like Semco's plant floor, might look chaotic to the casual observer, but a deeper look will reveal a self-organizing, self-managing, and self-coordinating dynamo with stunning productivity.

CONCLUSION

I had an intuitive flash in 1977 that emotions must be part of an elegantly designed system of social and biologic regulation. This book has been an exercise in bridge building to lead you, the reader, from the conventional notion that emotions are irrational to the radical notion that they are vital. I have tried to lead you step by logical step. I wanted you to think to yourself after each step, "Of course it works that way!"

The main scaffolding for my case has been the logic of survival. I have tried to reinforce this scaffolding with experimental data from fields such as neurobiology, psychology, and anthropology; statistics by the Gallup organization; empirical data from excellent and great company research; and the proof of concept provided by the three mavericks (Quadracci, Iverson, and Semler).

Although we have proceeded step by step, we have, in aggregate, traveled far from where we started. We started with the conventional notion that emotions are extreme, irrational, unbusinesslike, and generally a joke. We have ended up, hopefully, with a view that emotions are part of a vital system of social and biologic regulation that motivates every single action your employees take. We started out thinking about emotions as soft and ended up understanding that emotions rule in business and in life because they embody the fundamental needs of survival. I hope my explanation also harmonizes with your personal experiences as a day-to-day user of emotions and feelings.

Making a rational case for emotions is not enough. Tribal decisions are made on the basis of expected return on emotional investment. I therefore need to demonstrate to you, the jury, that the benefits of employee-centric management outweigh the costs. I believe that the benefits of working harmoniously with human nature are substantial for all parties. Employees win because their emotional take-home pay increases. They're also more secure because the company becomes a superorganism that dominates the marketplace. Management wins because the company is more productive, efficient, innovative, and profitable. Management also wins because the work environment is more exciting and rewarding. Customers win because they get faster, better service from people who radiate good feelings. Shareholders win because they make money. *Why wouldn't we want this?*

I think I have made a strong case in favor of people-centric management and against hyperrational, bureaucratic management. This idea will either get the thumbs up by the mass media, the book-reading public, the publishing industry, and Wall Street, or the thumbs down. If the mass media applauds by writing favorable reviews and if the business community applauds by buying and recommending the book, it will be magically imbued with value and spread through the tribe.

In summation, I want you, the jury, to vote in favor of emotions and people-centric management because this path leads to a bright future where everybody wins. I hope my emotional health survey, Horsepower Metric, and Tune-Up Metric will give Wall Street the tools it needs to identify and track superorganisms. I hope the tune-up suggestions presented in Chapters 5 through 9 will help CEOs to get their superorganisms up and running quickly, before investors get impatient.

I have taken a hard look at emotions by applying engineering principles, mathematical deduction, and the logic of survival. This hard approach leads, paradoxically, to a destination where everyone wins. My suggestion to employees, managers, supervisors, and executives is to build your businesses synergistically around nature's elegant design, rather than brutally on top of it. This is truly the rational and efficient thing to do.

A Parting Thought

Let's picture ourselves in retirement enjoying our yacht, villa, or tropical island retreat. We are relaxing and enjoying a margarita. So far, so good, but what about the emotions percolating beneath this tranquil scene? In other words, how do we feel?

If we purchased our yacht by victimizing our employees, shareholders, executive team, and customers, then we probably won't feel too good because the competency appetite won't let us. The competency appetite, as you may recall, is the one that forces us to hit society's target using powerful feelings of high and low self-esteem. Taking advantage of people does not qualify as hitting anybody's target, unless, of course, the target was programmed by a sick society or twisted parents. The competency appetite will detect the missed target and create festering wounds in our psyches. Nature's version of tough love does not respect the yacht or the villa or other surface appearances. It sees through these things to the reality underneath.

Here is another endgame that starts out like the first. Imagine that we are enjoying our yacht, villa, or tropical retreat. We are relaxing with a margarita and contemplating a life well spent in the service of our tribe.

Our minds are tranquil and pure because we did our best for the tribe. We left a noble legacy by helping employees find purpose, value, and success in their lives. We are remembered fondly and celebrated by the tribe, instead of reviled. And, by the way, our yacht is bigger than in the first scenario because we brought out the very best in our employees and our businesses prospered accordingly.

SHARE YOUR INSIGHTS ABOUT NATURE'S MOTIVATIONAL MECHANISM

As lifelong users of human nature, we each have personal theories about what makes human beings tick. If I've gotten something wrong, or if you'd like to share some data, insights, or case studies, please visit pri malmanagement.com to leave your suggestions.

AFTERWORD

My references to the biology of emotion are highly simplified. If you would like to explore the detailed neurobiology behind nature's regulatory systems, I highly recommend Antonio Damasio's trilogy, *Descartes' Error*, *Looking for Spinoza*, and *The Feeling of What Happens*. Damasio has received worldwide recognition for his revolutionary insights on emotions and has won numerous scientific awards for his work.

In regard to my designation of the five social appetites, the scientific community may take offense. There are lots of logical schemes categorizing human emotions and motivation into various appetites, subappetites, sub-subappetites, and so forth. This book isn't about the details of categorization but provides a sketch of the overall mechanism—which in my opinion is something the scientific community has been sadly lacking.

ACKNOWLEDGMENTS

Primal Management has been a labor of love for the past thirty years. During most of that time I felt as though I was on a lonely quest dragging a heavy sled through the wilderness. Most people just scratched their heads and wondered, "Where in the heck is he going?"

Family, friends, and colleagues who saw the value of my quest early on, and who offered their unconditional encouragement, deserve special mention. Here is a partial list of my steadfast supporters: my mother, Arline Herr, encouraged me to follow my dreams from childhood onward; Michael Felske was a loyal supporter way back in 1979; my brother, Mark Herr, was an early skeptic but is now a major booster; Brad Thompson, a business writer who stumbled across an early version of *Primal Management* on the Internet, thought I was on to something and encouraged me to finish and publish the book; my buddies Rob and William Ritter, Leo Burger, Ted Nelson, Tony Hartman, Jason Hewitt, and Dan Koval never wavered in their support; and my agent, John Willig, and editor, Christina Parisi, had the guts and good sense to take a newbie on as a client.

My wife, Britta, deserves high honors for giving me support and breathing room to research and write this book. My children, Christopher and Pauline, the joys of my life, keep me centered, amused, and motivated. I have endeavored to feed their social appetites from infancy onward and the results, in my humble opinion, are impressive.

A number of businesses in Madison, Wisconsin, and beyond agreed to be guinea pigs for my surveys, metrics, and methodology. Many thanks to Guy Van Rensselaer, City of Madison; Rich Horky, Precision Cable Assemblies; Dr. Tony D'Alessandro; Scott Ransom, Marshall Erdman and

Associates; Andy Laberge, Zimbrick BMW; and Ross Smith and Lori Ada Kilty, Microsoft Core Security, for agreeing to conduct demonstration projects. Special thanks also to Jeremy Clark from Gary Hamel's Management Innovation Lab for his thoughtful support and insights.

I would also like to thank the scientific community for the discoveries in neuroeconomics and neurobiology that helped me nail down my theory. Dr. Antonio Damasio and Dr. Michael McGuire deserve special mention for their groundbreaking work on the neurobiology of emotion.

On the business side, I'd like to acknowledge the three mavericks, Harry Quadracci, Ken Iverson, and Ricardo Semler, for breaking all the rules and showing us how to construct more humane and productive workplaces. Thanks to Tom Rath and the Gallup Organization for their enlightening research, statistics, and insights about human nature. Special thanks, also, to Gary Hamel and his inspiring book, *The Future of Management*, and to the Great Places to Work Institute, Inc., for its work in identifying companies that work harmoniously and productively with human nature.

My karate instructors at Kicks Unlimited deserve mention for their embodiment of motivational perfection. Anyone who can take a somewhat lazy, fifty-year-old couch potato and hone him into a lean, mean, fighting machine is a motivational genius.

As a first-time author, I greatly appreciate the assistance of the following authors for showing me the ropes: Deborah Blum, *Monkey Wars, Ghost Hunters, Love at Goon Park*; Dr. Sean Carroll, *Endless Forms Most Beautiful, Making of the Fittest*; Charlie Green, *The Trusted Advisor, Trust-Based Selling*; Paul Hawken, *How to Grow a Business, Natural Capitalism, Ecology of Commerce, Blessed Unrest*; Dave Logan, *Tribal Leadership*; Dr. Nigel Nicholson, *Executive Instinct*; and Dr. William Frederick, *Values, Nature, and Culture in the American Corporation*.

Last, but not least, are the reviewers who helped me hone my manuscript. The many comments were insightful and appreciated. Many thanks to Christine Flores, Jean Frank, Dale Evans, Wendy Cooper, Paul Wirtzfeld, Dr. Robert Mather, Kathryn Jeffers, Jeff Lyne, Jady Grad, Bruce Deadman, Sandy Schwartzberg, Mike Swita, Dr. Kurt Sladke, Deborah Sladke, Mary Paul, Ray Tierney, Faruk Oksuz, Dr. Ken Miller, and Emily Figueroa.

FOR MORE INFORMATION AND HELP

I believe that every company, profit or nonprofit, public or private, could benefit from monitoring and tuning their motivational engines. I hope to disseminate the ideas in *Primal Management* globally because I believe, deep down, that everyone benefits when companies align themselves with human nature. Even the naysayers, I believe, will eventually fall into line because the evidence is compelling and the logic is incontrovertible. If you'd like to align your company or work group with human nature, here are some resources that may help:

• *Book.* To order copies of *Primal Management* for your employees, managers, co-workers, or board members visit www.primalmanagement .com. You will also find my blog, a recommended reading list, and links to Web resources.

• *Metric.* If you'd like to implement the Horsepower and Tune-Up Metrics, a list of certified technology providers can be found at www .horsepowermetric.com. These technology partners can administer anonymous online surveys as well as crunch the numbers and provide monthly reports based on the Horsepower and Tune-Up Metrics.

• *Consulting.* If you'd like my help tuning your motivational engine, please refer to my consulting website, www.paulherrconsulting

.com, for a variety of consulting services. Paul Herr Consulting, Inc., is a management consulting firm dedicated to the people side of management. My mission is to grow trust-based superorganisms by bringing clarity, simplicity, and common sense to the people side of management.

NOTES

INTRODUCTION

1. The Gallup Organization has surveyed Americans about their views on human origins annually since 1982. The results of these surveys have varied only slightly over the years. Between 43 percent and 47 percent of Americans agreed with the strict creationist view. Between 35 and 40 percent agreed that human beings evolved, but with divine guidance. I refer to the midpoint of these ranges in the text. See Frank Newport, "Republicans, Democrats Differ on Creationism," June 20, 2008, retrieved from Gallup Organization website on October 11, 2008. http://www.gallup.com/poll/108226/Republi cans-Democrats-Differ-Creationism.aspx

2. I use the terms *tribe* and *tribal* to refer to our hunter-gatherer ancestors because these terms are familiar to most readers. The more accurate term, however, is *band*. A band is defined as a small egalitarian kin group no larger than an extended family. Tribes are larger groupings consisting of many families. Tribes are also more hierarchically structured and have more social institutions, such as chiefs and councils of elders.

3. Daniel Goleman, *Social Intelligence: The New Science of Human Relationships* (New York: Bantam Books, 2006).

4. Ming-Jer Chen, *Inside Chinese Business* (Boston: Harvard Business School Press, 2001).

5. Bruce S. McEwen, "Structural Plasticity of the Adult Brain," *Dialogues in Clinical Neuroscience: Neuroplasticity* 6, no. 2 (2004) (quarterly journal): 125.

6. You might be wondering how I came up with the figure of 150, or fewer, individuals as the natural group size for human beings. There are certainly no written records from the Ice Age; however, evolutionary biologists have come up with an innovative approach for determining this number. They noticed a relationship between social group size and brain size in primates. They concluded that group size in primates is limited by the information-processing ability of the primate brain. When this brain-size to group-size

relationship is graphed and extrapolated to the size of the human brain, the predicted maximum group size for humans is 148 (95 percent confidence limit ranges from 100 to 231). This finding is consistent with the clan sizes observed in the few hunter-gatherer societies that have survived into modern times, such as the San of the Kalahari, and with the sizes of the world's oldest-known villages in Mesopotamia. These villages were built 8,500 years ago and consisted of twenty to twenty-five dwellings and an estimated population of 150 to 200 individuals. For more information, see R. I. M. Dunbar, "Co-Evolution of Neocortex Size, Group Size and Language in Humans," *Behavioral and Brain Sciences* 16, no. 4 (1999): 681–735.

7. Ricardo Semler, "Managing without Managers," *Harvard Business Review*, September–October 1989, 2.

8. Ricardo Semler, *Maverick: The Success Story Behind the World's Most Unusual Workplace* (New York: Warner Books, 1993), 280.

9. "Harry Quadracci, 66; Printing Firm Made Him Among Richest in U.S.," *Los Angeles Times*, August 1, 2001, B-13.

10. Tom Daykin, "Quad/Graphics to Lease New Facility in Falls," JS Online, February 28, 2008, http://www.jsonline.com/story/index.aspx?id=723177 (accessed August 22, 2008).

11. Rebecca Ganzel, "Putting Out the Welcome Mat," *Training Magazine*, March 1, 1998, http://www.trainingmag.com/msg/search/article_display.jsp?vnu_content_id=1505740&imw=Y (accessed August 22, 2008).

12. Jim Collins, *Good to Great* (New York: HarperCollins, 2001), 136.

13. Semler, *Maverick*, foreword.

14. Ibid., 1.

15. Ricardo Semler, *The Seven-Day Weekend: A Better Way to Work in the 21st Century* (London: Century, the Random House Group Limited, 2003), 4, 11–12.

16. A recent critique of business school education supports my contention that MBA programs persist in emphasizing technical skill over leadership training, despite what their marketing flyers claim. Here is a quote by Khurana and Snook that supports my position:

> Recognizing that business schools have a responsibility that extends far beyond technical training is perhaps why so many business schools have come to describe their mission as one of educating leaders. While such mission statements make for attractive admissions copy or fundraising brochures, the actual business of educating leaders however, is not an easy pedagogical undertaking. Developing leaders is not the same as training our students in negotiations or the mechanics of financial engineering. Not only is the general process of leader development not well understood, but there is at least one essential element that business schools have not addressed very well, according to various surveys of

MBA programs and the continuing exodus of executives as a consequence of falsifying financial returns and backdating stock options. The art of educating society's business leaders then goes well beyond equipping students with technical skills in finance, marketing, and organizational behavior.

See Rakesh Khurana and Scott Snook, "Comments on Glenn Hubbard's *Business, Knowledge, and Global Growth,*" *Capitalism and Society* 1, no. 3 (2006).

CHAPTER 1

1. "Dilbert Is Right, Says Gallup Survey: A National Employee Survey Confirms That Uncomfortable Work Environments Do Make for Disgruntled Employees," *Gallup Management Journal*, April 13, 2006.

2. Tom Rath and Donald O. Clifton, *How Full Is Your Bucket?* (Omaha, NE: Gallup Press, 2004), 33.

3. Bryant Ott, "Investors, Take Note: Engagement Boosts Earnings," *Gallup Management Journal*, June 14, 2007.

4. Ibid.

5. Alex Edmans, "Does the Stock Market Fully Value Intangibles?" Social Science Research Network, http://papers.ssrn.com/sol3/papers.cfm?abstract_id =985735 (accessed January 31, 2008).

6. This quotation was obtained from the Great Place to Work Institute website, http://www.greatplacetowork.com/great/index.php (accessed May 26, 2008).

7. See Antonio Damasio, *The Feeling of What Happens, Body and Emotion in the Making of Consciousness* (New York: Harcourt Brace & Company, 1999), 39.

8. Colin Camerer, George Loewenstein, and Drazen Prelec, "Neuroeconomics: How Neuroscience Can Inform Economics," *Journal of Economic Literature* 43, no. 1 (March 2005); A. G. Sanfey, "Social Decision-Making: Insights from Game Theory and Neuroscience," *Science* 318 (October 26, 2007): 598–602.

9. Paul J. Zak, "The Neurobiology of Trust," *Scientific American* 298, vol. 6 (June 2008), 91.

10. Ibid., 92, 95.

11. In this paragraph I divide bioregulation into five basic categories or appetites: nutrition, energy conservation, protection of the body proper, breathing, and reproduction. While these categories capture a large swath of bioregulatory phenomena, they are in no way authoritative or comprehensive. In other words, my categories are meant to capture the basic architecture of biologic regulation for the lay reader, not the technical nuances.

12. Antonio Damasio wrote in *Descartes' Error* that the ventromedial prefrontal region contains personal, categorized information that he likens to a personal autobiography. This is similar to my view, except that I envision not just information storage, but investment storage and a sense of ownership over the investments. See Antonio Damasio, *Descartes' Error* (New York: G. P. Putnam's Sons, 1994, 2000; current edition Penguin Books, 2005), 183.

13. Jim Collins, *Good to Great* (New York: HarperCollins, 2001), 21.

14. Antonio Damasio, *Looking for Spinoza: Joy, Sorrow, and the Feeling Brain* (Orlando, FL: Harcourt, 2003), 95.

15. Zak, "The Neurobiology of Trust," 91.

16. Both Jim Collins in *Good to Great* and Thomas J. Peters and Robert H. Waterman, Jr., in *In Search of Excellence* (New York: HarperCollins), 2004, report a family feel inside high-performing companies. See Collins, *Good to Great*, 261.

17. Zak, "The Neurobiology of Trust," 95.

18. Peter D. Kramer, *Listening to Prozac* (New York: Viking Press, 1993), 197–222.

19. According to an article in *Journal of Neuroscience*, ecstasy blocks the reuptake of serotonin at serotonin 2b receptors by reversing the activity of the serotonin transporter (the serotonin transporter normally removes serotonin from the synapses, but ecstasy causes the transporter to release serotonin instead), thereby boosting the concentration of serotonin in the synapses. Rats that had their serotonin 2b receptors genetically deleted no longer responded to ecstasy. As a side note, other research involving rats indicates that ecstasy also increases the level of oxytocin, the relationship hormone, in the brain, thereby explaining the warm, interpersonal feelings reported by ecstasy users. See, Stéphane Doly, et. al., "Serotonin 5-HT2B Receptors Are Required for 3,4-Methylenedioxymethamphetamine-Induced Hyperlocomotion and 5-HT Release In Vivo and In Vitro," *Journal of Neuroscience* 28 (March 2008): 2933–2940.

20. Sheri L. Johnson, "Mania and Dysregulation in Goal Pursuit: A Review," *Clinical Psychology Review* 25, 2 (February 2005): 241–262.

21. Lisa Shulman, MD, "Apathy and Amotivation," Chapter 19 in *Parkinson's Disease: Diagnosis and Clinical Management*, eds. Steward A. Factor and William T. Weiner (New York: Demos Medical Publishing, 2002), 175.

22. According to a 1985 study, rats that are allowed to self-administer cocaine cease their grooming behavior, lose up to 47% of their pre-study body weight, and suffer a marked deterioration in health. The cocaine mortality rate over the course of this 30-day study was 90%. See Michael A. Bozarth and Roy A. Wise, "Toxicity Associated with Long-term Intravenous Heroin and Cocaine Self-Administration," *Journal of the American Medical Association*, 254 (1985): 81–83.

23. Liisa Keltikangas-Järvinen, Marko Elovainio, Mika Kivimäki, Dirk Lichtermann, Jesper Ekelund, and Leena Peltonen, "Association Between the Type

4 Dopamine Receptor Gene Polymorphism and Novelty Seeking," *Psychosomatic Medicine* 65 (2003): 471–476.

24. Irving Biederman and Edward Vessel, "Perceptual Pleasure and the Brain," Red Orbit website, http://redorbit.com/news/science/504251/perceptual_pleasure_and_the_brain/, May 15, 2006.

25. Scott Rauch and Lisa Shin, "Structural and Functional Imaging of Anxiety and Stress Disorders," in *Neuropsychopharmacology: The Fifth Generation of Progress*, ed. Kenneth L. Davis, Dennis Charney, Joseph T. Coyle, and Charles Nemeroff, American College of Neuropsychopharmacology (Philadelphia: Lippincott, 2002), Chap. 65.

26. This definition of hedonymy was obtained from the Psychobiology Website: http://psychobiology.ouvaton.org/textes.uk/uk-txt-p04.20-besoinspsychobio logiques.htm (accessed November 8, 2007).

27. The five social appetites shown in Figure 1-1 can explain the bulk of human social behavior, but there are actually more than five biologic appetites. The five biologic appetites (regulatory systems) listed in Figure 1-1 are the main players that we are most familiar with. There are many other regulatory systems that operate completely beyond our conscious awareness. These background systems regulate things like blood pressure, blood ion concentrations, hormone levels, and heart rate.

28. Keise Izuma, Daisuke Saito, and Norihiro Sadato, "Processing of Social and Monetary Rewards in the Human Striatum," *Neuron* 58 (2008): 284.

29. Damasio, *The Feeling of What Happens*, 78.

30. Dan Waldorf, Craig Reinarman, and Sheigla Murphy, *Cocaine Changes: The Experience of Using and Quitting* (Philadelphia: Temple University Press, 1991).

CHAPTER 2

1. Nikola Grahek and Daniel Dennett, *Feeling Pain and Being in Pain* (Cambridge, MA: MIT Press, 2007), 21, 54.

2. When I claim that the Horsepower Metric correlates with customer satisfaction, profitability, innovation, and growth, I am referring to research findings pertaining to employee engagement surveys. (See Gallup research cited in Chapter 1.) However, the Horsepower Metric has undergone preliminary validation testing at 150 companies and was shown to correlate with increased revenue, reduced employee turnover, and increased market share.

3. Game theorists have developed the concept of "entrance costs" that may explain why it takes four months to convince employees to trust management. An entrance cost in game theory is an investment that the partners in an exchange must make before reciprocal trading can commence. If either

party subsequently cheats, the relationship and the initial investment will be lost. This threat of loss keeps the relationship stable and prevents cheating. See Nick Szabo, *Shelling Out—The Origins of Money*, 2005, http://szabo.best .vwh.net/shell.html.

4. Telephone interview with Bob Carpenter in 2003.

5. Alex Edmans, "Does the Stock Market Fully Value Intangibles?" retrieved on January 31, 2008, from the Wharton School Website, University of Pennsylvania, Philadelphia, http://papers.ssrn.com/sol3/papers.cfm?abstract_id= 985735.

CHAPTER 3

1. William M. Baum, *Understanding Behaviorism: Behavior, Culture, and Evolution* (New York: HarperCollins, 2004); B. F. Skinner, *About Behaviorism*, (New York: Knopf, 1974).

2. Recent research indicates that the anterior cingulate cortex, a pain-sensing area of the brain (in conjunction with portions of the anterior and posterior insula), is activated during effortful activities like clenching one's fist or doing mental arithmetic and may be the primary brain area responsible for the sensation of effort. See J. W. Williamson, R. McColl, and D. Mathews, "Evidence for Central Command Activation of the Human Insular Cortex During Exercise" *Journal of Applied Physiology* 94 (2003): 1726–1734. First published January 31, 2003; 10.1152/japplphysiol.01152.2002.

3. Antonio Damasio, *Descartes' Error* (New York: G. P. Putnam's Sons, 1994, 2000, current edition Penguin Books, 2005), 34–51.

4. Mary Francis Robinson and Walter Freeman, *Psychosurgery and Self* (New York: Grune & Straton, 1954), 31.

5. E. Stengel, "A Follow-Up Investigation of 330 Cases Treated by Prefrontal Leucotomy," *Journal of Mental Science* 96 (1950): 633–662.

6. Damasio, *Descartes' Error*, 45.

7. Robinson and Freeman, *Psychosurgery and Self*, 23.

8. Damasio, *Descartes' Error*, 36–37.

9. Ibid., 49.

10. Ibid., 51.

11. Recent research indicates that this emotional cost-benefit analysis takes place at the anterior prefrontal cortex at the very front of the brain. See E. Koechlin and A. Hyafil, "Anterior Prefrontal Function and the Limits of Human Decision Making," *Science* 318 (October 26, 2007): 594–598.

12. Nigel Nicholson, *Managing the Human Animal* (London: Texere, 2000), 137.

13. Aristotle, *Nicomachean Ethics*, Book 2.

14. Daniel Goleman, *Emotional Intelligence: Why It Can Matter More than IQ* (New York: Bantam Books, 1995).

CHAPTER 4

1. For an excellent book dealing with cathexis, see Scott Peck, *The Road Less Traveled: A New Psychology of Love, Traditional Values and Spiritual Growth* (New York: Simon & Schuster, 2003), 95.

2. Most of the research studies dealing with the neuropeptides oxytocin and vasopressin have been conducted on two related species of prairie voles. I attended the Twelfth Annual Wisconsin Symposium on Emotion in April 2006. One of the speakers was Dr. Larry Young. He gave a fascinating talk titled "The Molecular Neurobiology of Social Bonding" that described the crucial roles oxytocin and vasopressin play in regards to bonding behavior.

3. Antonio Damasio proposes that sense of self, or what he calls "autobiographical self," resides in the ventromedial prefrontal region. See Antonio Damasio, *The Feeling of What Happens, Body and Emotion in the Making of Consciousness* (New York: Harcourt Brace & Company, 1999), 17.

4. Elliot S. Valenstein, *Great and Desperate Cures* (New York: Basic Books, 1986).

5. See Mary Francis Robinson and Walter Freeman, *Psychosurgery and Self* (New York: Grune & Straton, 1954).

6. Walter Freeman and James Watts, *Psychosurgery in the Treatment of Mental Disorders and Intractable Pain*, 2nd ed. (Springfield, IL: Charles C. Thomas, 1950), 190.

7. Ibid.

8. See Robinson and Freeman, *Psychosurgery and Self*, 192; and Antonio Damasio, *Descartes' Error* (New York: G. P. Putnam's Sons, 1994, 2000, current edition Penguin Books, 2005), 37.

9. See Robinson and Freeman, *Psychosurgery and Self*, 23.

10. See Freeman and Watts, *Psychosurgery*, 192.

11. Ibid., 187.

12. Ibid.

13. See Robinson and Freeman, *Psychosurgery and Self*, 28–29.

14. See Freeman and Watts, *Psychosurgery*, 204.

15. Ibid., 228.

16. Ibid., 238.

17. Jim Collins, *Good to Great* (New York: HarperCollins, 2001), 27.

18. Ibid., 25.

19. "Dilbert Is Right, Says Gallup Survey: A National Employee Survey Confirms That Uncomfortable Work Environments Do Make for Disgruntled Employees," *Gallup Management Journal*, April 13, 2006.

20. "Employee Engagement—A Concept Clean Up," BSI Consulting White Paper, http://www.bsiconsulting.com.au/pdfs/Engagement%20Clean%20Up%2003.pdf (accessed April 22, 2008).

21. Peck, *The Road Less Traveled*, 140, 141–142, 149.

22. Ibid., 146.

23. Telephone interview with Bob Carpenter, 2003.

24. Ming-Jer Chen, *Inside Chinese Business: A Guide for Managers Worldwide* (Boston, MA: Harvard Business School Press, 2003), 42.

25. Y. H. Wong and Thomas K. P. Leung, *Relationship Marketing in a Chinese Context* (Binghamton, NY: International Business Press, an imprint of Haworth Press, Inc., 2001), 4.

26. Jon P. Alston, "*Wa, Guanxi* and *Inhwa*, Managerial Principles in Japan, China and Korea," *Business Horizons* (March–April, 1989): 28.

27. Chen, *Inside Chinese Business*, 33.

28. Tom Peters and Robert Waterman, Jr., *In Search of Excellence* (New York: Warner Books, 1984), 75–76.

29. "Quad/Graphics: Business as Social Experiment," *Business Ethics* 7, no. 3 (May/June 1993).

30. Ken Iverson, *Plain Talk: Lessons from a Business Maverick* (New York: John Wiley and Sons, 1998), 177.

31. Scott Hovanyetz, "10 Days Later, Firefighters Head Home," DMNews online, July 24, 2002, http://www.dmnews.com/10-Days-Later-Firefighters-Head-Home/article/78182/ (accessed August 22, 2008).

32. "Quad/Graphics Recovers from Fire in its Big Plant," Graphic Arts online, August 1, 2002, http://www.graphicartsonline.com/article/CA239225.html (accessed August 22, 2008).

33. Chen, *Inside Chinese Business*, 92.

34. Charles Darwin, "The Descent of Man, and Selection in Relation to Sex" (Appleton and Company, 1871), 166.

35. Iverson, *Plain Talk*, 51–56.

36. Ibid., 23.

37. Alston, "*Wa, Guanxi* and *Inhwa*," 26.

38. Frederick Reichheld profiles a number of we-based CEOs in his book *Loyalty Rules*. See Frederick F. Reichheld, *Loyalty Rules: How Today's Leaders Build Lasting Relationships* (Boston: Harvard Business School Press, 2001).

39. Iverson, *Plain Talk*, 16–17.

40. Reichheld, *Loyalty Rules*, 117.

41. Tom Rath, *Vital Friends* (New York, Gallup Press, 2006), 62–63.

42. Tom Rath and Donald O. Clifton, *How Full Is Your Bucket?* (Omaha, NE: Gallup Press, 2004), 97.

43. Iverson, *Plain Talk*, 5.

44. Ricardo Semler, *Maverick: The Success Story Behind the World's Most Unusual Workplace* (New York: Warner Books, 1993), 139–140.

45. Ibid., 138.

46. Iverson, *Plain Talk*, 11–24.

47. Alan G. Sanfey, "Social Decision-Making: Insights from Game Theory and Neuroscience," *Science* 318 (2007): 600.

48. Ernst Fehr, Urs Fischbacher, and Michael Kosfeld, "Neuroeconomic Foundations of Trust and Social Preferences," *Discussion Paper Series IZA DP No. 1641*, Institute for the Study of Labor, June 2005.

49. Sanfey, "Social Decision-Making," 601.

CHAPTER 5

1. On a technical note, the cooperation and competency appetites are probably both expressions of the same underlying cathexis, or investment-tracking, phenomenon. The cooperation appetite motivates human beings to invest in relationships and bring them inside and the competency appetite motivates human beings to invest in skills and other socially valued assets and bring them inside as well. Deep down, the same investment-tracking mechanism mentioned in Chapter 3 probably governs both appetites.

2. Peter D. Kramer, *Listening to Prozac* (New York: Viking Press, 1993), 41.

3. Gary Hamel, *The Future of Management* (Boston: Harvard Business School Press, 2007), 185–212 and 229–237.

4. Ibid., 232–236.

5. James Surowiecki, *The Wisdom of Crowds* (New York: Random House, 2004).

6. Constance Holden, "Global Survey Examines Impact of Depression," *Science* 288, no. 5463 (2000): 39–40.

7. "Quad/Graphics: Business as Social Experiment," *Business Ethics* 7, no. 3 (May/June 1993).

8. Tom Peters and Robert Waterman, Jr., *In Search of Excellence* (New York: Warner Books, 1984), 104–105.

9. Ibid., 105.

10. Ricardo Semler, *The Seven-Day Weekend: A Better Way to Work in the 21st Century* (London: Century, the Random House Group Limited, 2003), 214–225.

CHAPTER 6

1. In order for this reward mechanism to make survival sense, the size of the reward should be commensurate with the difficulty and status of the task. Logically, the tasks most valued and applauded by the tribe should provide more joy than the routine tasks of everyday life. In other words, we should feel better after winning a hard-fought game of skill, say, than after successfully brushing our teeth in the morning.

2. Bethany Sotak, et al., "Dysregulation of Dopamine Signaling in the Dorsal Striatum Inhibits Feeding," *Brain Research* 1061, no. 2 (2005): 88–96.

3. Michael J. Frank, Lauren C. Seeberger, Randall C. O'Reilly, "By Carrot or by Stick: Cognitive Reinforcement Learning in Parkinsonism," *Science* 306, no. 5703 (2004): 1940–1943.

4. Katherine Unger, "Addicted by Sex?" *Science NOW Daily News*, May 18, 2006.

5. Peters and Waterman in their book *In Search of Excellence* noted that hoopla is a common characteristic of excellent companies. See Tom Peters and Robert Waterman, Jr., *In Search of Excellence* (New York: Warner Books, 1984), 263.

6. John Gottman, *Why Marriages Succeed or Fail . . . And How You Can Make Yours Last* (New York: Fireside, 1994).

7. Tom Rath and Donald O. Clifton, *How Full Is Your Bucket?* (Omaha, NE: Gallup Press, 2004), 39.

8. Rebecca Saxe and Johannes Haushofer, "For Love or Money: A Common Neural Currency," *Neuron* 58, 2 (April 24, 2008): 164–165.

9. Peters and Waterman, Jr., *In Search of Excellence*, 71–72.

10. Ricardo Semler, *Maverick: The Success Story Behind the World's Most Unusual Workplace* (New York: Warner Books, 1993).

11. Ken Iverson, *Plain Talk: Lessons from a Business Maverick* (New York: John Wiley and Sons, 1998), 23–24.

12. Ricardo Semler, *The Seven-Day Weekend: A Better Way to Work in the 21st Century* (London: Century, the Random House Group Limited, 2003), 192.

CHAPTER 7

1. I attended a lecture presented by Dr. Harry Davis at the 54th Annual Management Conference at the University of Chicago in 2006. This is where I first encountered the terms *incremental* and *disruptive* innovation.

2. Irving Biederman and Edward Vessel, "Perceptual Pleasure and the Brain," Red Orbit website, http://redorbit.com/news/science/504251/perceptual_pleasure_and_the_brain/, May 15, 2006.

3. Mihaly Csikszentmihalyi, *Flow, The Psychology of Optimal Experience* (New York: HarperCollins, 1991).

4. Susan Russell, et al., "Benefits of Undergraduate Research Experiences," *Science* 316 (2007): 548–549.

5. Robert Root-Bernstein, "Roger Sperry, Ambicerebral Man," *Leonardo* 38, no. 3 (2005): 224–225.

6. The pleasure of a win is regulated by dopamine-1 and dopamine-2 receptors in the striatum (part of the limbic system). Novelty-seeking pleasures are regulated by dopamine-4 receptors in the mesolimbic branch of ascending dopamine projections (dopamine receptors in the left side of the brain). See Liisa Keltikangas-Järvinen, et al., "Association Between the Type 4 Dopamine Receptor Gene Polymorphism and Novelty Seeking," *Psychosomatic Medicine* 65 (2003): 471–476. See also R. Tomer and J. Aharon-Peretz, "Novelty Seeking and Harm Avoidance in Parkinson's Disease: Effects of Asymmetric Dopamine Deficiency," *Journal of Neurology, Neurosurgery, and Psychiatry* 75 (2004): 972–975.

7. J. Kagan, N. Snidman, and D. M. Arcus, "Initial Reactions to Unfamiliarity," *Current Directions in Psychological Science* 1 (1992): 171–174.

8. Keltikangas-Järvinen, et al., "Association Between the Type 4 Dopamine Receptor," 471–476.

9. T. L. Falzone, et al., "Absence of Dopamine D4 Receptors Results in Enhanced Reactivity to Unconditioned, but not Conditioned, Fear," *European Journal of Neuroscience* 15, no. 1 (2002): 158–164.

10. Ricardo Semler, *The Seven-Day Weekend: A Better Way to Work in the 21st Century* (London: Century, the Random House Group Limited, 2003), 235–252.

11. Antonio Damasio, *The Feeling of What Happens: Body and Emotion in the Making of Consciousness* (New York: Harcourt Brace & Company, 1999), 24.

12. Roger N. Shepard, "Externalization of Mental Images and the Act of Creation," in *Visual Learning, Thinking and Communication*, eds. Bikkar Randhawa and William Coffman (New York: Academic Press, 2002).

13. Damasio, in *The Feeling of What Happens*, proposes the idea that consciousness evolved from the brain's image-making circuits. See page 24.

14. Antonio Damasio, *Descartes' Error* (New York: G. P. Putnam's Sons, 1994, 2000, current edition Penguin Books, 2005), 89–113; S. M. Kosslyn, et al., "Visual Mental Imagery Activates Topographically Organized Visual Cortex: PET Investigations," *Journal of Cognitive Neuroscience* 5 (1993): 263–287; A. Sirigu, et al., "The Mental Representation of Hand Movements After Parietal Cortex Damage," *Science* 273 (1996): 1564–1568.

15. Damasio, *Descartes' Error*, 101.

16. In this paragraph I throw down the gauntlet to the hyperrational naysayers who claim mental imagery does not exist. Antonio Damasio eloquently takes on the naysayers in *The Feeling of What Happens*. See page 108.

17. Gail A. Carpenter and Stephen Grossberg, "Adaptive Resonance Theory," in *The Handbook of Brain Theory and Neural Networks,* 2nd ed., ed. Michael A. Arbib (Cambridge, MA: MIT Press, 2002).

18. Michael Gazzaniga, "The Split Brain Revisited," *Scientific American* 279, no. 1 (1998): 50–55.

19. Ibid.

20. Roger N. Shepard, "Externalization of Mental Images."

21. For exercises to tune out the logical left hemisphere of the brain and tune into the nonverbal right hemisphere, see Betty Edwards's classic book, *Drawing on the Right Side of the Brain* (Los Angeles: J. P. Tarcher, 1979).

22. Gary Hamel suggests that, "for every 1,000 oddball ideas, 100 will be worth experimenting with; out of those, only 10 will merit a significant investment, and only two or three will ultimately produce a bonanza." See Gary Hamel, *The Future of Management* (Boston: Harvard Business School Press, 2007), 45.

23. Mihaly Csikszentmihalyi, *Flow, The Psychology of Optimal Experience* (New York: HarperCollins, 1991).

24. R. Anderson, "Honoring Human Experiences," in *Transpersonal Research Methods for the Social Sciences* (Thousand Oaks, CA: Sage, 1998), 81.

25. Roger N. Shepard, "Externalization of Mental Images," 138–139.

26. Ap Dijksterhuis and Loran F. Nordgren, "A Theory of Unconscious Thought," *Perspectives on Psychological Science* 1, no. 2 (2006): 95–109.

27. Roger N. Shepard, "Externalization of Mental Images," 139–140.

28. Scott G. Isaksen and John P. Gaulin, "A Reexamination of Brainstorming Research: Implications for Research and Practice," *Gifted Child Quarterly* 49, no. 4329 (2005): 315–329.

29. Presentation titled "Leading Innovation" by Dr. Harry Davis at the 54th Annual Management Conference at the University of Chicago in 2006.

30. "Kelly Johnson's Skunk Works® Created the World's Most Amazing Planes," *Popular Mechanics*, September 1999.

31. Tom Peters and Robert Waterman, Jr., *In Search of Excellence* (New York: Warner Books, 1984), 67.

32. Ricardo Semler, *The Seven-Day Weekend*, 6.

33. Hamel, *The Future of Management*, 90.

34. Ibid., 95.

35. Ibid., 148.

36. Ibid., 148–49.

37. Donald N. Sull and Yong Wang, *Made in China: What Western Managers Can Learn from Trailblazing Chinese Entrepreneurs* (Boston: Harvard Business School Press, 2005), 56.

38. This quotation was obtained from a description of Quad/Graphics on the fundinguniverse.com website, http://www.fundinguniverse.com/company -histories/QuadGraphics-Inc-Company-History.html (accessed August 22, 2008).

39. Ken Iverson, *Plain Talk: Lessons from a Business Maverick* (New York: John Wiley and Sons, 1998), 98–99.

CHAPTER 8

1. Laura Helmuth, "Fear and Trembling in the Amygdala," *Science* 300 (2003): 568–569.

2. Naomi I. Eisenberger, Matthew D. Lieberman, and Kipling D. Williams, "Does Rejection Hurt?: An fMRI Study of Social Exclusion," *Science* 302 (2003): 290–292.

3. John Byrne, "How Al Dunlap Self Destructed," *BusinessWeek*, July 6, 1998, 58–65.

4. John Byrne, *Chainsaw: The Notorious Career of Al Dunlap in the Era of Profit-at-Any-Price* (New York: HarperCollins, 2003), 352.

5. Ibid., 357.

6. Ibid., 358.

7. Corporations may achieve a similar result to my oil industry fieldwork when they send employees to ropes courses for team-building sessions. I have witnessed quality ropes courses that achieved the same sort of rapport building I experienced in Alaska.

8. Daniel Goleman, *Social Intelligence: The New Science of Human Relationships* (New York: Bantam Books, 2006), 117–132.

9. Ibid., 118.

10. Daniel Goleman, Richard Boyatzis, and Annie McKee, *Primal Leadership: Learning to Lead with Emotional Intelligence* (Boston: Harvard Business School Press, 2004), 80.

11. *Diagnostic and Statistical Manual of Mental Disorders,* Fourth Edition (Washington, DC: American Psychiatric Association, 2000), 714–717.

12. See prevalence data for narcissistic personality disorder on Internet Mental Health website, http://www.mentalhealth.com/dis/p20-pe07.html.

13. *Diagnostic and Statistical Manual of Mental Disorders,* 660.

14. Willem Martens, "A Multicomponental Model of Shame," *Journal for the Theory of Social Behavior* 35, no. 4 (2005).

15. Michael Maccoby, "Narcissistic Leaders: The Incredible Pros, the Inevitable Cons," *Ideas with Impact:* Harvard Business Review *on Leadership at the Top* (Boston: Harvard Business School Publishing Corporation, 2003), 75.

16. Jim Collins, *Good to Great* (New York: HarperCollins, 2001), 36.

17. Ibid., 29.

18. Lao Tzu, *Tao Te Ching.*

19. Collins, 70.

20. Telephone interview with Bob Carpenter in 2003.

21. Tom Peters and Robert Waterman, Jr., *In Search of Excellence* (New York: Warner Books, 1984), 121–125.

22. Kevin Freiberg and Jackie Freiberg, *Guts!: Companies That Blow the Doors off Business-as-Usual* (New York: Doubleday, 2004), 7–8.

23. The spool of paper, or web, moves through the printing press at a speed of up to 3,000 feet per minute, or 34 miles per hour. Any mistake in machine alignment or ink application rate quickly adds up to tons of wasted paper.

24. Ellen Wojahn, "Management by Walking Away," *Inc. Magazine,* October 1983, 68.

25. Tom Peters and Nancy Austin, *A Passion for Excellence* (New York: Random House, 1985), 270.

26. Leadership presentation by Bill McComb at the 55th Annual Management Conference at the University of Chicago in 2007.

27. Johnson & Johnson has consistently ranked at the top of Harris Interactive's "National Corporate Reputation Survey." J&J was ranked number 1 in this survey for seven consecutive years! J&J is also ranked as one of the 100 Best Companies to Work For by the Great Places to Work Institute.

28. Ken Iverson, *Plain Talk: Lessons from a Business Maverick* (New York: John Wiley and Sons, 1998), 23.

29. Ibid., 60.

30. Ibid., 51–77.

31. Ibid., 54–55.

32. Ibid., 59.

33. Ibid., 55–56.

34. Collins, *Good to Great*, 136.

35. Ibid., 139.

36. Iverson, *Plain Talk*, 137.

37. Nucor's 2006 revenue figure was obtained from a Standard and Poor's–Compustat® report dated June 17, 2007. The information regarding headquarters staff and layoff history were obtained from a description of Nucor on the website www.thevault.com.

38. Taken from Ricardo Semler, "Managing without Managers," *Harvard Business Review* (September–October 1989), pp. 1–10 of reprint 89509, and Ri-

cardo Semler, *Maverick: The Success Story Behind the World's Most Unusual Workplace* (New York: Warner Books, 1993), 2, 72, 162, 310, 330–335.

39. Semler, *Maverick*, 7.

40. This reference was obtained from a description of Quad/Graphics on the fundinguniverse.com website, http://www.fundinguniverse.com/company-histories/QuadGraphics-Inc-Company-History.html (accessed August 22, 2008).

41. Tom Peters and Nancy Austin, *A Passion for Excellence* (New York: Random House, 1985), 274.

42. Collins, *Good to Great*, 190.

43. Gary Hamel, *The Future of Management* (Boston: Harvard Business School Press, 2007), 64.

44. Ibid.

CHAPTER 9

1. Nigel Nicholson, *Managing the Human Animal* (London: Texere, 2000), 256.

2. Ibid., 46.

3. Ibid.

4. Joseph S. Nye, Jr., "Soft Power, Hard Power, and Leadership," unpublished manuscript available on the Harvard University website, http://www.ksg.harvard.edu/netgov/files/talks/docs/11_06_06_seminar_Nye_HP_SP_Leadership.pdf.

5. Ibid., 1.

6. Among the San hunter-gatherers of the Kalahari, the archer who kills a large animal is awarded the choice back portion of the animal and the hide. See Jiro Tanaka, *The San, Hunter-Gatherers of the Kalahari*, trans. David Hughs (Tokyo: University of Tokyo Press, 1980).

7. Dan Goleman reviews the literature pertaining to stress and health in Chapter 16 of his *Social Intelligence: The New Science of Human Relationships* (New York: Bantam Books, 2006), 223–237.

8. Tanaka, *The San*, 112–113.

9. Ibid., 108.

10. Richard G. Wilkinson, "Health, Hierarchy, and Social Anxiety," *Annals of the New York Academy of Sciences* 896 (1999): 48–63.

11. Ibid.

12. Ibid.

13. Ibid.

14. K. Fleissbach, et al., "Social Reward Affects Reward-Related Brain Activity in the Human Ventral Striatum," *Science* 318 (2007): 1305–1308.

15. Gregory T. Huang, "The Economics of Brains: A Collection of Research Papers Touts the Promise of Neuroeconomics," *Technology Review* (Cambridge, MA: MIT Press, 2005), http://www.technologyreview.com/biomedicine/14439/page 1/.

16. See Alan G. Sanfey, "Social Decision-Making: Insights from Game Theory and Neuroscience," *Science* 318, no. 5850 (2007): 599; Keise Izuma, Daisuke Saito, and Norihiro Sadato, "Processing of Social and Monetary Rewards in the Human Striatum," *Neuron* 58 (2008): 289.

17. Sanfey, "Social Decision-Making," 600.

18. As quoted in Huang, "The Economics of Brains," 1–3.

19. Herman Krommendam, "Cross-Border Mergers and Acquisitions: Success Stories and Best Practices," *Point of View* 2, 2002, Spencer Stuart Consulting, www.spencerstuart.com.

20. Leslie Norton, "Merger Mayhem," *Barron's*, April 1998.

21. Colin Cook and Don Spitzer, "World Class Transactions: Insights into Creating Shareholder Value Through Mergers and Acquisitions," KPMG (2001), 9–10, http://www.us.kpmg.com/RutUS_prod/Documents/8/kpmg%20ma%202001%20web.pdf.

22. M. Bekier, A. Bogardus, and T. Oldham, "Why Mergers Fail," *McKinsey Quarterly* 4 (2001): 6–9.

23. David Henry, "Mergers: Why Most Big Deals Don't Pay Off," *BusinessWeek*, October 14, 2002.

24. E. J. Bruner, "Stress and the Biology of Inequality," *British Medical Journal* 314 (1997): 1472–1476.

25. Ricardo Semler, *Maverick: The Success Story Behind the World's Most Unusual Workplace* (New York: Warner Books, 1993), 7.

INDEX